IN THE
COMPANY
OF SAGES

"A clear, reasoned exposition that will help seekers of all persuasions."

YOGA JOURNAL

"Bogart calls upon his expertise as a psychotherapist and his experience as a mature spiritual seeker to discuss issues that are crucial for Western students of inner pathways. This is a must-read for all spiritual seekers and their teachers."

JUDITH HANSON LASATER, PH.D., P.T.,
COAUTHOR OF *WHAT WE SAY MATTERS*

"This book is valuable for anyone who has been a student of a spiritual teacher or who is contemplating becoming one, and it helps prevent misconceptions so that a mature teacher-student relationship can develop."

YOGA INTERNATIONAL

"Bogart's book is a clear and detailed map of the experience of self-unfoldment under the guidance of a guru or spiritual guide—including its difficulties, dangers, joys, and ultimate value. Highly recommended."

JOHN WARREN WHITE, AUTHOR OF *WHAT IS ENLIGHTENMENT?*

"If the recurring stories of gurus gone egregiously astray have you wondering whether teachers still have relevance on the spiritual path, I encourage you to read this wise and balanced book. Bogart makes a cogent case for the perennial value of awakening to who we are in relationship with one who already knows and can point the way."

STEPHAN BODIAN, AUTHOR OF *WAKE UP NOW*

"In this volume, which I regard as his best, Bogart brings an integrated psychospiritual perspective to his description of the guru-disciple relationship. I welcome this book and will recommend it frequently to clients and students of my own."

BRYAN WITTINE, LMFT, PH.D.,
TEACHING AND SUPERVISING ANALYST,
C. G. JUNG INSTITUTE OF SAN FRANCISCO

"Based on decades of firsthand, inspiring, and life-changing experiences and scholarly research, Greg Bogart's *In the Company of Sages* astutely and caringly steers you through the winding terrains of the spiritual mentor and student relationship."

STUART SOVATSKY, PH.D., AUTHOR OF
ADVANCED SPIRITUAL INTIMACY

"This is an excellent practical guide for anyone seeking a spiritual teacher and for those who are teachers. Bogart's openness and forthright storytelling may benefit parents or loved ones who are concerned about friends and family members who invest themselves in spiritual practice. I highly recommend this book. Well researched and documented, readable, and personal, it lights the way for those navigating the journey of transformation."

LAUREL CLARK, AUTHOR OF *INTUITIVE DREAMING*

"This uniquely insightful book is a new classic of contemporary spiritual literature."

MASTER CHARLES CANNON, ORIGINATOR OF
SYNCHRONICITY HIGH-TECH MEDITATION

"Full of wisdom and insights, this book is an essential guide for students and teachers at all levels of their spiritual journeys. Highly recommended."

SANDY SEE, MEDITATION TEACHER,
ASHTANGA YOGA STUDIO, OKLAHOMA

IN THE
COMPANY
OF SAGES

The Journey of the
Spiritual Seeker

GREG BOGART

Inner Traditions
Rochester, Vermont • Toronto, Canada

Inner Traditions
One Park Street
Rochester, Vermont 05767
www.InnerTraditions.com

Library of Congress Cataloging-in-Publication Data
Bogart, Gregory C.
  [Nine stages of spiritual apprenticeship]
  In the company of sages : the journey of the spiritual seeker / Greg Bogart.
    pages cm
  Originally published under title: The nine stages of spiritual apprenticeship : understanding the student-teacher relationship, c1997.
  Includes bibliographical references and index.
   ISBN 978-1-62055-384-8 (pbk.) — ISBN 978-1-62055-385-5 (e-book)
  1. Spiritual life—Miscellanea. 2. Guru worship (Rite) 3. Disciples. I. Title.
  BF1729.S64B64 2015
  204'.4—dc23

                                                    2014017151

Printed and bound in the United States

10 9 8 7 6 5 4 3 2

Text design by Debbie Glogover and layout by Virginia Scott Bowman
This book was typeset in Garamond Premier Pro and Gill Sans with Jenson Pro and Gill Sans used as display typefaces
Photography by Greg Bogart and Leo Bogart

To send correspondence to the author of this book, mail a first-class letter to the author c/o Inner Traditions • Bear & Company, One Park Street, Rochester, VT 05767, and we will forward the communication, or contact the author directly at **www.gregbogart.net**.

Contents

Preface

*When the cry of the disciple has reached a certain pitch, the
teacher comes to answer it.*

Hazrat Inayat Khan

*In order to achieve the Accomplishment, one should depend upon
a Guru for the Initiation, Instruction, and Inner Teaching.*

Milarepa

I received initiation from a great yogi at age sixteen, sparking my life-long interest in the subtle, mystical pedagogy that aids seekers on the spiritual path. This book offers a reasoned discussion of this process, but it's also a highly personal work. I describe the lasting resonance of my encounters with several provocative spiritual mentors, openly sharing my interior journey, expansive states, doubts, and occasional foolishness. I've distilled the nine stages of this path from my own experiences, from the teachings of various religions and spiritual practice lineages, and from the stories of people I have interviewed.

I believe this book will be of interest to anyone involved in the process of spiritual initiation and tutelage, including those searching for a spiritual guide, those who already have a teacher, and those who are themselves guides and teachers. I wrote this for both students and teachers of yoga, meditation, and other paths of the Spirit, to provide a clear description of the role of a teacher in a student's life, which changes over time. I see an arc of development in this process that makes it meaningful as a sacred life passage. It's my hope that mapping these stages will prove helpful to anyone whose fiery inner urge for transformation prompts a search for spiritual mentoring.

First published in 1997, now updated and revised, this book is dedicated to the goal of increasing our capacity to receive and convey liberating knowledge.

WILDCAT CANYON
JULY 2014

Acknowledgments

I'm indebted to Nancy Carleton, whose editorial guidance helped me clarify the vision of this book. I warmly thank Jon Graham and the editors of Inner Traditions for their enthusiastic support and collaboration. A bow of thanks to ten gentle sages who offered comments and suggestions: Georg Feuerstein, John White, Judith Lasater, Master Charles Cannon, Bryan Wittine, Dan Millman, Laurel Clark, Stephan Bodian, Sandy See, and David Frawley. I also thank Linda Cogozzo for her wise counsel.

I'm grateful for the positive influence of these friends, teachers, and allies: Chris Abajian, Rick Amaro, Robert Bartner, Ken Bowser, Betsy Cohen, Richard Cook, Brant Cortright, Jorge Ferrer, Michael Gelbart, Michael Gliksohn, Vern Haddick, Amar and Sahib-Amar Khalsa, Karl Knobler, Stanley Krippner, David LaChappelle, Colleen Mauro, Laurel McCabe, Thomas Miller, Shelley Montie, Tricia Moore, Girija Moran, Geri Olson, Claude Palmer, Gayle Peterson, Robert Powell, Richard Rosen, Donald Rothberg, Pat Russell, Bill Sargent, Laura Shekerjian, Swami Shankarananda, Monica Singh, Stuart Sovatsky, Andres Takra, Nandini and Basava Weitzman, Janice Willis, Miles Vich, and Jeremy Zwelling. I gratefully acknowledge Chakrapani Ullal, the luminous astrologer, who has been a guide and companion throughout my life since we first met in Bombay in 1978.

My father, Leo Bogart, was a kind of secular mahatma who spoke eight languages, traveled the whole world, authored many learned books,

The author at Tanjore Temple, Tamil Nadu, January 1996.
Built of golden granite in the eleventh century by Raja Raja Choala I,
Tanjore is an exquisite monument of the Tamil siddhas.

and was once described as "the guru's guru of marketing research." In 1996, while I was writing this book, we traveled together in Kerala, Karnataka, and Tamil Nadu, South India. All my life I'd struggled to explain to my father, a skeptical and highly rational person, my predilection to seek the company of yogis and gurus. So it was amazing when he came to India with me to see for himself—and ended up falling in love with India. I'm grateful we got to share that soulful journey as this work was taking form.

I thank my mother, Agnes, for her laserlike editing and steady encouragement. I also thank my nephew, Nick Pauly, and my sister, Michele Bogart, my lifelong friend; you can look up her books on

Amazon. I thank my fabulous wife, Diana Syverud, for her graceful presence and healing energy. And a special thank you to Charles Mintz, advisor and enlightened elder brother.

I thank all of the people I interviewed for the book. I've changed most of their names and identifying details to preserve anonymity; others requested that their real names be included.

For some years I lived in close proximity to two spiritual teachers, Sangye Drolma and Sheikh Nur Richard Gale. I've been richly rewarded by our friendships and gratefully acknowledge all the wisdom they've shared with me. Drolma led women's spiritual pilgrimages in India and Kashmir and studied with Muktananda, Pir Vilayat Khan, and Dilgo Khyentse Rinpoche. We meditated together for more than a decade. Drolma passed away in 2004, but her wisdom lives on in several stories recounted in these pages.

I offer loving thanks to Swami Muktananda, my root guru, powerful and mysterious as a jaguar; to my hatha yoga guru, Allan Bateman; to Judith Lasater, who taught me the meaning of balance in yoga; and to Dane Rudhyar, mystic philosopher, poet, and composer, who guided me across a crucial threshold on the path. I offer this work with reverence for the spiritual teachers of all lineages, whose wisdom illuminates the many paths to truth.

An old saying is just as valid today as ever: When the pupil is ready, the Master appears. But he may appear in many disguises. What matters is not the Master, but the Mastery he "reveals." It is veiled in his person. It has to be contacted through his person, rather than in his person. Devotion to a guru may be the way, but sooner or later it should be transmuted into reverence: the truth within the disciple saluting in true humility the truth in the Teacher. . . . [This] is the essential, withal rather mysterious process of transmission.

DANE RUDHYAR

The spiritual pedagogy that initiates the soul into itself cannot be limited to a single form or to the Active Intelligence alone. Thus some souls learn only from human masters; others have had human and superhuman guides; others have learned everything from invisible guides, known only to themselves. This is why the ancient Sages, those who had the gnosis of direct vision, having been initiated into things that the sensible faculties do not perceive, taught that for each individual soul, or perhaps for a number of souls with the same nature and affinity, there is a being of the spiritual world who, throughout their existence, adopts a special solicitude and tenderness toward that soul or group of souls; it is he who initiates them into knowledge, protects, guides, defends, comforts them, brings them to final victory.

HENRI CORBIN

The Catalyzing Role of Teachers

In many contemplative traditions, learning from an enlightened teacher is considered an important means of advancement on the spiritual path. In India, for example, it is common for an aspirant to seek a guru at a young age and to remain devoted to that teacher for many years. Many illumined beings and mystics, especially those from Hindu, Sufi, and the Zen and Tibetan Buddhist lineages, have maintained lifelong connections with their teachers and are in agreement that the student-teacher relationship is essential to the alchemy of transformation. It is also customary in the Jewish, Christian, and Islamic traditions to learn from wise spiritual teachers and ecstatic mystics. Although it's common in some contemporary Western intellectual circles to ridicule gurus and spiritual teachers and to view those who associate with them as naive or immature, many people continue to pursue the age-old tradition of spiritual apprenticeship. A perennial rite of passage, training under the guidance of a spiritual teacher can be a powerful initiatory experience.

The major religious texts of humanity are based on the teachings of illumined men and women of the Spirit, many of whom instructed students. Indeed, the student-teacher relationship goes to the heart of religious and spiritual life. Humanity has always acknowledged the influence of great spiritual teachers and religious leaders, from Zoroaster, Patanjali, Buddha, Moses, Jesus, and Mohammed, to Martin Luther, Meister Eckhart, Rinzai, St. Theresa of Avila, Ibn 'Arabi, Chaitanya, and the Baal Shem Tov; from Ramakrishna, Yogananda, Joseph Smith, and Crazy Horse, to Martin Luther King, Satya Sai Baba, and the fourteenth and current Dalai Lama.

Spiritual apprenticeship is the path of training under the guidance of spiritual teachers to achieve inner awakening, enlightenment, or realization of the Self, a state of pure consciousness or spacious awareness that is transpersonal, nonegoic, and beyond the boundaries of the individual self.

I use the term spiritual apprenticeship to denote the relationship we have to those who guide us on the path of sacred knowledge and inner wisdom, as opposed to teachers of secular subjects. In this book I explore how associating with a spiritual guide can aid a seeker on the path, as well as detail the challenges and difficulties that can arise.

In this book I examine nine stages of the student-teacher relationship:

- *Stage one, choosing a teacher:* a look at what impels us to search for a genuine teacher, and how we know when we've found one
- *Stage two, initiation:* the prerequisites and transformative power of initiation; the link to a lineage of awakened beings
- *Stage three, discipleship:* developing a person-to-person relationship with a teacher, receiving skillful instruction, and finding a spiritual practice that leads to inner freedom
- *Stage four, testing:* examination of the student's character, motives, and purity of thought and action; the exposure of one's imperfections
- *Stage five, grace and guru yoga:* the mysterious infusion of blessings experienced in the company of some teachers; balancing

grace with self-effort; contemplation of the teacher's qualities and state of consciousness

- *Stage six, at the threshold of awakening:* achieving the goal of spiritual apprenticeship, the experiential knowledge of the real, Self-realization in moments of illumination
- *Stage seven, separating from a spiritual teacher:* reestablishing an independent life; resolving emotional conflicts of discipleship; unhealthy merging; facing a teacher's shadow side; individuation from the teacher
- *Stage eight, finding the teacher within:* accessing inner sources of guidance, such as dreams, symbols, and disembodied teachers
- *Stage nine, teaching others:* with appropriate intention and ethics, sharing what we know; tests of character for teachers; guidelines for spiritual teachers

Stages one, two, and three describe the process of entering into a relationship with a teacher. Stages four, five, and six describe the ways we begin to be transformed within the relationship. And stages seven, eight, and nine describe the process of integrating the relationship and internalizing the teacher. It's important to note that these aren't linear stages. Some people might not pass through all nine stages or experience them in the order discussed here. These stages often intersect, blend together, and unfold concurrently. Nevertheless, I believe that taken as a whole, they describe the full cycle of the student-teacher relationship in all of its complexity.

SPIRITUAL APPRENTICESHIP
IN ADULT DEVELOPMENT

The student-teacher relationship in spiritual apprenticeship has much in common with the apprentice-mentor relationship more generally, while also being different in some important respects. Mentoring relationships focus on acquiring particular kinds of skills and expertise, especially those required to learn a trade such as plumbing, carpentry, nursing, Tibetan *thangka* painting, or the practice of homeopathic medicine. In mentoring relationships the student sets out to master a certain skill or body of knowledge with the understanding that eventually he or she will leave the teacher to practice this skill, art, or discipline independently.

However, in spiritual apprenticeship, matters can become somewhat more complex. Here the goal is for the student to undergo a profound change of consciousness and character. This may require challenging the student to overcome fears, attachments, and limiting personal beliefs. The methods may be unorthodox or shocking, such as those used by the Buddhist crazy-wisdom teachers, whose sometimes unconventional or outrageous conduct cuts through fear and ignorance to help others reach liberation.[1] The relationship challenges the student on the deepest levels and can activate intense conflicts. Further complicating matters, discipleship often involves a certain degree of deliberate psychic merger or union with the teacher, especially in the practices of *guru yoga*. One may be encouraged to surrender, to offer oneself to the teacher in body and mind, to meditate on the teacher, and, in this way, to become one with the guru. Such a practice may enable the student to more swiftly achieve spiritual elevation, but may also make the student's eventual separation from the teacher more complex to navigate than in secular forms of apprenticeship, where the boundaries between student and teacher are drawn more clearly.

Despite these differences, mentor-apprentice and spiritual teacher–disciple relationships have much in common. Both types of relationships involve a collaboration that fosters the student's learning and growth. Both involve instruction given by a teacher and some form of service offered by the student, as well as effort toward task mastery on the student's part, whether this means learning to hit a target with an arrow or to focus the mind in meditation. Most relationships of both types involve some degree of commitment between the student and the teacher. Finally, all types of guru-disciple, teacher-apprentice, or mentor-student relationships seem to carry certain inherent tensions and difficulties, which we'll examine in this book.

Psychologist Daniel Levinson views a period of apprenticeship as an important stage in the personal and career development of many adults.[2] Levinson believes that mentors serve many functions: they act as *teachers,* to enhance the novice's skills and intellectual development; as *sponsors,* who use their influence to facilitate the apprentice's social or professional advancement; as *counselors;* and as *exemplars* whom the apprentice can admire and emulate. Most importantly, mentors foster the development of their students by believing in them and supporting the realization of their own dreams and aspirations. These characteristics of mentoring relationships also apply to relationships between spiritual teachers and their students. The spiritual guide provides personal guidance, instructs the student in techniques of self-transformation, and is an exemplar of an expanded, enlightened state that the seeker can emulate and aspire to. The guide recognizes the student's innermost potential and aids the student in achieving the goal of enlightenment, or Self-realization. Thus the spiritual guide is a mentor who guides the seeker toward awakening, holding the vision of the student as a luminous, enlightened being, and transforming the student through mysterious vibrational influence.

DISCIPLESHIP AND
SPIRITUAL APPRENTICESHIP

I use the term *spiritual apprenticeship* deliberately to counterbalance what I perceive as the heaviness implicit in the word *discipleship. Disciple* implies a master, a concept that often creates mistrust in Americans, who have been bred on a tradition of autonomy and freedom from bondage to masters of any kind. I don't believe the notion of masters and servants is intrinsic to the process of spiritual training; this is only one way of framing the power relations that emerge on this path. Yet it's a conception that leads to two related problems: exaggerated attempts at surrender, sometimes leading to loss of will and autonomy; and the need to angrily repudiate a figure to whom one may have given too much power in the first place.

I believe we're better served by viewing spiritual tutelage as a process of apprenticeship wherein we undergo deep transformation, as well as acquire knowledge of spiritual doctrines or disciplines, master this knowledge, and then practice what we've been taught independently. The term *spiritual apprenticeship* also more accurately reflects the varied levels of commitment that are called forth in seekers by teachers of varying levels of wisdom and realization. Some teachers who have reached the highest levels of attainment deserve our deepest reverence, one-pointed attention, and devotion. In such cases the term *discipleship* may be properly applied. In discipleship there's an enduring commitment between student and teacher and conscious acceptance of the teacher's guidance and authority in one's life.

However, *discipleship* doesn't accurately describe the relationship we have with other teachers who aren't fully enlightened but who nevertheless can serve as important guides for us on the path, even though they may only be a few steps ahead of us. We may respect such teachers and honor what they teach us, but we wouldn't say we're their disciples. We choose to study with them to acquire specific knowledge. In such cases it's not appropriate to speak of discipleship, which implies a much more solemn commitment to a teacher. The idea of *spiritual apprenticeship* suggests that our involvement with a teacher may include stages of committed discipleship as well as phases of growth beyond the student-disciple role and a teacher's direct influence. This term leaves greater room for our instincts toward individuation and normalizes the process of approaching a teacher to learn for a period of time and then becoming independent.

To illustrate why I've coined this term for the student-teacher relationship, consider the example of David, a man of fifty-five who spent a decade as a committed student of a spiritual teacher until he began to feel uncomfortable with trends within his teacher's community. He was grateful for the teachings he'd received, but David eventually left the group, realizing that the teacher was fallible and made mistakes; he wasn't perfect. David then experienced a period of confusion because as he put it:

> I've been a devoted disciple for years and now I'm on my own and I'm not living as his disciple anymore. But I also don't view myself as a "former disciple." So what am I? I'm still engaged in the process of training and spiritual practice, but I'm doing it on my own now. It's different. It feels like a natural maturation to me, more than the loss of what I once had.

Reimagining himself as a spiritual apprentice helped David understand that he'd evolved through his period of discipleship and had now reached a stage where he was learning to rely on his inner teacher. Otherwise, he was left with the belief that his discipleship had failed to achieve its intended purpose. It was reassuring for David to understand that spiritual training may naturally include a stage of liberation from the teacher following the earlier, nurturing stages of devotion and surrender.

Spiritual apprenticeship is a term encompassing many types of relationships with spiritual teachers and their students, involving varied levels of commitment. At times I'll also use the term *discipleship*. Yet *spiritual apprenticeship* implies a greater independence of spirit. We seek out teachers to learn something that we can apply in our own lives, not to sit at their feet forever.

A PATH WITH MANY LINEAGES

As I describe the stages of the student-teacher relationship, I'll introduce some ideas from various religions and lineages. While not an exhaustive historical survey, this material will highlight the unique vocabulary each tradition has used to describe the student-teacher relationship. I hope to convey respect for every tradition. We'll see that the student-teacher relationship has been a central concern of most spiritual paths, and that guru yoga—focusing one's attention on an enlightened teacher's consciousness and presence—is a practice found in many traditions. In Judaism widely revered wise rebbes, tzaddiks, and ecstatic mystics are legendary. Christianity is centered around the faith of disciples whose attunement to the presence and teachings of Jesus draws them toward salvation. Those who follow the way of Islam are directed to find a mullah, sheikh, or dervish to guide them on the path.

The student-teacher relationship, and specifically the practice of guru yoga, has been described in particular depth in the Hindu, Buddhist, and Islamic traditions. The teachings of Zen Buddhism and Hindu yoga emphasize the student-teacher relationship and recount many stories of encounters between teachers and their students. Kashmir Shaivism, Sufism, and Tibetan Buddhism are other traditions whose teachings on this topic we'll discuss.

As I was working on this book, I came across a large number of prior writings on this subject, including accounts by authors who have experienced either profound transformation or deep emotional trauma as a result of contact with a spiritual teacher. Rather than trying to review at length the vast literature on the student-teacher relationship, I focus here on the stories of people I've interviewed who have followed the path of spiritual apprenticeship. Their stories vividly portray the nine stages, including some of the peaks and valleys through which one travels on this path. I also describe my own experiences with several teachers, especially Swami Muktananda, who profoundly influenced my life. I'll recount my memories of Muktananda, as well as discuss some of the controversy that has surrounded him since his death.

PROBLEMS OF DISCIPLESHIP
AND SEPARATION

This book explores a variety of emotional and interpersonal issues that often arise for contemporary Western students of spiritual teachers. This discussion isn't intended to cast doubt on the validity, value, or importance of the teacher-student or guru-disciple relationship, nor do I disparage those who enter into devotional relationships with spiritual teachers. I'm interested in the factors conducive to successful transmission of the awakened state of consciousness from teacher to student. I also explore the question of why, for many people today, a relationship with a spiritual teacher frequently proves to be problematic and why the process of separation from such a relationship can be treacherous.

I examine general features of spiritual apprenticeship as well as some of its inherent tensions and paradoxes. I'm particularly interested not only in those instances where a teacher's gross misconduct precipitates a student's departure, but also in cases where the student, in a healthy and almost inevitable process, needs to separate from the teacher—whether this means severing the relationship altogether or simply leaving the teacher's immediate physical presence. My purpose is to deepen our understanding of the disturbances and difficulties that often arise.

I celebrate the student-teacher relationship and discuss its many facets so that those who travel this road will understand both its possibilities and its challenges. I refer to pertinent historical examples and stories describing my therapeutic work with people striving to clarify their relationships with spiritual teachers. I also refer to ideas drawn from psychoanalytic and Jungian thought.

In recent decades countless thousands of Westerners have flocked to spiritual teachers, particularly those from Asia. Some have gone to Asia: to India, Burma, Nepal, or Japan. Others attend weekend courses or meditation retreats held in the West. With this widespread public interest in spirituality and enlightenment, there have also been casualties and instances where students have split from their teachers, feeling bitter and disappointed. While my own contacts with spiritual teachers have been exceedingly positive, I'm aware that many other people have been bruised by their experiences, and some of them carry lasting feelings of disillusionment and cynicism about teachers and the spiritual path in general. While it can be a great blessing to study with a spiritual guide, the process can sometimes go astray and result in confusion and desolation instead of clarity and enlightenment. I think it can be immensely healing to understand the cycle of spiritual apprenticeship, including the stages of separation from a teacher and finding the teacher within.

IMAGES OF SPIRITUAL TEACHERS IN WORLD RELIGIONS

Many of our conceptions of spiritual teachers derive from the cultural traditions of the East. Western fascination with Eastern gurus goes back to the late nineteenth century, when scholars such as Max Muller and Paul Deussen began translating into German and English the classics of Eastern spirituality such as the Vedas, the Upanishads, and the Dhammapada. The Theosophical writings of Helena Blavatsky and Alice Bailey and works by authors such as Alexandra David-Neel, Walter Evans-Wentz, Sir John Woodroffe, Paul Brunton, and Lama Govinda stirred westerners' interest in the wisdom of Eastern sages and masters. In the early twentieth century, Asian teachers such as Swami Vivekananda, Paramahansa Yogananda, and the Zen master Nyogen Sensaki began arriving in the West. By the 1950s the doctrines of Hinduism, yoga, Taoism, and Zen and Tibetan Buddhism were drawing widespread attention through the influence of such writers as Aldous Huxley, D. T. Suzuki, Alan Watts, Jack Kerouac, Allen Ginsberg, and Gary Snyder. In the 1960s Eastern spiritual teachers influenced the humanistic psychology movement and captured the interest of the youth subculture and then American and European society at large. In subsequent decades large numbers of westerners embraced the teachings of Eastern spiritual leaders, and many became serious and dedicated practitioners of yogic and meditative disciplines.

Some commentators consider devotion to gurus alien to western religious traditions. Yet our own western cultures and religions deeply respect the guidance of spiritual teachers. For example, there's a long tradition of spiritual direction and mentorship in Christianity. Two of the great Christian mystics, St. John of the Cross and St. Teresa of Ávila, had a transformative teacher-student relationship. John was Teresa's confessor (even though she was his elder), and they profoundly impacted each other; they would both go into an ecstatic state while discussing spiritual matters.

Thus, it's not only people in the East who revere and follow spiritual teachers, nor do the problems in such associations only arise in the case of Asian teachers and their western students. No matter what religious tradition we follow, we recognize that there are both true and false teachers, those who are venerable and wise, and those who are untrustworthy. But the basic human need to seek guidance from those who know the mysteries of Spirit is universal.

CULTS, CHARLATANS, AND SPIRITUAL TEACHERS

It's common for discussions about spiritual teachers to turn into talk about dangerous, fanatical groups and the coercive activity of cults. Indeed, some spiritual teachers do practice techniques of mind control and manipulate the lives of their students. The world has seen people such as Jim Jones, Marshall Applewhite, and David Koresh lead their followers into disaster. But while there are undoubtedly corrupt spiritual leaders, many authentic teachers engage in transformative and positive relationships with their students. Some people adopt a skeptical and cynical attitude toward all spiritual teachers by virtue of the fact that some of them have had a destructive influence on people's lives. As a result some observers view all spiritual teachers and their communities with suspicion. In noting this I don't mean to denigrate the important work that cult critics and exit counselors are doing. I simply want the reader to know from the outset that this book is written from a different perspective, one quite comfortable with the idea of the student-teacher relationship.

Of course, some charlatans do use their power and influence over others to gain access to sex, power, and money. One such notorious teacher, Rama, aka Frederick Lenz III, was accused by a number of female ex-followers of forcing them to have sexual relations at gunpoint, in some cases after being coerced to ingest LSD. The women were told that they'd be possessed by the devil if they didn't submit and that this was the only way they could be protected from the forces of evil. This deluded person Rama later committed suicide. Another notorious female self-proclaimed guru hired several Tibetans to dress up in monk's robes and proclaim that they had discovered through divination that she was the incarnation of Tara, one of the most powerful and beloved deities of the Tibetans. The Tibetans had the last laugh, however: they demanded a large fee for perpetrating this fraud, and when the teacher borrowed the money and presented it to the Tibetans, they tore the money into pieces and flushed it down the toilet, telling her, "Sometimes even Tara has to learn a lesson."

Many exposés have been written, complete with juicy gossip, salacious allegations, and, in some cases, well-documented evidence of financial or sexual improprieties. The tacit discourse of many such exposés is to show that most spiritual teachers are frauds and aren't to be trusted. Cynicism and suspicion of the student-teacher relationship often inform such reports. Instead, I believe it better serves us to examine realistically some of the complexities implicit in spiritual apprenticeship, so that those who choose this path can be uplifted, not hurt, by their experience. With this in mind, I offer this book to anyone considering studying with a spiritual teacher; anyone currently connected to a teacher and hoping to mature in this relationship; those who wish to discontinue their involvement with a spiritual teacher; and those who've already left a teacher and are striving to forge their own path.

I hope to show that the process of separation from a teacher can be worked out in such a way that it results in a higher level of integration and realization of our potentials. I'm especially interested in inner sources of guidance and intuition, such as dreams, which at certain stages can begin to supplant the role of an external teacher, as we learn to rely increasingly on the teacher within. At some point we may even find ourselves teaching and guiding others in some capacity on their path of sacred knowledge or in meditation practices. Thus, the final chapter addresses some challenges encountered by those who are openly sharing their knowledge and realizations. As a renewed spiritual culture emerges in the West, there's a growing need for dedicated, emotionally balanced people to assume the role of spiritual guides, instructing and initiating others.

This book develops the idea that learning spiritual doctrines or techniques from a teacher gives us tools and experiences we can utilize to mature in our lives and refine our awareness. As we absorb these teachings and allow their message to transform us, we must eventually depart from the messengers who guided us and learn from life in some different way or from some other person. We'll see that this path reaches its fruition when we unfold our own destinies as spiritually awakened individuals. At culminating stages we focus all our efforts on fulfilling what C. G. Jung calls the individuation urge, the drive to actualize the totality of who I am, to realize the complete potentials of the Self in a uniquely faceted personality. All of this was foreshadowed in the final instructions of the Buddha, who told his students right before he died, "Be a light unto yourself."

CRITICS OF AUTHORITARIAN POWER DYNAMICS

Several commentators have criticized the nondemocratic, authoritarian power structure they believe is inherent in the traditional teacher-disciple relationship and the whole concept or institution of spiritual teachers. For example, social activist Michael Rossman, commenting on the growth of large spiritual movements in the 1970s, observes that the "pedagogy of the guru" is often bestowed in an authoritarian learning environment that contradicts, or negates altogether, the message of empowerment, enlightenment, or liberation that a teacher may espouse:

> What the student learns about learning, through engagement with
> the Guru and his Organization, is no new lesson at all, but a

reinforcement of the metalessons taught by the usual workings of the society. . . . The student learns that to learn involves being treated as an object. . . . The student learns that to learn he or she must sacrifice autonomy—not simply by joining in something collective, but by letting another define what is of value and how to learn it. . . . The student learns not to question or to interfere with the Guru's purposes and judgments, but instead to accept the centralization of power. . . . The student learns not to question the social structure and processes of the Organization, substantively and spiritually, by reinforcing their terms by recreating them within himself or herself, . . . identifying himself or herself with the [the Organization's interests]. In all of this, the student learns . . . to accept the operation of authoritarian social forms and to integrate himself or herself in their operation. . . . This schooling is disastrous for citizens of an age of social and personal chaos and crisis; for in the absence of reliable, authoritative answers, we must depend increasingly on self-directed and genuinely cooperative skills of learning to determine our futures, or even to survive.[3]

In a similar vein, Joel Kramer and Diana Alstad's book *The Guru Papers* argues that the student-teacher relationship involves implicit dynamics of control and obedience. Gurus attempt to keep control over students and devotees by manipulating fear and desire and by getting them to surrender control. The authors call the guru-disciple relationship, "the most extreme, clear-cut, and sophisticated example of a bond of dominance and submission not based on physical coercion."[4] They question "the great myth that external authority can be the source of inner freedom," and they contend that gurus use "the absolute power of active mind control . . . to make people who are being callously manipulated believe they are freer than everyone else."[5]

Expressing similar views the mystical scholar and poet Andrew Harvey has written that we no longer need spiritual teachers because "most of the masters and gurus are actually the patriarchy's most brilliant way of keeping [the] always-revolutionary truths of divine identity and equality under wraps. . . . [T]he guru systems have nearly always been indirect servants of power. . . . [Gurus] have conspired with that infantilism and that incessant desire for authority that has kept the human race trapped and unempowered."[6]

While I think these commentators make important points, the direction I pursue here is different. I believe that we very much need the wisdom of spiritual teachers. Spiritual apprenticeship is the setting in which gnosis—enlightened knowing, knowledge of the sacred—is passed from one person and one generation to the next. The illumined being of today inspires and guides the illumined person of tomorrow. We have a natural need to apprentice and to be mentored, and so, too, we have an intrinsic urge to learn from evolved men and women, to receive their blessings, and to be transformed in their company.

According to transpersonal psychologist and author John Welwood, there's nothing intrinsically wrong about the exercise of authority by spiritual teachers. What we must examine in each specific case is how authority is defined and exercised in the student-teacher relationship, and the source from which a teacher derives that authority.

> A given teacher has [spiritual] authority only for those who respond to his or her presence and teachings. A disciple (Latin for "learner") is one who recognizes that he or she has something essential to learn from a given teacher. . . . Just as one would turn to an acknowledged master in any field one wants to pursue in depth, so a person who longs to overcome the limitations of egocentricity would feel drawn to someone who has mastered how to do that. The role of an effective teacher is to instruct, encourage, provide feedback, and inspire through personal example. Moreover, the more effective teachers tap and nurture the inherent potential of students, rather than imposing their own style and agenda.[7]

The student-teacher relationship can indeed be complicated by issues of domination, hierarchy, and authoritarianism. At the same

May all who take refuge in a spiritual guide find strength and serenity
as they approach the temple of the Spirit through meditation.
On the banks of the river Tunga, in Karnataka, the sacred temple at
Srinageri houses the first monastery established by Adi Shankaracharya,
the great Advaita Vedanta yogi and philosopher.

time, contending with power, hierarchy, obedience, and the maturation and expression of one's own inner authority are essential concerns for any person in our era. We face these same issues in our jobs and careers and in our marriages and family relationships. We don't shy away from these relationships just because they involve complex power dynamics or imply hierarchical relations. Inevitably, these same issues are also faced in the student-teacher relationship. While it's always possible that we'll fall prey to authoritarian power and exploitation, associating with a spiritual guide can be transformative if we're informed about the challenges implicit in the relationship. We need to develop a clear understanding of the stages of spiritual apprenticeship so we can navigate this path wisely. That's the purpose of this book.

༈

Choosing a Teacher

In Search of a Trustworthy Guide

I know all the scriptures which are like the sea
All five branches of learning I have mastered
With grammar and epistemology
Yet without a competent Guru
The fire of my craving will not die.
If my yearning not be stilled
By the Guru's grace which is like
The nectar stream of Tantra essence
Wide as the ocean, despite my attainments
Virtues and supersensible cognitions
I have not seen Reality.
Therefore I shall rely on Hevajra
And seek firmly for the true Guru.

THE LIFE AND TEACHING OF NĀROPA

At certain stages on the spiritual quest, we need a teacher to guide us on the path. Just as we seek a teacher to learn a foreign language or a musical instrument, if we wish to be enlightened, then we need to find a guide to instruct and inspire us. As Milarepa, Tibet's most accomplished and celebrated yogi, stated, "You need a qualified and dependable Guru."[1]

Throughout human history, there have been people who have demonstrated signs of spiritual realization, mystical illumination, or intimacy with God. The idea spans nearly every culture and era, that certain people are able to awaken higher consciousness and become conduits for healing and spiritual truths: yogis, shamans, prophets, illuminated saints, ecstatic mystics. These are individuals who have been entrusted by others with the mantle of spiritual leadership. Many cultures revere the figure of the shaman, who enters trance states, returns with insights from the spirit world, and initiates apprentices.[2] In ancient China people sought out the Taoist sages Lao Tzu and Chuang Tzu to question them about the meaning of life. In ancient Greece philosophers such as Pythagoras, Socrates, Plato, and Plotinus taught doctrines and techniques to lift students beyond ordinary consciousness into mystical experience and contemplation of higher realms of existence.

All spiritual traditions acknowledge the aspirant's need for a teacher. The teacher holds the highest place of respect in Sufism, the mystical branch of Islam, which has many orders of practitioners that gather for spiritual instruction by sheikhs, *pirs,* and *murshids.*

> The Sheikh is the master of spiritual alchemy. . . ; thus he can transform the base material of the novice's soul into pure gold. He is the sea of wisdom. The dust of his feet gives the blind eye of the beginner sight. . . . He is the ladder toward heaven, so completely purified that all the virtues of the Prophet are visible in him as in a mirror.[3]

Describing contemplative training among the Sufis, orientalist Annemarie Schimmel writes:

> In order to enter the spiritual path, the . . . *murīd,* "he who has made up his will" (to enter the Path) is in need of a guide to lead through the different stations and to point the way toward the goal. . . . The

mystics . . . saw in the constant supervision of the disciple's way by the mystical guide a *conditio sine qua non* for true progress.[4]

In a similar vein, Gershom Scholem, the renowned scholar of Jewish mysticism, notes:

A mystic requires a spiritual guide, or *guru,* as he is called in India. On the face of it the function of the *guru* is primarily psychological. He prevents the student who sets out to explore the world of mysticism from straying off into dangerous situations. For confusion or even madness lurk in wait; the path of the mystic is beset by perils. It borders on abysses of consciousness and demands a sure and measured step. The yogis, the Sufis, and the Kabbalists, no less than the manuals of Catholic mysticism, stress the need for such a spiritual guide, without whom the mystic runs the risk of losing himself in the wilderness of spiritual adventure.[5]

The spiritual teacher instructs the student in powerful methods of self-transformation, such as meditation, mantra, yogic breathing, and visualization, and teaches the student how to use these methods safely. The teacher helps the student find the most beneficial practices, prescribing techniques that are best suited to that aspirant's personality and level of maturity. And the teacher observes and supervises the student's progress in practicing these techniques, offering encouragement, advice, or actively intervening at certain stages, particularly when someone is beset by doubts or frightening experiences. The teacher also protects the student from dangers and pathologies of the spiritual path such as ego inflation or preoccupation with visions and psychic phenomena.[6]

SPIRITUAL TEACHERS IN HINDUISM

In the Hindu tradition, a guru is considered essential, for only one established in knowledge of the Self, the changeless reality, can transform our perceptions and remove the darkness of ignorance from our eyes. Innumerable realized saints in India have sung the praises of their gurus. The sage Narada said, "The association of the great souls is hard to acquire, hard to be had completely, but is always fruitful. For gaining even that association one requires God's blessing; for between God and His men there is no difference. So try to acquire the company of the holy soul."[7]

The Bhagavad Gita (IV. 34) states, "Those who themselves have seen the truth can be thy teachers of wisdom. Ask from them, bow unto them, be thou unto them a servant."[8] Commenting on this verse, Krishna Prem, a British-born mystic who lived in India for many years, writes:

> The disciple must resort to the feet of a wise teacher, one who is an embodiment of that Teacher Who is already in his heart, the Eternal Wisdom. . . . [H]e needs the guidance of one who, because his whole being has become one with the Wisdom, can speak with the same voice as that Teacher in the heart and yet can do so in tones which can be heard with the outer ear. . . . But it is not by wandering . . . , by searching out the remoter corners of the earth, that the Guru can be found. The Path which leads to the feet of the Guru . . . is an interior path, and only by treading the preliminary steps by oneself can one reach the outer guide. It is only when this stage has been reached, the stage in which the disciple is ready to offer up his self in sacrifice to the Self in all, that the Guru can and does manifest himself. . . . When . . . the disciple has found his Guru, he must, by the obedience of self-effacement, and the service which consists of putting the will at the disposal of the Teacher, so unite his being with that of the latter that the Wisdom which shines in him may light up in the disciple too.[9]

The student-teacher relationship is an integral part of the traditional culture of India, where the first of four stages of the life cycle is that of the *brahmacharin,* the pure and disciplined student. In this stage a youth studies Vedic hymns and the branches of yoga under a teacher's tutelage.[10] The guru gives the student initiation in mantra, sacred sounds and chants; instruction in *shastra,* sacred scriptures and teachings; and may also teach meditation. In some cases the teacher bestows *shaktipat,* a transmission of spiritual power that awakens the student's dormant kundalini energy.[11]

The Hindu tradition contains a wealth of stories about the guru-disciple relationship. In *The Autobiography of a Yogi,* Paramahansa Yogananda describes how his parents and entire family were devoted to a saintly guru named Lahiri Mahasaya, and how during his childhood a photo of this teacher healed him from a life-threatening bout of cholera. He met many yogis, including one reputed to be over a thousand years old, one known as the "Levitating Saint," and the muscle-bound "Tiger Swami," who subdued tigers with his bare hands, reducing them to pussycats. Finally, he was psychically drawn to his guru, Sri Yukteswar, when the two instantly recognized each other. Yogananda's timeless book details how Yukteswar initiated him and carefully guided him, revealing everything to his worthy disciple.

Thousands of years of Hindu meditation on the significance of the guru are summed up in the Sanskrit verse "Om namah shivaya gurave, satchidananda murtaye"—"I bow to Lord Shiva, the Guru, Being-Consciousness-Bliss in the form of a human being" (or "the embodied form of Being-Consciousness-Bliss"). The guru is the *murti,* the sacred form of perfect being, consciousness, and bliss. The teacher rests in a state beyond the flux of changing forms, abiding in the changeless reality, the Atman, the Self, merged with all-pervasive consciousness. And the teacher is blissful, no longer bound by the ignorance, suffering, and limitation of ordinary human life. Such an illumined being emanates the power of love and the light of consciousness. In the company of such a sage, we experience ourselves as limitless being, consciousness, and joy.

It's the presence of the teacher that communicates to us most deeply, more than the words the teacher speaks. The teacher's gaze, demeanor, wisdom, and loving emanation affects us emotionally and energetically. We may feel an inner awakening of dormant forces and enter a different state of consciousness as a result of encountering the teacher's clear mind.

ILLUMINATION AND SKILLFUL INSTRUCTION

A spiritual teacher exhibits illumination and enlightenment, as well as skill in transmitting consciousness to others. Such a person is a buddha, one who is awake, who can also awaken others from their sleep of ignorance. A guide who perceives the Self, the inner light or omnipresent Spirit, and uses skillful means to communicate the taste of this experience to others: that is a captivating teacher. One teacher might be quite illumined but an inept guide—irresponsible, surly, exploitative, indifferent. Another teacher might not be a fully realized or fully seasoned practitioner but might be quite gifted in sharing knowledge with others and leading them with positive impetus. An effective teacher combines *prajna* (wisdom and realization) with skill in the art of spiritual direction, leading to the awakening of the student. In identifying skill in awakening others as one mark of an effective teacher, I leave open the question of what tools are appropriate for teachers to use, allowing room for the use of unorthodox, crazy-wisdom methods.

TYPES OF TEACHERS

There are different kinds of spiritual teachers and teachers of different stature. One may be a teacher of physical yoga postures, another may teach us how to train our minds through meditation, while another may be a great pundit, able to give profound intellectual discourses. But there are some rare teachers who can awaken us and lead us into expanded consciousness by their mere presence. In the words of David Frawley:

Gurus are not all of one type. There are great gurus, ordinary gurus, and false gurus. . . . Great gurus may be sages of superhuman capacity. Ordinary gurus may be able to teach us something even though they have many ordinary human limitations. False gurus may exploit and deceive people. Some false gurus have great powers but use them wrongly. They can do great damage to their followers' minds and hearts.[12]

A fully enlightened spiritual teacher is more than just a teacher of meditation or yoga techniques; he or she embodies expanded human potentials and exudes a palpable love, compassion, or power. The clearest sign that we're in the company of a great teacher is the way we're deeply, often inexplicably moved by this person's presence. Sometimes a teacher demonstrates extraordinary abilities, such as healing, materializing objects, or clairvoyant knowledge of details about the past, present, and future lives of devotees. Some rare beings such as Ram Dass's guru Neem Karoli Baba exhibit perplexing and unfathomable powers such as being reported (on several occasions) to be in two different and geographically distant locations at the same time. Or there are stories about the blissful yogi Nityananda and his reputation for miracles and cures. Once when he started building an ashram near Kanhangad (in Kerala), the local police thought he must be producing counterfeit money to pay for the construction, so Nityananda took them to a crocodile-infested pool in the jungle, where he dove into the water and produced stacks of money, which apparently satisfied the police. These kinds of exploits and capacities captivate the public's attention and evoke feelings of awe and devotion. Indian and Tibetan cultures acknowledge the existence of rare beings known as *siddhas,* "perfected ones." Siddhas are beings who possess *siddhis,* powers transcending conventional human faculties. Siddhas have been transformed through spiritual practice and realization to such an extent that extraordinary powers manifest through them. They exhibit visible signs of having achieved advanced, metanormal stages of human development.[13]

According to Esalen co-founder Michael Murphy, some extraordinary capacities associated with metanormal functioning include enhanced sensory perception of external events such as extraordinary powers of seeing or hearing; self-mastery and control over autonomic bodily processes; ability to perceive internal somatic events such as awareness of cells and molecules within the body; perception of the numinous in the physical world; perception of auras or scintillae, or sparks of light, around people or objects; clairvoyant perception of distant events, precognitive perceptions, and telepathic communication with others; self-existent delight; ability to directly transmit states of illumination to others; ability to awaken the kundalini shakti, the "serpent power," in others; and "modification of some portion of space by mental influence, as in the apparent creation by mystics and saints of a special joy or presence in their place of contemplation."[14] In short these are the amazing psychic powers and miraculous actions attributed to great saints. Although these capacities are no guarantee of complete enlightenment, they're visible evidence of spiritual attainment, and they may elicit the faith and devotion of others.

Those who spend time in the company of enlightened beings often experience spontaneous deep meditation, awakening of an irridescent joy, or a rousing of the kundalini energy. Their presence tangibly affects other people's inner states, stirring emotional catharsis, feelings of profound serenity, visions, and sometimes waves of tears. Such teachers exhibit an elevated love, wisdom, power, or radiant emanation that generates in others a strong desire to be in their presence as much as possible.

Ideally, a spiritual teacher is someone quite advanced on the path, one who has achieved a state of enlightenment, or Self-realization. But teachers of lesser attainment can also guide us. These are what Frawley calls "ordinary teachers." I call them "helpful guides," emphasizing their positive contributions as well as recognizing their limitations. Those with a commitment to spiritual practice and with sufficient experience may teach others, even if they aren't completely enlightened. Fully illumined teachers and siddha gurus are rare, and seekers are often led forward by someone just a few steps ahead of themselves on the path. Thus teachers of various levels of accomplishment play a role at different stages of the journey. Along the way our main concern should be to avoid becoming entangled with a false teacher, who is generally much more of a conceited and manipulative rogue than the ordinary teacher, who acknowledges limitations.

I believe that the psychological and interpersonal issues involved in forming, sustaining, and dissolving relationships with spiritual teachers of varying levels of attainment are basically the same. Teachers of all levels are susceptible to certain predictable pitfalls of the student-teacher relationship. Regardless of the teacher's stature, the process of training and guiding others is always complex. Even highly realized mystics still have lessons to learn about human relationships and how to be of service to others.

The teacher is never perfect, because the teacher is human. The teacher is a stand-in for the eternal archetype of the Teacher, the Guide, the Initiator. All teachers and gurus are challenged in their own development to embody this archetype as fully as possible. Some do so more adequately than others. In this book we're going to look at both sides of this relationship—how students learn to be receptive and disciplined students, and how teachers evolve as teachers, hopefully with sufficient humility and openness to learn from their students. It's a coevolving path.

ATTRIBUTES OF THE SPIRITUAL GUIDE AND THE QUALIFIED STUDENT

In many traditions the character traits of the spiritual guide and the qualified student are explicitly described. For example, Islamic texts say the authentic guide is supposed to possess the following attributes:

> [S]ervitude to God alone, reception of truth directly from God, privileged access to God's mercy, a heart purified of all non-divine

forms of knowledge, rebirth into knowledge of the essence of God's presence, . . . correct belief, intelligence, liberality, courage, chastity, lofty aspiration, compassion, forbearance, forgiveness, sweet temper, selflessness, contentment with one's lot, dignity, tranquility, steadfastness, and a presence worthy of reverence.[15]

In short the teacher is expected to be a person of extraordinary power, purity, clarity, and personal integrity. The student is also expected to possess certain characteristics:

[R]epentance, renunciation, abandonment of family ties, proper belief, fear of God, patience, struggle against the lower self (the "greater struggle" [*jihad*] as compared to struggle against external foes), courage, readiness to sacrifice, chivalrousness, sincerity, knowledge, active searching, willingness to suffer reproach without giving occasion for it, intelligence, even disposition, submission to the shaykh "as a corpse in the hands of the corpse washer," and utter abandonment to God. . . . The seeker must strive to counteract the tendency to egocentricity through the attitudes of "servanthood" or "worshipfulness," and gratitude.[16]

Furthermore, qualified students dedicate themselves to the quest for realization or enlightenment and make this a priority in life, even when it means deemphasizing other desires and ambitions.

In the classical yoga traditions of India, a student's readiness for initiation is carefully assessed. One is expected to meet some high standards of personal competency and must be prepared for the rigors and challenges of training. While there are practices for less prepared students, the Shiva Samhita (a Sanskrit treatise on yoga) states that the fully qualified practitioner possesses these attributes:

[G]reat energy, enthusiasm, charm, heroism, scriptural knowledge, the inclination to practice, freedom from delusion, orderliness, youthfulness, moderate eating habits, control over the senses, fearlessness, purity, skillfulness, liberality, the ability to be a refuge for all people, capability, stability, thoughtfulness, the willingness to do whatever is desired by the teacher, patience, good manners, observance of the moral and spiritual law (dharma), the ability to keep his struggle to himself, kind speech, faith in the scriptures, the willingness to worship God and the guru (as the embodiment of the Divine), knowledge of the vows pertaining to his level of practice, and, lastly, the practice of all types of knowledge.[17]

Most people who meditate on these desired traits realize that they still have a long way to go in character development. Thus, the seeker is presented with a task even before a teacher has appeared—the task of self-examination and striving for self-betterment. Most students don't possess many of these noble qualities when they first approach teachers. But these can be benchmarks of the kind of mature demeanor and virtues that hopefully will develop over time as the student's character and motives are examined, tested, and reshaped. It's important to recognize that teachers also may fall short on many desirable traits, and they too will go through tests of character.

The main attribute of the student qualified to meet a mystic guide is a longing to attain the state of awakeness and clarity, to know and experience enlightenment, Spirit, or inner awakening. Something seems to guide us on the path before we ever meet our teacher face to face. As Baba Ram Dass explains, "When you reach the stage of asking, 'God, know me,' or 'let me be enlightened,' or 'I want Nirvana,'. . . at that moment you call forth your spiritual guide or Guru. . . . That . . . may be any one of a number of beings, and it is not necessarily on the physical plane."[18]

BEING GUIDED TO A TEACHER

Being a spiritual seeker means we actively seek out a teacher to guide us; we're like bees in search of pollen, eager to make honey from it. We may travel many roads and great distances to visit a teacher, or the guide may appear right where we are, without going anywhere. The teacher usually appears when we're inwardly calling out for guidance and searching for the light. Then it may not be long before a teacher appears to help us find our way. As the well-known saying goes, "When the disciple is ready, the guru appears." A woman named Pamela reports:

> One day I was in a bookstore, and for some reason I picked up a magazine off a shelf that I'd never seen before. I opened it up and it had this picture of this beautiful woman saint from India. I was completely drawn to her from the moment I set eyes upon her. *Who is that?* I wondered. I read all about her and it gave a phone number. I called it and there was a retreat happening in our city that month. I signed up and went to see her. And the first time I was introduced to her she acted like she already knew me. I've never been drawn to a teacher before but I was drawn right to her. I'd been interested in finding a teacher for a while, but I'd given up. Then it just happened.

While a seeker can be influenced by teachers who are no longer physically alive, a living guide is the most potent catalyst for awakening. But to meet a highly evolved teacher in this lifetime, one needs to have exceptionally good fortune. According to Annamalai Swami, a disciple of Ramana Maharshi, "One only comes into contact with a sage when one's good *karmas* bear fruit. Only those who've accumulated good karma from many lives get the chance to meet and love a sage."[19]

One can be drawn to a teacher in a variety of ways—through a captivating picture or reading about a teacher in a book or magazine or attending a workshop. Or an interest may be stirred by speaking with someone who has been affected or transformed through contact with a certain teacher. In first encountering a teacher, there's often a distinct moment of recognition. Jim, a student of kundalini yoga, describes meeting his spiritual teacher in 1978:

The moment I saw him I felt an electric shock go through my body, then the whole room seemed to be illuminated. As I listened to his lecture, I felt my heart opening and a sensation of an overflowing love. I was in ecstasy. Since then, I often feel his presence with me, even though I'm far away from him physically.

One may feel this type of immediate connection to a teacher, or the connection may grow slowly over time.

The first contact with a teacher can deeply affect us as we observe the teacher's enlightened attributes. Consider this description of Shirdi Sai Baba, a mysterious saint who slept on a narrow plank inside a delapidated mosque and tended the flame of a seemingly eternal fire. He was a benevolent source of solace and blessing to all who approached him and was also a healer who used herbal remedies to cure the ailments of others. Govind Dabholkar writes:

He whose mind reflects upon nothing except on Allah Malik, the Fountain of Life; who is unruffled and calm; has no desires or expectations and looks upon all equally, how can he have an identity separate from the Supreme Being?. . . . Inwardly, he was as tranquil as the sea. . . . His state of Self-absorption was constant. . . . By nature unconceited and very humble, he strove to please all. The words 'Allah Malik' were constantly on his lips. He disliked arguments and unprofitable wranglings. . . . Somebody's deeds, good or bad, or his innermost secrets were all known to him and he used to astonish devotees by giving a sign or an indication of them. . . . Inwardly detached and ascetical; yet outwardly there was a strong desire to guide people on the right path. . . . He was calm and self-restrained, detached and patient, forever in deep meditation; one with the Self and totally absorbed in It; pleased and gracious to his devotees. . . . Without the least desire for wealth or fame, and alms collection as the sole means of subsistence, he passed his days in this yogic state of withdrawal of all the senses. Whoever went to have his *darshan* would be told the whole secret of his past, future, and present, without his asking for it. . . . He expected nothing from anyone, but treated them all alike and showered blessings even on those who were ungrateful. Fortune or misfortune did not disturb his equilibrium, nor was he ever touched by doubts or misgivings.[20]

When we come into the presence of someone such as this, we feel an irresistible urge to be in their presence, which spreads the mood of enlightenment. But where do we find such a person? This is our quest, our story, which begins with a longing to find someone who embodies the next stage of our evolution, the one who can be our soul's captain.

MY SEARCH FOR A TEACHER

I learned about the importance of finding a teacher right from the beginning of my journey. I first became interested in yoga when I was fourteen years old. I felt a curious excitement about the topic and was especially intrigued by the concept of kundalini, the serpent power. I read everything on yoga I could find and began practicing asanas, pranayama, and meditation. I studied books by Ernest Wood, Richard Hittleman, Mircea Eliade, Paramahansa Yogananda, and Swami Satchidananda. Then, when I was sixteen, I read B. K. S. Iyengar's *Light on Yoga,* which hit me with the force of a thunderbolt, and I began to follow the systematic courses of hatha yoga postures recommended in that book. Each night I started my yoga practice several hours after dinner and continued until past midnight. I lay there on the floor with Iyengar's book, imitating the pictures. I especially liked the ones where he was in lotus posture, meditating. Sometimes I fell with a thud while coming down from a headstand or handstand, and downstairs neighbors complained about the disturbing noises I was making at all hours. As I felt the effects of this discipline, my previous habits were overturned. I loved the standing poses and did them for hours. I felt an intense vitality doing these practices. I moved through as many of the poses as I could manage and felt energy and heat being released inside me. I practiced the *maha mudra,* the great seal. I learned the *uddiyana* and *jalandhara bandhas,* contracting and pulling up the abdominal muscles, gently containing energy as it moved through the throat, learning to direct and enervate the breath.

Several months after starting this regimen, I learned why practicing yoga without proper guidance can be dangerous. One night I overzealously practiced *bhastrika pranayama,* the "breath of fire." I felt a flash of light within my body, then lost consciousness. My mother found me at two o'clock in the morning, passed out on the living-room floor. This experience frightened me. I'd succeeded in rousing a powerful internal energy, yet I had no idea how to do this safely. I wasn't adequately prepared for such an intense practice. It was then that I realized the importance of finding a teacher.

I read books about great beings such as Ramana Maharshi, Ramakrishna, and the amazing Shirdi Sai Baba. I was especially interested in reading everything by Ram Dass, particularly the stories of his life-transforming encounters with Neem Karoli Baba, known simply as Maharaji, and I attended a meditation group where I received a thread of Maharaji's blanket that was distributed by devotees when he left his body. The thread, attached to a *mala,* a string of prayer beads, had a peaceful emanation. I began to feel an invisible guidance quietly assisting me.

My longing to know a spiritual teacher grew intense. I was looking for a person of wisdom to show me how to move forward on my path. At the time, on the Upper West Side of Manhattan where I lived, there were many yoga centers springing up, and I visited a number of teachers and learned much from them about yoga, meditation, and spiritual life. But none of these teachers were right for me. One demanded a large amount of money and an immediate commitment of volunteer time to assist his organization. Another encouraged me to confront my parents, reject their values, and leave home when I was sixteen. Another was vain and totally preoccupied with himself. One beautiful being, Muni

Chitrabhanu, a Jain yogi, had a magnetic presence that affected me. But I kept searching, because in my heart I knew there was another teacher.

I saw two great beings whom I loved but didn't accept as my guide. I remember the expectancy in the air one summer evening at the Cathedral of St. John the Divine, where the Tibetan teacher Chögyam Trungpa Rinpoche was scheduled to give a lecture titled "The Dawn of the Age of Enlightenment." The audience members seemed enthused and were probably expecting a confirmation of their imminent spiritual realization. However, Trungpa was late in arriving, and the crowd began to get restless and impatient. When he finally arrived, an hour and twenty minutes late, he walked up on stage fantastically drunk. I had rarely seen a person so completely soused. He had a noticeable limp because half his body was paralyzed after an auto accident. Later I saw how he was like the mythical Chiron, the wounded healer, a limping sage. Trungpa's first words were, "To talk about enlightenment at this stage is completely ridiculous." Then he burst out laughing. The entire audience deflated at once! With a single stroke he was messing with everybody's egos.

Another great teacher I saw was Pir Vilayat Inayat Khan. Before his lecture one evening, he sat quietly on stage looking around the room, silently making contact with each person present. When his eyes fell on me for a moment I felt a wave of peace and inner joy. He gently smiled and I smiled back. Although he wasn't to be my teacher, I received a wonderful blessing from him that evening. When you were in his presence you felt he could see your higher being, your angelic soul. Years later I formed a strong connection with two of his students, Sangye Drolma and Nur Richard Gale, among my closest friends in this lifetime.

Mysterious karmic factors lead us to choose a particular teacher. We feel a deep inner connection that can't be forgotten or denied, and we know intuitively that we have something important to learn from this person. The first test of spiritual apprenticeship is to exercise discernment when choosing a teacher. As Pir Vilayat once wrote, "Before you attach yourself to a master, make sure he is the master for you."[21]

I was sixteen when I first met Swami Muktananda, a meditation teacher and siddha from India. I met him the day he arrived in New York City in the fall of 1974, at the beginning of his second world tour. I'd read about Muktananda in several books by Ram Dass, Swami Rudrananda, and Da Free John, all of whom described him as a highly evolved being, so I was excited to learn that he was staying three blocks away from my high school. It was easy to go there early in the morning to meditate before school started, and after school there was *darshan,* a chance to spend time in his presence and listen to questions and answers.

Muktananda was a short, potbellied yogi wearing bright orange robes and a maroon sweater. He was magnetic, moving like a restless cat, and had a strangely fascinating and powerful emanation. He didn't look like any other human being I had ever seen, and I couldn't take my eyes off of him. His face assumed innumerable expressions, darting glances all over the room, momentarily seeming irritable, then bubbling with throaty laughter, then quiet and blissful, humming to himself, appearing to move in other dimensions. Even behind dark sunglasses, his mysterious eyes shone like bright suns. You can ask anyone who met him and they will agree there was something so radiant and captivating in this man's eyes; they conveyed the ray of his Self-realization.

The first time I met Muktananda, I had the intuition that I was in the presence of an ancient being whose true nature was fire. At first I wasn't sure I liked him. He scared me, plus he seemed grouchy and intense, not the serene holy man I'd anticipated finding. Yet he affected me in a mysterious way, and after he left New York to continue his tour, I thought about him, and I yearned to meditate and began to practice diligently. Muktananda's influence became evident through an intensification of my inner life. I soon shed the desire to drink alcohol and take drugs and became a disciplined meditator and yogi.

HOW WE KNOW WE'VE FOUND A TEACHER

Meeting a teacher can impact us so powerfully that we're seized by a desire to change our lives and embrace the quest for mystical realization. When Rumi, a highly respected scholar, met his teacher, Shams of Tabriz, Shams took a book Rumi was writing about philosophy and threw it into a well. Rumi became an ecstatic devotee of Shams and abandoned all else, including scholarship and family responsibilities.

After finding a teacher, a person may begin to undergo a noticeable transformation and change of habits and lifestyle. One may experience deeper meditations or feel a blissful energy or an opening of the heart, the kindling of an inner fire. Rumi said:

> *What draws Friends together*
> *does not conform to Laws of Nature.*
> *Form doesn't know about spiritual closeness. . . .*
> *A hand shifts our birdcages around.*
> *Some are brought closer. Some move apart.*
> *Do not try to reason it out. Be conscious*
> *of who draws you and who not.*[22]

A common experience after meeting a teacher is for everything in our lives to fall apart. In the Koran it is said, "I am with those whose hearts are broken for My sake."[23] Old interests fall away, and old friendships become less compelling as a seeker turns toward the path of spiritual awakening. The disciples of the Indian guru Ramakrishna underwent a profound transformation as a result of their contact with their saintly master. Many were filled with a feverish devotion and burning for enlightenment. Many of them renounced worldly life soon after Ramakrishna's death and became monks committed to pursuing Self-realization.[24]

We accept a teacher who inspires us to attain the enlightened state through meditation, yoga, and other consciousness-enhancing practices. In deep meditation the mind quiets down and awareness turns inward, becoming self-reflective, becoming aware of itself as awareness. The diligent practitioner experiences the growth of tranquility, contentment, and wisdom. In Buddhist terms meditation reveals our *dharmakaya* nature—the truth body, the pure mind, like a clear mirror. In the Hindu tradition this is known as realization of the Self, or Atman, which is one with Brahman, the Absolute.

We need a teacher not only to teach us techniques and doctrine, but also to embody the enlightened state so that we can recognize it in ourselves and attain it. We may also choose a teacher to learn a particular method, such as meditation, yoga, or shamanic journeying. Even in cases where a teacher isn't a fully enlightened buddha, sage, or siddha, we could still grow by studying with that person for a period of time, as long as the teacher seems clear and balanced, and we feel confident that this person can guide us effectively through a stage of our transformation. It's enough that the teacher embodies a quality of freedom that we wish to emulate.

Teachers appear in many guises. When I met my hatha yoga teacher, Allan Bateman, in 1979, I found that he was quite an unusual person. Self-taught in yoga, Allan looked like a muscle-bound jock. He moved around his studio in a bikini, sang opera arias, and held in the palm of his hand an enormous cat named Godzilla, who lay on his back stretching out his paws in a magnificent backbend, in full spinal extension. Allan bragged modestly about this and that, and talked about his cattle ranch in upstate New York, where he had a herd of beefalo. I learned so much yoga from this man that I didn't care if he was some great pundit or intellectual. He wasn't trying to be saintly. He used his body in his teaching. He was very graceful and respectful and supportive of your intelligent movement. He was a free and sexy guy, very confident, and a positive male role model.

John Welwood notes, "Since genuine spiritual teachers come in many different shapes and forms, we'll no doubt fail if we try to spell out how a good guru should behave."[25] David Frawley echoes this view, saying, "Great gurus may be saints with impeccable characters and lifestyles. However, they may also look like madmen and refuse to conform to any social norms. Society may consider them scoundrels."[26] We shouldn't accept a teacher just because everybody else says this is an enlightened sage, nor should we immediately reject all teachers who don't conform to our expectations or conceptions of holiness. The teacher doesn't have to be famous, or an impoverished ascetic, or surrounded by eager disciples. What's important is that the teacher's personal example inspires us, the teacher's words speak to us deeply, and the teacher's presence affects us intensely. The guide shows us glimpses of the goal of the spiritual journey, as well as a path we can follow to reach this goal.

In this book we'll consider how spiritual teachers have been described in a number of world religions. From the insights derived from these traditions, we'll reach a number of conclusions:

1. Spiritual apprenticeship begins with a personal relationship with a teacher who tangibly affects our awareness and inspires us to practice a contemplative discipline in order to attain enlightenment.

2. Initiation connects the student to the influence of a spiritual lineage that transcends the individual teacher.

3. The student-teacher relationship involves the mutual meditation of the student and teacher on each other, and may entail the deliberate cultivation of a form of psychic merger or unity, which can have a transformative effect on the student.

4. The relationship may involve experiences of grace in which the teacher functions as a conduit for transmission of transpersonal forces.

THE GURU PRINCIPLE

In India the spiritual teacher has played a central role in the culture since ancient times. A Sanskrit verse reads "Gurubrahma gururvisnur gurudevo mahesvarah"—"The guru is Brahma and Vishnu, and Lord Shiva too." Like Brahma, the Creator, the guru creates a new life within us, molds our character, initiates us, and kindles the light of consciousness inside us. Like Vishnu, the preserver, the guru sustains and protects us over the course of time until we reach the final goal. And like Shiva, the destroyer, the guru destroys our limitations, our identification with the ego and the physical body, our fears, and our cravings, so that we can experience a state of freedom and expansiveness.

In the Indian yogic tradition of Kashmir Shaivism, the guru or enlightened teacher is a being who embodies and incarnates a cosmic principle called the *guru tattva,* the guru principle or the guru function. According to Shaivism God, or Shiva, has five activities or functions: The first three are the *creation* or manifestation of forms; the *sustenance* of those forms, and their *destruction.* Within the eternal cycle of creation-sustenance-destruction, Shiva engages in *concealment,* hiding so

Shiva with serpents, Tamil Nadu.

that only the transient show of forms is evident, not their eternal origin and source. The culminating function of Shiva is *revelation,* divine self-disclosure through the *bestowal of grace.* The guru tattva, the guru principle, is this power to bestow grace. The guru is one through whom the concealed power and splendor of Shiva, the Supreme Light, is revealed and unfolded within a human being. The word *guru* literally means "one who takes us from the dark to the light"; thus the guru transforms the night of ignorance into the dawn of inner vision and oneness. According to Hindu tantra scholar Paul Eduardo Muller-Ortega:

> The primary characteristics of the *guru* are the achieved condition of realization . . . and his capacity to transmit realization directly to his disciple. . . . The [Siva Sutra Vimarsini] states: "*Gurupayah,*" that is, "the *guru* is the way," and he is the only method that is needed. This *sutra* can be read in two different ways. In its first interpretation, "the *guru* is the method," it means that a willing attendance upon the teacher is the sole prerequisite for the achievement of liberation. On a surface level, this means that the *guru* will then make himself responsible for the training of the disciple, and will lead him through the various disciplines and practices that will secure for the disciple the realization of liberation. On a deeper level, however, the statement that the guru is the method reflects the idea that the *guru* represents the embodied wholeness that is the goal of the *sadhaka.* The face-to-face meeting of the disciple and the *guru* does not represent merely an encounter between two separate beings, one of whom happens to be enlightened and can thus aid and help the other in the search for enlightenment. Rather, by entering into a relationship of service the disciple places his finite awareness in direct confrontation with the enlightened consciousness of the *guru,* which is the same unbounded consciousness the disciple wishes to attain.[27]

We form a connection with a spiritual teacher in order to attain the teacher's state of freedom. The Hindu yogic traditions, and Shaivism in particular, view the guru not just as a person, but as a universal principle embodied by evolved teachers who awaken students to the inner light of consciousness. The teacher functions as a conduit through which the concealed power of Shiva, the all-pervading, ever-expanding Source, is revealed to us and directly experienced. We choose a teacher who vibrationally entrains us to the enlightened state and draws us toward it.

SPIRITUAL TEACHERS IN BUDDHISM

Buddhism strongly emphasizes the role of the guru. After Guatama Buddha attained enlightenment, he was surrounded by disciples who listened attentively to his teachings on suffering, impermanence, clinging and attachment, the nature of *samsara* (this world of birth, death, and eternal rebirth), and the path to enlightenment and nirvana. The Buddha explained how the human mind can create bondage or freedom, fear or confidence, misery or equanimity. He taught the preciousness of human birth, the importance of striving for enlightenment in this lifetime, and the Noble Eightfold Path that leads to enlightenment. According to Lama Govinda:

> The germ of Enlightenment is ever present in the world, and just as . . . Buddhas arose in past world-cycles, so Enlightened ones arise in our present world-cycle and will arise in future world cycles. . . . The historical features of Buddha Guatama, therefore, recede behind the general characteristics of Buddhahood, in which is manifested the eternal or ever-present reality of the potential Enlightenment-consciousness of the human mind. . . . The Buddha, who is worshipped, is not the historical personality of the man, Siddhartha Guatama, but the embodiment of the divine qualities, which are latent in every human being. Therefore, the Buddhas and Bodhisattvas are . . . the prototypes of those states of highest knowledge, wisdom, and harmony which have been realized in humanity and will ever have to be realized again and again.[28]

Countless beings have followed the path shown by the Buddha and found enlightenment. Some of them, known as *bodhisattvas,* delay their own final liberation to dedicate themselves to service and relieving suffering; and some of these, such as Avalokitesvara and Tara, can be invoked and supplicated by aspirants to enlightenment. As Buddhism evolved in Tibet, accomplished yogis such as Marpa, Nāropa, Milarepa, and Padmasambhava achieved buddhahood through various meditations, visualizations, mantra, and energy practices. In some lineages practitioners meditate on these beings as symbols of enlightenment. But Buddhism has always emphasized the relationship between a student and a living, embodied spiritual teacher. Buddhism also cultivates the attitude that buddha nature is present in all beings, and in the many teachings life gives us. Even our enemies are our teachers because they teach us patience and compassion. Yet a teacher's guidance is necessary to guide us through the fires of purification and transformation; we need a qualified lama, *roshi, bhikkhu,* or *bhikkhuni.* The teacher inspires the student to develop *bodhicitta,* the intention to develop a clear mind and great compassion and to strive for enlightenment for the benefit of all sentient beings.

In Tibetan Buddhism the lama serves as preceptor, instructor in Buddhist doctrine, officiant at rituals and initiations, and the focus of devotional practices. Lamas are conduits for blessings through their *sadhanas,* ceremonies, and empowerments, which feature loud horns and vibrant chanting of mantras that raise the energy. The lama becomes a vehicle for powerful transmission of energies beyond the ego, a rain or stream of blessings, a sense of heightened spaciousness and luminosity. I once saw the Sixteenth Gyalwa Karmapa give the Black Hat ceremony, wherein the lama becomes the instrument of intense transpersonal forces. Tibetan Buddhist initiates invoke and visualize the presence of the lama though the practice of guru yoga, which we'll discuss later.

It's not just the teacher or the Buddha to whom one becomes committed. It's also the dharma teachings that can be followed by anyone seeking peace and harmony. These teachings illuminate impermanence, a fact of life that affects every being, causing suffering. Buddhism emphasizes the cultivation of tranquillity, equanimity, mindfulness, nongrasping, and opening of the meditator to *sunyata,* the space of emptiness, openness, spaciousness beyond the ego, wherein one perceives a union of form and emptiness. Through its doctrine of dependent origination, Buddhism asks us to consider our interdependence, the effects of karma, and the effects our actions have on others, and with this awareness to strive to create a more enlightened world.

The practices of Buddhism have produced many enlightened beings, including beautiful teachers such as Thich Nhat Hanh. I once heard Thich give this talk:

> Breathe into sorrow, regret, fear about the future. Say to yourself, *I have arrived. I am home.* This is our practice. Mindful breathing, mindful waking. Learn to live deeply each moment of daily life. I have arrived in the here and now. Chew your food with happiness and freedom. A piece of bread is a wonder of life. The piece of bread is there for you; you need to be there for it. When you brush your teeth, don't be carried away by your projects, thinking, and worries. Don't be a slave of the past, the future. Rest. Do nothing. Learn how to be here without doing anything. At Plum Village we have "lazy day," where we have no schedule. The practice is to not be busy. Enjoy your breathing, enjoy the fact that you are alive.

In Buddhism the inspiring presence of a teacher inspires us to undertake an arduous process of self-observation, moral training, and meditative discipline. The guru isn't a magical savior whose bestowal of grace will liberate us. The teacher points the way, but we have to practice, to follow our breath, to chew our food mindfully and walk mindfully. And to accelerate the process of seeking enlightenment, we may wish to practice more intensive meditation in a retreat setting. The various Buddhist practice lineages all recommend that practitioners meditate with great focus and energy to achieve a clear mind. Here the presence of an experienced teacher is crucial because practitioners typically go through periods of exhaustion, despair, physical discomfort, and emotional upset. This process has been described at length in the excellent writings of Jack Kornfield, Joseph Goldstein, Ram Dass, Daniel Goleman, Sylvia Boorstein, Donald Rothberg, John Welwood, Mark Epstein, Pema Chödrön, Lama Surya Das, Lama Ole Nydahl, and other Buddhist luminaries.

A fascinating account of somebody who went for broke in a quest for the peaks of meditation is found in Eric Lerner's book *Journey of Insight Meditation.* Lerner describes how several Theravadin Buddhist teachers guided him through harrowing ordeals during extended *vipassana* meditation retreats in India, Burma, and Ceylon.[29] Lerner experienced stages of mental obsession and fixation and physical and emotional exhaustion, and was often overwhelmed by despair, sadness, overpowering memories, anxiety, and fears of the future. On several occasions he became so mentally and emotionally unbalanced that he feared he was verging on insanity. He describes his meditative journey as an ego-wrenching experience, a personal holocaust, a process of watching himself unravel while observing an unceasing stream of sensations, perceptions, and thoughts, experiencing torturous inner doubts. His teachers taught him to witness, examine, and gain insight into each micromoment of physical pain, fear, and emotional neediness. He experienced desperate clinging—to the past, to people, to ideas about the future. There were periods when he became completely unglued. Lerner reached a critical point in his practice when he experienced an agonizing knot in his spinal column the size of grapefruit, which grew more and more intense over long days of sitting meditation, causing extreme pain and discomfort. He became physically ill and resolved to give up meditation forever. His teacher instructed him to mentally move his awareness into this energetic block instead of running away from it, and to observe its impermanent, constantly changing nature. When he worked through the physical pain and his tendency to recoil from pain, and as he developed mindful awareness of the mental states that gave rise to the unpleasant sensations, the knot disappeared.

On several occasions Lerner had glimpses of enlightenment while meditating on retreat. He had visions, raptures, and experiences of expanded awareness that led him to believe he was on the verge of nirvana. However, when he reported these experiences to his teacher, she reprimanded him for becoming distracted by the snares of blissful trance states and losing sight of the goal of enlightenment, which is the awareness of *anicca,* impermanence. He was getting carried away; there was too much ego and drama in his high mystical experiences. This teacher took charge of his practice and set him on a path of simplicity in following his breath and being in the bare nakedness of this moment. This teacher's assistance kept him on the right path at a time when he was gripped by the illusion that he'd reached enlightenment. Lerner's book vividly portrays the ordeals of an aspirant during a period of courageous effort in intensive spiritual training.

In Japanese Zen Buddhism a relationship with a spiritual teacher, or *roshi,* is considered a foundation of the path.

> In the person of a genuine roshi, able to expound the Buddha's Dharma with a conviction born of his own profound experience of truth, is to be found the embodiment of Zen's wisdom and authority. Such a roshi is a guide and teacher whose spirit-heart-mind is identical with that of all Buddhas and patriarchs, separated though they may be by centuries in time. . . . Zen, as a transmission from mind to mind, cherishes pulsating, living truth. . . . Like sound imprisoned in a record or tape, needing electrical energy and certain devices to reproduce it, so the Heart-mind of the Buddha, entombed in the sutras, needs a living force in the person of an enlightened roshi to re-create it.[30]

In Zen practice students meet regularly with their roshi to report their experiences in meditation and their progress in solving perplexing *koans,* paradoxical questions intended to short-circuit the rational mind and jolt the practitioner into a state of sudden enlightenment, called *kenshō* or *satori.* A roshi rouses the assembled to rigorous zazen meditation and meets privately with students for *dokusan,* an interview where the teacher examines the student's experiences in meditation and tests the student's understanding of the dharma. According to Roshi Philip Kapleau:

> Dokusan (individual instruction) . . . is the time allotted for bringing all problems pertaining to practice before the roshi in private. This tradition of individual teaching started with the honored Shakyamuni himself and has continued unbroken until today. . . . This "eyeball to eyeball" encounter with the roshi within the privacy of his inner chambers can be anything from an inspiring and wonderfully enriching experience, giving impetus and direction to his practice, to a fearful ordeal of mounting frustrations. . . . An accomplished roshi will not scruple to employ every device and strategem, not excluding jabs with his ubiquitous baton (*kotsu*), when he believes it will jar and rouse the student's mind from a state of dormant unawareness to the sudden realization of its true nature. . . . The teacher may repeatedly frustrate the student by summarily dismissing him, rebuking him for not solving a koan, or cracking the student with the baton while he is prostrating. . . . This strategy of placing the student in a desperate situation where he is relentlessly driven from the rear and vigorously repulsed in front often builds up pressures within him that lead to that inner explosion without which true awakening seldom occurs.[31]

This tradition of private meetings provides what is perhaps an ideal model for the relationship of teacher and student, where there is much personal contact and continuity of instruction. In contrast one may also come under the influence of spiritual teachers who are more remote figures, constantly surrounded by large throngs of students and devotees.

It is possible to experience transformation through attention and devotion to such teachers, as the teacher's charismatic presence or lucid public discourses are sometimes sufficient to answer our inner questions and resolve our doubts. We also learn to find answers from within ourselves, through meditation.

Nevertheless, a personal relationship with a teacher can be inspiring and uplifting for the aspirant. Even if the teacher has hundreds or thousands of devotees and disciples, there needs to be some setting in which we can communicate directly with the teacher. Contact with the enlightened consciousness of the guide inspires us to intensify our spiritual practices and helps us break through into deeper clarity. With a living teacher one has more opportunities for personal instruction and more prodding to fan the flames of purification. The teacher observes our progress on the path. Later, as we mature, it will be time to become more independent. But at certain stages, relying on a teacher aids the process of transformation.

It is a blessing and a triumph to find a teacher who offers a clear, convincing articulation of the truth, who describes the experience of enlightenment and the means to attain it. At this stage a spiritual seeker willingly affiliates with a teacher who demonstrates skill and compassion in guiding others in the practice of consciousness-enhancing disciplines and yogic lifestyles. Such a teacher demonstrates the ability to guide the inner journey.

EXERCISING DISCERNMENT

In choosing a guide, proceed with care. Take sufficient time to examine the teacher's character and note any internal changes or shift of consciousness you may feel as a result of contact with this person, which may prompt you to seek further contact and instruction.

The path of spiritual apprenticeship begins with discrimination in choosing a teacher. Let your feelings and intuition be your guide in determining whether a teacher has something important to offer you.

Of course, there's no guarantee your intuition won't mislead you. There are many cases of seekers who have been preyed on by magnetic, persuasive, but misguided people who exploit or hurt their followers. There's always some risk that comes with trusting someone in this way, but it's a risk that we accept, as all mystical traditions emphasize the importance of finding a teacher. This is a moment when we choose to proceed with openness and receptivity to the teacher's instruction or transmission. At this early stage it's not necessary to commit one's life to the teacher, to surrender fully. Self-giving, trust, and devotion may emerge in the course of time, as the teacher proves worthy and as our doubts are addressed.

At this stage we observe the teacher's character and personality in order to appraise whether this is someone we can admire and emulate. Ask yourself: How do I feel if the teacher is someone with notable idiosyncrasies? Do I feel any change of consciousness in this person's presence? Will the teacher listen to my questions and address these directly and lovingly? Is this person able to responsibly lead a community of students? Is the teacher a convincing embodiment of purity, serenity, and truth, someone who inspires me to develop my potential?

In approaching a teacher, assess whether you're subjected to any cultish dynamics and pressures. Will you be expected to go out on the streets to sell flowers or newspapers to raise money? Does the teacher demand that you sever all other ties with family and friends? Traditionally, willingness to renounce worldly ties and attachments is considered a necessary attribute of a sincere aspirant, yet in our era we seek a more integrated spirituality that can be pursued amidst complex relationships, family roles, and occupational challenges. Renunciation may develop spontaneously, but shouldn't be forced or demanded in the beginning.

Be sure to examine the teacher's other students. Do they look healthy and radiant or haggard and undernourished? Do they seem balanced and genuine or unbalanced and contrived? Pay attention to any vague discomfort you might feel in the presence of some teachers and their communities. These feelings could be a keen intuition that something is amiss and that this isn't a place where your growth will be furthered. Daniel Goleman has described the "early warning signs for the detection of spiritual blight":

> Taboo topics: Questions that can't be asked, doubts that can't be shared, misgivings that can't be voiced. For example, "Where does all the money go?" or "Does Yogi sleep with his secretary?" Spiritual Clones: In its minor form, stereotypic behavior, such as people who walk, talk, smoke, eat and dress just like their leader; in its more sinister form, psychological stereotyping, such as an entire group of people who manifest only a narrow range of feeling in any and all situations; always happy, or pious. . . . Groupthink: A party line that over-rides how people actually feel. "You've fallen, and Christ is the answer"; or "You're lost in samsara, and Buddha is the answer"; or "You're impure, and Shiva is the answer." The Elect: A shared delusion of grandeur that there is no Way but this one. The corollary: You're lost if you leave the group. No Graduates: Members are never weaned from the group. Assembly Lines: Everyone is treated identically, no matter what their differences. Loyalty Tests: Members are asked to prove loyalty to the group by doing something that violates their personal ethics; for example, setting up an organization that has a hidden agenda of recruiting others into the group, but publicly represents itself as a public service outfit. Duplicity: The group's public face misrepresents its true nature. Unifocal Understanding: A single world-view is used to explain anything and everything; alternate explanations are verboten. Humorlessness: No irreverence allowed.[32]

Then there's the question of the teacher's lineage. Who were this teacher's teachers? Or is the teacher self-taught and self-proclaimed? The latter, in itself, isn't always the sign of a charlatan, and there are certainly many examples of well-qualified teachers with the full authorization of great lineages who abuse their position as teachers. But be especially careful with teachers who say your evolution is solely dependent on them, that there is no other path to realization than to become their student. I'm mistrustful of teachers who make grandiose claims to have a mission or role of unique importance in the course of history. In forming an association with a spiritual guide, we should be aware of the tendency to place messianic hopes on teachers. To explore these issues, let's briefly examine the role of spiritual teachers in Judaism and compare two remarkable examples.

SPIRITUAL TEACHERS IN JUDAISM

In the Jewish tradition, rebbes (rabbis) are greatly respected and revered figures, guiding others on the path of moral action, righteousness, and commitment to biblical teachings and commandments. In contrast to Hinduism, where it's often said that an enlightened teacher merges with God and becomes divine, in Judaism it is believed that while a mystic may have a vision of God or angelic realms, it's not possible to ever attain actual union with God. Even the most enlightened teacher is always seen in human terms. Nevertheless, a teacher may be considered close to God and able to lead others toward God through his example and moral influence.

Medieval Hasidic Judaism featured the emergence of the *tzaddik,* "the righteous one," to whom great powers and healing abilities were often attributed. The tzaddik was a charismatic figure said to be in constant communion with God, a visionary possessing extraordinary powers who provided spiritual and prophetic leadership to his community.[33] Like the siddha guru in India, the Jewish tzaddik was viewed as an instrument for an influx of divine energy and vitality that streamed through him from God down to his contemporaries. Tzaddiks were holy men little concerned about formal religious services and scriptural study, and more interested in the living spirit of prayer, devotion, song, and community.

In Judaism the perception that a spiritual leader can play a redemptive role in the world has been filtered through two lenses that even to this day color our perceptions of teachers: messianism and apocalypticism. *Messianism* is the hope for the advent of a religious and political leader who will be the savior and liberator of the exiled Jewish people. The great spiritual leaders of ancient Israel were patriarchs and prophets who provided leadership in times of crisis and made prophecies regarding the future destiny of Israel: the hope for the reestablishment of the House of David, the future glory of an Israel returned to God, the beginning of an era of everlasting peace, and the turning of all nations toward the One God. The role of spiritual teachers in the Jewish tradition is interwoven with the collective hope for changes in social conditions. Thus, messianism is concerned with the collective historical destiny of the Jewish people, not with the attainment by individuals of special mystical knowledge achieved through states of inwardness.

But messianism isn't exclusively a feature of Judaism. It seems to be an intrinsic part of human psychology to look for an external savior who will liberate us. Every religion has the myth of the expected return of a universal teacher. Hinduism has Kalki, the next avatar of Vishnu. Buddhism has Maitreya, the future Buddha who is to appear on Earth. Christians await the return of Jesus. Shiite Muslims expect the return of Mahdi, the twelfth son from Ali, nephew of Mohammed. This expectancy of return is closely connected to the recurrent mythic theme of hope in the return of a paradise on Earth and the restoration of a once sacred world.

Messianism often appears in connection with *apocalypticism,* the belief in the imminent end of the world. According to Gershom Scholem, messianism is both "a content of religious faith . . . and also living, acute anticipation."[34] This apocalyptic expectancy is heightened during moments of communal suffering and desperation, in which people begin to believe that the end of the world is imminent.

Even today many people view spiritual teachers through the lens of messianic expectation, placing on them the burden of redeeming the entire world. We look to spiritual teachers not only to instruct us in contemplative techniques, but also to provide leadership for a community or social movement and to liberate us from the sufferings of history. This desire for leadership and salvation is often filled with the "living, acute anticipation" that Scholem notes. Some students or devotees fervently believe that their teacher has a uniquely important historical mission and is indeed the long-awaited savior of humanity. Some teachers also believe this about themselves.

A case in point from the history of Judaism is Sabbatai Sevi, the seventeenth-century "mystical messiah." Sevi was a complex figure— an ecstatic mystic with an illuminated gaze who also periodically fell into states of deep depression; he appears to have suffered from bipolar personality disorder. Born in August 1626, he began to live ascetically and study Kabbalah from youth, practicing frequent ritual baths, fasts, and mortifications. Often called a fool, a lunatic, and a madman, he exhibited recurring cycles of anguish and depression followed by manic euphoria, ecstasies, and illumination. In these latter phases his face would turn red and was said to "burn like fire" while he was in prayer or song.[35]

In 1648 agitation swept the Jewish community due to the mass murder of Jews in Poland. This crisis coincided with one of Sevi's phases of inner euphoria, during which he heard a voice proclaiming him the Savior of Israel. He began to act as if this were so and to proclaim that he was beyond the authority of rabbinic Judaism, subject to a higher law. Nobody paid any attention to him; people thought he was crazy. He had himself wedded to the Torah in a public ceremony. Rabbis flogged him and drove him out of town.

Then a man named Nathan had a vision and began announcing publicly that Sevi was the Messiah. Sevi denied it. Nathan spent weeks trying to convince Sevi of his messianic mission. In May 1665 Sevi went into a manic rapture and proclaimed himself "the anointed one," giving rise to an acute public frenzy and a flock of followers. He was later excommunicated and banished from the cities of Smyrna and Salonika and fled to Aleppo, where his following grew due to the feverish activity of Nathan, Sevi's prophet. Sevi's life reached a climax when he was captured by the Muslims, whereupon he converted to Islam, the ultimate apostasy for a Jew. His followers were left desolate and disillusioned. Many tried to interpret the secret logic of his bizarre actions through the doctrine of "the holiness of sin." Such a doctrine posed a grave threat to the rabbinic orthodoxy, which spared no effort to suppress the nascent movement. The Sabbatian movement thus ended in catastrophe for thousands of Sevi's followers, who desperately tried to explain his actions.

The story of Sabbatai Sevi is a classic example of how a teacher's psychological imbalance and delusions of grandeur, coupled with the messianic hopes of followers, can lead to devastating outcomes for disciples. Later I'll cite examples of contemporary false teachers who caused great harm to others.

The history of Judaism also informs us about spiritual teachers who have worked selflessly for the benefit of others and exercised a positive and uplifting influence. Consider the life of the Baal Shem Tov, an ecstatic wise man who taught a celebratory spirituality and whose movement revitalized the Jewish communities of Eastern Europe. The Baal Shem Tov was the original tzaddik. Whereas the Jewish tradition tends to be strongly intellectual, the Baal Shem Tov brought spirituality into the body, encouraging others to express the love of God and the spirit of joy through ecstatic songs, dancing, and renewal of the living spirit of religious community. The noted Jewish author and activist Elie Wiesel, in his book *Souls on Fire,* writes:

Historically speaking, the character barely emerges, his outlines blurred by contradictions. Nothing about him can be said with certainty. Those who claim to have known him, to have come close to him or loved him, seem incapable of referring to him in terms other than poetic. . . . [He was] a man who almost single-handedly opened the soul of his people to a new creativity, a creativity heretofore unexplored, of man come to grips with what crushes or lifts him toward infinity. The man who left his mark on so many survivors of so many massacres in Central and Eastern Europe . . . [t]he master who gave song to despairing communities managed to disappear without leaving . . . even a fragment of valid autobiographical material. Obsessed by infinity, he neglected history and let himself be carried by legend.[36]

Born either in 1698 or 1700, the Baal Shem lived his early life in obscurity as an impoverished innkeeper in the country. One day a "madwoman" told him, "I know who you are. . . . I know that you possess certain powers. I also know that you may not use them before the age of thirty six."[37] At age thirty-six, observers witnessed the Baal Shem flooded with light, thus launching his public work. He was said to be able to see into a person's soul and to respond to the unspoken thoughts of others. He exhibited an unusual, prolonged trembling, as if he was continuously aware of some fear- and awe-inducing presence.[38] He traveled constantly, appearing here and there, accosting strangers, making followers of them all. Generous and kind, he showed interest in the details of every person's life; every human being deserved his attention.

A man of contagious intensity, he changed all who approached him. The most mediocre of men vibrated at his contact; an encounter with him was the event of a lifetime. To have his gaze rest on you meant feeling his fire run through you. . . . He wished to remain accessible to all who came to him to share their worries, their anguish. . . . What he wanted was to end all waiting, personify all hope. If one believed his legend, he succeeded. He belonged to all.[39]

The Baal Shem loved peasants, ruffians, sinners, and drunkards, and brought hope to those who had no hope. The movement he spawned sustained communities through the devastation of exile, pogroms, and the Holocaust—despite the fact that he himself possessed no notable ancestors, no exalted social status, no official titles or influential friends, no material possessions, and no talmudic learning.

> He explained . . . that abstract erudition is not the sole vessel of truth or the sole path leading to saintliness. And that saintliness is not the only link between man and the eternity he carries inside him. Song is more precious than words, intention more important than formulas. . . . [W]hy despair? Why give up the fight? One tear, one prayer can change the course of events; one fragment of melody can contain all the joy in the world, and by letting it go free, influence fate. . . . When he died in 1760 . . . there remained in Central and Eastern Europe not a single Jewish town that was left unaffected. He had been the spark without which thousands of families would have succumbed to gloom and hopelessness— and the spark had fanned itself into a huge flame that tore into the darkness.[40]

The life of such a teacher confirms our belief that there are rare beings who can inspire and liberate the hearts of others, lifting them beyond suffering into joy. While there are false teachers who bring about their own downfall and bring disaster on their followers, there are also true teachers who serve humanity and leave an indelible mark on all they touch. When we meet a being aflame with the light of truth, we feel it in our bodies. In their presence our own souls are set on fire.

Spiritual apprenticeship begins with the recognition that we have found a trustworthy guide to show us a path to enlightenment. The kindness, peacefulness, and powerful intensity apparent in the teacher

A gentle guide accompanies us into the sanctuary of spiritual life.
Temple priest, Kanchipuram.

inspires us to meditate and experience refinement of consciousness
through a life of contemplation. The guide is the harbinger of spiritual awakening, becoming our model of greatness and the focus of our
reverent attention. Led forward by a courage that will be tested and
strengthened over time, we take a breath and step forward.

❧

Initiation

The Kindling of Spiritual Life

There is a trust between the murshid (master) and the mureed (disciple) which establishes a link between them. . . . The initiation is the outward sign of that link, a link which can only be maintained by the faith that a mureed has and by the confidence which the murshid returns in answer to that faith. Initiation by a spiritual teacher means both a trust given by the teacher to the pupil and a trust given by the pupil to the teacher.

HAZRAT INAYAT KHAN, *THE SACRED LINK*

In most traditions the student approaches a teacher to receive initiation, which is a specific introduction to a transformational technique, an investiture of grace, or an acknowledgment by the teacher that the student has been accepted for instruction. It may involve either a formal ceremony or a quiet, private exchange between teacher and student. It may involve instruction in meditation or prayer, a vow to serve the teacher, or a ceremonial initiation into a contemplative order.

Before the student is allowed to take initiation, there's often a preliminary period of preparation and purification, which may range from a few days or weeks to several years. It's by fulfilling these conditions without complaint that the student demonstrates genuine readiness. Teachers often put students through various trials to test their courage, resolute intention, and commitment to practice the teachings that will be given. Through these preliminary tests, the teacher examines the student to determine whether he or she is a suitable candidate for initiation. The student may be asked to refrain from consuming intoxicants, to avoid certain foods, or to observe celibacy for a certain period. One may also be asked to offer service to the teacher for some time prior to receiving initiation. Traditionally, an aspirant might spend several weeks, months, or years tending the teacher's fields or working in a barn shoveling cow manure or some similar laborious task prior to receiving initiation. The student may be asked to pay a fee or make a financial contribution to support the teacher's work. In Native American cultures, those seeking instruction from a medicine man or woman offer tobacco and blankets as payment. In these varying ways, the student proves genuine worth, sincerity, and persistence.

A practitioner of Transcendental Meditation (TM) gave this account:

I clearly remember my initiation into TM twenty-five years ago. I listened to the preliminary lectures closely and absorbed their meaning. I paid my fee. I was asked to avoid using alcohol or drugs for two weeks prior to the event. The day of my initiation I received the mantra and chanted prayers of thanks to the teachers of the TM tradition. My first meditation was peaceful and deep. It felt so calm I didn't want to come out of meditation. All through the day afterward I felt a soft glow throughout my body.

In some cases initiation is a relatively simple matter. The student may have a private meeting with the teacher in which instructions are given. In some traditions the teacher places his or her hands on the novice's head to bestow a blessing. Or it may involve a more elaborate rite of passage. One woman gave this account of her initiation:

> We were told to spend the two days before initiation observing silence, reflecting on what we were about to undertake. We were to be absorbed inward, to fix our minds on God, and to eat lightly. Then on the morning of the ceremony, we were each given a special robe to wear and we were asked to take off our own clothes and leave them by the banks of the river to signify our leaving behind of our old lives and former selves. We put on these beautiful sky blue robes, which were called robes of glory, representing our renewal and purity of spirit. We put on the robes and walked in a procession from the river into a lush forest, accompanied by drumbeats. Finally we were called one by one to come before the teacher. She wore a special velvet robe we had never seen before, and a silver necklace shaped like a coiled serpent; she looked very powerful. Quietly she spoke to each one of us, explaining our lineage and the importance of the practice she was now teaching us. She instructed me in meditation and prayers I was to offer every day. I was asked to not tell anyone about the specifics of these practices.

The initiate is often sworn to secrecy to preserve the sanctity of the experience and the customs surrounding it. Secrecy is a way of honoring the specialness of this experience, which is a sacred event, not a profane or everyday occurrence. It preserves the power of the initiation. To speak about our initiation experiences may dissipate their power. It may also expose us to the doubts and cynicism that others might display toward our experience. This can cause us either to devalue the experience or to feel anger toward others—which is not the purpose of receiving initiation. In other words speaking too soon or too openly about such experiences and divulging secret instructions creates a variety of mental and interpersonal distractions. It's better to keep silent and allow the initiation to work inside of us.

SUFI INITIATION

To explore this subject further, I'll describe the meaning of initiation among the Sufi mystics of Islam. In the Mevlevi order of Sufis, the novice first learns to perform various kitchen functions, learns to recite and interpret Rumi's *Mathnawi,* and learns the technique of the whirling dance, thus fulfilling a preparatory period of 1,001 days prior to formal initiation.

> After the [novice] had performed the three years of service he might be considered worthy of receiving the *khirqa,* the patched frock, "the badge of the aspirants of Sufism." The relation of the novice to the master is threefold: by the *khirqa,* by being instructed in the formula of *dhikr* (recollection), and by company, service, and education. In investing the murid with the patched frock, Sufism has preserved the old symbolism of garment: by donning a garment that has been worn, or even touched, by the blessed hands of a master, the disciple acquires some of the mystico-magical power of the sheikh. . . .
>
> During the initiation ceremony—a festive day in the dervish community—the adept had to pronounce the *bay'a,* the oath of allegiance, and was invested with the *khirqa,* the Sufi frock. An essential part of the ceremony consists of the novice's putting his hand into the sheikh's hand so that the *baraka* is properly transmitted. Another important act is the bestowing of the *taj,* the dervish cap.[1]

Initiation is often a joyous event, a celebration of connection to a lineage of awakened beings, an expression of gratitude for the blessings and instruction being offered, and an expression of hope that we can travel the mystic path toward its goal. Having made offerings of gifts or service to the teacher, we're ready to receive the gifts offered by the teacher as a symbol of initiation. The teacher may give a special blanket, a piece of clothing, a pair of sandals, or a cap—objects invested with the teacher's energy that become a continuing reminder of the teacher's blessings and inner psychic influence. Receiving a gift from the teacher as a mark of acceptance of the student is found in many traditions. The objects are empowered by the teacher's *shakti* or *baraka*. The one object I received from my teacher Swami Muktananda's hand was a shawl he gave me in 1978. I have worn that shawl while meditating for more than thirty-five years. To me it's more than a piece of cotton cloth; it's a reminder of his presence.

The real garment of initiation is a subtle but tangible blessing the disciple receives that he or she feels as a tingling or bliss in the crown of the head, an inner stillness, a descent of peace, exhiliration, or a feeling of love and connection with everything. This is the real event of initiation. An electricity is kindled, a sense of connection to Spirit, the Absolute. Something new comes alive and begins to grow within us—especially as we intensify our practices and experience an inner awakening that propels us into a new life. This is the interior event of which external initiation is the occasion and the symbol.

Sufi sage Pir Vilayat Inayat Khan has explained the deeper significance of initiation:

> What is the meaning of initiation given at the hands of a human being? The initiator is like a catalyst who sets in motion the forces that have been building up in that process of incubation. We find the same principle in alchemy: there is a process of transformation taking place, and it takes just that spark to trigger it off. . . . You cannot say the guru does it for you, but you can say that if you are in a state of readiness, that action upon you can really trigger off something that is on its way very intensely.[2]

THE SPIRITUAL POWER OF LINEAGE

The teacher is the catalyst we need to grow. Our intense desire for illumination makes us ready to catch a single spark of the awakened mind that sets the process of self-transformation on fire. This spark that awakens us is a gift, a blessing not just from the teacher, but from an unending lineage of awakened beings. In Sufism it is said that the student-initiate is linked, through the teacher, to the *silsila,* the chain of initiation and spiritual guidance. Thus the aspirant who becomes connected to a teacher also becomes connected to the teacher's teacher, to Mohammed, and to all the other great prophets, and ultimately to God.

The fact is that if an initiator is a genuine initiator, he is never alone. According to the tradition of the Sufis, the initiator who is always present behind any initiator is Khidr, the same being as Elijah. . . . The initiation links you up with the masters of that particular line through the whole hierarchy, . . . and in so doing it links you with all the masters of all the other religions. . . . A karmic connection is established, which means that from the moment Murshid gives you *bayat* (initiation) he feels responsible for you.

One looks for a guide who is suffiently in harmony with the hierarchy of masters to act as a go-between or even lift the consciousness of the pupil to the point where he is able to reach some measure of guidance directly. If such a master is authentic, he will refer to the one hierarchically above him (whether incarnated or not) for his briefing. This is the chain of transmission which reaches to the source of all initiation, the One beyond, of whom naught can be said. . . . Initiation is the reiteration of the covenant which was made at the birth of one's soul, the vow to proclaim the divine sovereignty. . . . According to the Zoroastrian Gathas, when we were still in the angelic state we vowed to incarnate upon earth in order that we might become channels for the transfiguration of the world, to insure the victory of light over darkness. Our struggle on earth is the enactment of this pledge. The bayat (initiation) is the renewal of the pledge we made in eternity. . . . One is linked . . . to the whole hierarchy of masters, saints, and prophets, who form the spiritual hierarchy of the government of the world, the embodiment of the master, the spirit of guidance.[3]

Fiery guardians of the lineage, from the temple at Srinageri.

Hindu and Buddhist traditions also emphasize a belief that the spiritual power and awakened consciousness of lineages of enlightened beings—many of them no longer physically alive—supports and guides sincere seekers of truth. Thus, as we receive initiation, we may wish to acknowledge and celebrate our connection to those who have preceded us on the path, their instructions to us, and the mysterious blessings and assistance that flows to us from the lineage of knowledge.

As Pir Vilayat asserts, the transmission of truth passes to us through an unending chain of illumined souls. The lineage of ancient Indian yoga descended from Shiva down to sages such as Matsyendranath, Goraknath, Patanjali, Narada, Shankara, Guadapada, and Ramanuja, and continues through the chain of instruction to contemporary practitioners. In Tibetan Buddhism there's a vast lineage of buddhas and bodhisattvas: from Shakyamuni Buddha to Lokeshvara, Tara, and Manjushri; to Padmasambhava, Atisha, and Tsongkhapa; to the great yogis Tilopa, Nāropa, Marpa, Milarepa, and Gampopa; and to the fourteen Dalai Lamas, the Karmapas, and other *tulkus,* or reincarnated teachers.

Often, in the course of initiation, one is asked to learn about the great practitioners of the teacher's lineage. At later stages some people come to realize the power of lineage when they experience guidance from their "grandparent gurus," that is, their teachers' teachers. One man reported:

After I had open-heart surgery, I felt the presence of Bhagwan Nityananda, my guru's guru, at my bedside. He left his body in 1961, but there he was with me. He rubbed my forehead and told me to meditate on the sound of *Om.* I felt completely peaceful. The apparition left me in a state of ecstasy that continued unabated throughout my period of recuperation. Now I feel a deeper reverence for my teacher but also for his entire lineage, because I could so clearly feel the greatness of his teacher.

A woman who had been initiated into techniques of meditation had a vision of a famous teacher of her lineage:

Several months after my initiation I was grappling with my desires for sex and beer and pot and I didn't feel like meditating anymore. I resisted it for weeks. One day I sat in front of my altar, on which sit the pictures of the gurus of my lineage. I prayed to them for assistance and guidance. I felt Swami R (my teacher's teacher) was there with me. He repeated my meditation instructions to me very slowly and softly. My third eye began to throb and I saw a brief flash of light. Then my mind became silent and I glided into a long, peaceful meditation. I feel that Swami R's spirit blessed me and helped me meditate. This experience definitely increased my desire to meditate more regularly.

This example illustrates that sometimes an aspirant receives initiation from a teacher who isn't in a physical body. Many Christians report visions and visitations of Christ. Hindus have visions of avatars and saints such as Krishna, Babaji, Shirdi Sai Baba, or Ramakrishna. A friend of mine described how Meher Baba once appeared to him and instructed him; it was as if he were physically in the room. In Islam there's a long tradition of initiation by the Prophet Mohammed or other saints and masters:

> A final possibility of initiation from a source other than a human master was through Khidr. Khidr, identified with the mysterious companion of Moses mentioned in Sura 18 [of the Koran], is the patron saint of travelers, the immortal who drank from the water of life. Sometimes the mystics would meet him on their journeys; he would inspire them, answer their questions, rescue them from danger, and, in special cases, invest them with the *khirqa,* which was accepted as valid in the tradition of Sufi initiation. Thus, they were connected immediately with the highest source of mystical inspiration.[4]

PROGRESSIVE INITIATIONS

In some traditions the student takes a series of initiations that mark the different stages of the student's understanding and commitment to the teachings. In Buddhism the first, most basic initiation is that of taking refuge, in which one takes refuge in the Buddha, the dharma (the teachings), and the sangha (the community of practitioners). This is followed by subsequent empowerments or initiations such as the bodhisattva vow or the Tibetan Vajrayana foundational or preliminary practices, called *ngöndro* (pronounced *noon-dro*). Later on further initiations are given depending on the student's personality and needs. Each initiation articulates another piece of the vast teachings of Buddhism and also introduces the student to a new mantra, prayer, visualization, or meditation practice. In Tibetan Buddhism initiation isn't just a single event; it's a process of gradual transmission to the student. Periodic empowerments revitalize the student's commitment to practice and awaken increasing determination to attain enlightenment. A student may also periodically reaffirm vows or commitments made during the original initiation.

Initiation marks a transition into a new condition or way of being. As in all effective rites of passage, its goal is to transform the initiate so that he or she will be deeply and permanently changed by the experience.

SHAKTIPAT INITIATION

In the Indian yogic traditions, the most transformative and auspicious initiation is called *shaktipat diksha*. According to Indologist and yoga scholar Georg Feuerstein, *diksha* is "a form of spiritual transmission by which the disciple's bodily, mental, and spiritual condition is changed through the adept's transference of spiritual energy."

> By means of initiation, which may occur informally or in a more ritual setting, the spiritual process is either awakened or magnified in the practitioner. It is always a direct empowerment, in which the teacher effects in his disciple a change of consciousness, a turnabout, or metanoia. It is a moment of conversion from ordinary worldliness to a hallowed life, which alters the initiate's state of being.[5]

In the Hindu tantric tradition, the supreme form of diksha, or transmission, is called *shaktipat,* which translates as "descent of the power." Feuerstein describes it as "the event and the experience of the descent of a powerful energy current into the body. . . . Shakti-pata can be inaugurated by the adept through a verbal command, his touch, his glance, or . . . even his mere presence."[6] Through shaktipat, the teacher awakens the aspirant's dormant kundalini energy, which begins to unfold and expand. This may occur rapidly in the case of a highly prepared aspirant, or more gradually in others. Shaktipat can be bestowed through the teacher's touch, gaze, or thought. It may occur spontaneously in a vision or a dream, or simply by being in the teacher's presence. The teacher's enlightened awareness and spiritual power begin to awaken and transform the aspirant.

The effects of shaktipat can be quite varied and are often dramatic. According to Swami Vishnu Tirth, the symptoms of an awakened kundalini include involuntary bodily movements, trembling, shaking, laughing, weeping, states of intoxication and bliss, involuntary retention of the breath (*kumbhaka*), spontaneous bhastrika pranayama (deep, rapid inhalation and exhalation, a cleansing and stimulating form of pranayama), speaking in strange and unknown languages, frightening or blissful visions, smelling inexplicable aromas, currents of energy rising up the spine, spontaneously assuming yogic postures or making animal sounds, vibrations in the chakras (energy centers), and experiences in which the mind stops and plunges into an ocean of bliss.[7]

A woman named Dorothy reported this shaktipat experience:

I was sitting there listening to his lecture when his eyes fell on me. They were dark and intense and open wide. The next thing I knew, I felt this pain at the base of my spine. Then I felt something explode inside me, and all this energy started rushing up my spine. My body began to move violently. Soon my head started rotating very fast. Later my eyeballs began to spin and to look upward into the crown of my head. I felt like I was moving up into higher centers of my brain. I started hyperventilating and then I don't know what happened but I just disappeared. I sat there meditating for over two hours. Later I learned that yogis call this state *nirvikalpa samadhi,* which means meditative absorption without form.

In some yogic schools, shaktipat is considered the key to spiritual liberation because it makes it possible to proceed much more rapidly toward awakening. Shaktipat can give us an immediate experience of the goal of the spiritual path, a taste of enlightenment. This increases our enthusiasm for the inner quest and increases our faith in the teacher who bestows this transmission. Shaktipat may even precede our consciously choosing a teacher. Indeed, one might not be ready to accept a teacher until after experiencing this initiation, which provides convincing evidence of the teacher's stature and transformative power.

Receiving shaktipat can be problematic for some people who aren't psychologically balanced. Awakening powerful inner energies can stimulate underlying emotional problems and mental disorders, bringing these tendencies rapidly to the surface. That's why anyone with an active kundalini should ideally remain under a teacher's guidance during periods of active energetic awakening. This is also a reason why some teachers believe that shaktipat is not advisable. Consider this brief discussion with the Indian guru H. W. L. Poonja, also known as Papaji:

> I have had shaktipat from a Guru and it made me feel very quiet and stoned, as if I just smoked three chillums.
>
> So why go to a guru when you can have some hash for one rupee behind the Gandhi ashram in Hazrat Ganj? This high will stay for three hours and then you can have more. In this same way shaktipat of power without knowledge of Truth will turn the guru-disciple relationship into dealer-addict dependence. Don't cultivate a habit which is dependent on anything. You have nothing to do and you will not get anything. Here there is no transmission or shaktipat but all that happens is within you. I don't transmit anything. I don't give shaktipat. All that I do is remove your dependence on anything else. . . . Just remove your dependence on God and on methods and everyone else and It will shine and reveal itself without any method. Don't depend on gurus.[8]

These provisos aside, shaktipat can be a powerful catalyst for inner transformation for the spiritual aspirant. In shaktipat initiation the awak-

If the gift of shaktipat is received and well integrated, this transmission matures in the practitioner who reaches the inner pinnacle of meditation and evolves into a citadel of divine embodied consciousness. Brihadeeswara Temple, Tanjore.

ened consciousness of the teacher is transmitted to the student, offering an immediate connection to the enlightened state. The guru gives us a jolt that assists and uplifts us, showing us our true potential. The ecstatic, expansive, blissful experiences that follow shaktipat can ignite a fire of sadhana and an urge to transform the self, to develop the strength of body, mind, and character needed if we are to be worthy receptacles for this bestowal of grace. This is the ongoing work of discipleship. After shaktipat initiation, the awakening kundalini energy subtly evolves the student from within. Shaktipat is the planting of a seed within us. If properly watered and tended through devotion and meditation, in the course of time it flowers into the tree of spiritual attainment.

MY INITIATION

The occasion of one's initiation is a moment to remember with love and gratitude. After my teacher left New York, I felt drawn to spend more time with him, and I resolved to visit him again soon. In the summer of 1975, when I was seventeen, Muktananda was to conduct a retreat in Arcata, California. To be able to attend, I needed to pay the registration fee and buy a plane ticket. I bused dishes in a restaurant for several months to earn the money. Right before I flew out to California, I learned that Baba had been very ill, and he missed the first several weeks of the retreat while he recuperated in the hospital. For many of us present it was a test of faith to remain there despite his physical absence. I even thought about asking for a refund and leaving. He didn't arrive until two days before I was scheduled to fly home to the East Coast to begin my first year of college. I came to California despite the strong disapproval of my parents, who were horrified as they watched me pursue this Indian swami, whom they feared was possibly a dangerous cult leader. And some of my friends had told me that my plans for summer vacation sounded very strange. So it was agonizing waiting around for several weeks to see if he was going to actually show up. At times I became distressed, thinking that perhaps I'd made a big mistake spending all this money and traveling such a distance. I worried that I wouldn't receive the transmission that had motivated my journey. I was afraid that I'd return home without receiving shaktipat. This turned out to be one of those situations I'd read about where the seeker has to work really hard or overcome some obstacle to be able to come into the presence of a great being, and then when it finally happens, it is better than the seeker ever could have imagined.

The morning before I was scheduled to depart, I was called before Muktananda's throne by his secretary, Arjuna (now known as Master Charles Cannon). Muktananda pulled my hair to draw me close to him. He tapped on my glasses, indicating that I should remove them. He grabbed me by the nose, right between the eyes. With the palm of his hand he slapped my forehead, then pounded me hard on the top of my head four or five times. He ran his hand up and down my spine. He pulled me next to him, practically into his lap, looked into my eyes, and repeated "Guru Om Guru Om Guru Om Guru Om Guru Om Guru Om." His eyes were bright and powerful. I repeated the mantra back to him. Then he told me to sit next to him with my eyes closed. While I sat beside him I felt as if I were sitting next to a furnace; he emanated intense heat and palpable energy. After meditating next to him for about fifteen minutes, he told me to return to my seat. I walked through the crowd of devotees, giddy and wobbly-legged and completely spaced out.

I was expecting something really intense to happen. After receiving shaktipat, some people begin to sway, tremble, or burst into tears; others have visions of saints or distant places, or quaking energies of kundalini. For me there were no thunderbolts. What I felt was a soft glow in the top of my head and a soft electrical current running through my spinal column.

The next day I flew back to New York. My father, whom I love dearly, was grouchy when I got into the car at the airport. He didn't want to hear anything about the retreat; he only wanted to know that I was okay and ready for school. Later my father revealed to me how upset he was that I'd turned myself over to this man from India. He felt I'd rejected him and it hurt him deeply. Perhaps some of my father's pain would have been alleviated if I had been able to explain to him that it was an ageless tradition in India for a young man or woman to seek out the guidance of a guru and to seek instruction. It would take twenty years before I was finally able to explain that to him so he finally understood. At age seventeen I experienced a strong tension of forces as I struggled to break away from my father for the summer so I could be in the company of this intense yogi. And I was leaving for college and it was time to begin classes. Now, having made some effort and overcoming some logistical obstacles to receive initiation, I felt an intense urge to meditate and follow a yogic life path.

STAGES OF INITIATION AND DISCIPLESHIP

At this point it will be helpful to gain an overview of the unfoldment that occurs as a result of initiation. In his book *The Path of Initiation,* Sufi master Hazrat Inayat Khan details the process that begins when the student finds a guide on the path.[9] The student's faith is central, and even if the teacher proves to be false or not fully enlightened, the student's sincerity of purpose will itself be sufficient to lead to spiritual advancement. The student must then go through various tests, which are often confusing. The teacher tests the student's faith, sincerity, and patience by doing things that appear strange, bizarre, coldhearted, meaningless, or unjust. Inayat Khan contends that only students who endure the stage of testing will reach the next stage, in which they receive knowledge attentively, meditate on it patiently, and assimilate it fully.

According to Inayat Khan, the external teacher's primary role occurs relatively early in the process of spiritual unfoldment and will soon end. The seeker still has a long road to walk.

> Several initiations may be given to the pupil whom the teacher has taken in hand, but his progress depends upon the pupil himself. . . . There is another kind of initiation which comes afterward, and this initiation is also an unfoldment of the Soul. It comes as an after-effect of the initiation that one had from the teacher. It comes as a kind of expansion of consciousness.[10]

In the next stage of discipleship, the seeker is initiated by his or her own ideal, the ideal of his or her imagination and highest aspirations. But Inayat Khan emphasizes that the student must strive to become the embodiment of this ideal. As he puts it, "The savior will not save him." The student who has reached this stage begins "to radiate his initiator who is within him as his ideal."[11] Discipleship becomes an interior process of dedication to spiritual practice and the refinement of one's own consciousness and character, rather than focusing primarily on devotion to the teacher.

One begins to discover the teacher as a living entity within oneself, present at all times, especially in times of trouble and difficulty. The subtle link between teacher and apprentice grows stronger and is discovered in a variety of life situations.

Finally, Inayat Khan says, the disciple undergoes the initiation in God. The student "rises above the ideal he has made, to that perfect ideal which is beyond the human personality, which is the perfect Being. . . . One sees no other than God."[12] The student now communicates with God, who becomes to the initiate a living presence. Discipleship or spiritual life isn't just a matter of belief in God or service to a human teacher. It's a process through which we're actually transformed, assimilating that knowledge and power felt in the presence of the guide, until we're one day raised to the same state of exaltation and freedom.

> No one can give spiritual knowledge to another, for this is something which is within every heart. What the teacher can do is to kindle the light which is hidden in the heart of the disciple. . . . The work of the teacher is most subtle. It is like that of a jeweller who has to melt the gold first in order to make an ornament out of it. . . . When the pupil has received the initiations that the teacher has to give, then the teacher's task is over, and he sends him on. The teacher does not hold the pupil indefinitely; he has his part to perform during the journey on the path, but then comes the inner initiation. This comes to the disciple who has become meditative.[13]

🌿

External initiation received from the teacher activates an internal process of awakening. The aspirant's priorities and lifestyle change, becoming focused on attainment of Self-knowledge—the knowledge of the heart as a temple in which a living Spirit dwells and unfolds. Initiation is like the sounding of a gong that resonates for weeks, months, years, even decades, until the student's whole life has been transformed.

❧

Discipleship

Absorbing Instruction and
Developing a Spiritual Practice

Look with unswerving faith and love
At the Jewel of a Guru:
Drink the pure water of instruction.
THE LIFE AND TEACHING OF NĀROPA

Spiritual apprenticeship is based on the aspirant's desire to associate with a person who has traversed the mystic way, who has achieved some degree of illumination (if not complete enlightenment) and has the skills and motivation to guide students on the path. Having made the effort to approach a teacher and receive initiation, now the student strives to assimilate the teacher's message and transformative influence, building a life that's nourished by the teacher's inspiration. This may entail some heroic effort to find a way to be in the teacher's presence.

The commitment to discipleship is an outgrowth of encounters that demonstrate a teacher's wisdom and evoke respect, gratitude, devotion, and a desire to receive instruction. The student becomes a follower of the teacher's way, accepting the teacher's authority, inviting the teacher's influence. In some cases a single encounter with an enlightened being leads to an awakening. The Indian poet-saint Kabir is an example of this. Kabir sought the blessing of the great Hindu guru Ramananda, but feared he'd be rejected because he was a Muslim and the adopted son of a weaver. Kabir hid under the steps at the River Ganges, where Ramananda used to bathe. Stepping on Kabir's head, the startled guru spontaneously uttered the name of Ram. Kabir felt that Ramananda had initiated him into the mantra and adopted it as his own, and he held a firm conviction that the guru's foot touching his head for a moment had tangibly transferred his shakti. That single encounter was enough to liberate Kabir, who became drunk with devotion.[1]

In other cases, such as that of the Tibetan yogi Milarepa,[2] the disciple engages in extended study and service to the teacher. Others become devoted students of teachers who are no longer physically alive. Any of these paths may serve us. Regardless of the form it takes, the relationship is sought and chosen by the student who desires to attain a state of pure consciousness, to awaken from the sleep of ignorance into the dawn of truth. At certain times prior goals may pale into insignificance as we feel a burning desire for transformation in the teacher's company.

According to Georg Feuerstein, the aspirant to enlightenment who approaches a teacher begins as a student inspired by the teacher's presence and discourses, but is not yet seriously engaged in spiritual practice, still wavering in commitment and often pulled by worldly desires and interests. Gradually, the student advances to the stage of the disciple, more aware of the subtle, nonphysical, psychospiritual link to the teacher and willing to honor and cultivate this link. Finally, the aspirant reaches the stage of the devotee, in which the teacher is experienced as a spiritual reality rather than as a human personality, giving rise to a devotional attitude toward the teacher.[3]

For some discipleship means performing direct service to the teacher or living in the teacher's community, ashram, or monastery. For others it means practicing meditative, yogic, or other contemplative techniques, following vows or precepts, and carrying the spirit of the teachings into daily life. Some students accept a teacher they've never met on the physical plane and pursue discipleship by meditating on the teacher's words or pictures and through inner remembrance. At different times we may live all of these paths. This is a stage when we willingly embrace a reverent or devotional relationship with a spiritual teacher who is a positive guiding influence. The many emotional and interpersonal issues that arise in student-teacher relationships will be memorable features of this journey.

As the relationship unfolds, a warm devotion between teacher and student grows. At its core this is a relationship of love—not a romance, but a mutual acknowledgment. The teacher's presence and energy transmission can elicit in the student a natural gratitude and willingness to accept the teacher's discipline and authority. Clare, a student of a Zen teacher for over twelve years, reports, "His sanity and clarity of mind are a beacon for me. He teaches me how to live with dignity, simplicity, and humor. I'll always honor him for that."

Beth, a student of a teacher with an international following, says, "My guru has shown me my own divine essence. For me, he's the final destination, my deity, my Beloved. There's nothing else for me to accomplish beyond this relationship. I feel most fulfilled just being his devotee."

Such statements illustrate a pure state of devotion. The relationship with a teacher who provides the guidance needed for spiritual illumination can become all-important, the fulcrum on which the student's entire life is balanced. One woman describes her experience: "In the ashram, the daily pattern of our lives was that when we got up in the morning we raised prayers to Guruji, meditated in front of his pictures, and got totally absorbed in the chanting. In the evening we waved lights to his picture just as if he were present with us in the room and the atmosphere became charged with an atmosphere of love and devotion. Our lives were completely those of devotees."

A young man named Ted offers, "I was grateful to receive such lucid instruction in Buddhist doctrines, and I was so inspired by the lama's presence that there was no way I wasn't going to practice a lot. I wanted to follow his example, to wake up and become an enlightened buddha like him."

For some people recognizing the cord of love linking them to a teacher is the beginning of a lifelong commitment. They may follow the spiritual mentor's teachings toward the goal of enlightenment without experiencing any significant disturbance in the relationship; for them the teacher is a trusted companion on the spiritual path. For example, I've talked to members of the Mount Madonna community, who have lived for decades with their guru, Baba Hari Dass. Some of them grew up with him and are now growing old with him. Hari Dass is a yogi who observes silence, a serene but powerful being whose example inspires students to follow a yogic way of life. He is a guru and a gentle spiritual friend.

In this chapter I describe how we develop an ongoing relationship with a teacher, listen to instruction, receive individualized guidance, embark upon a new yogic or meditative practice, and seek out opportunities to meet the teacher in person to receive guidance and to encounter and carefully observe someone radiating a clear, enlightened way of being. In India this is known as receiving a teacher's darshan. Regular visits to the teacher are very helpful at this stage. This in itself requires effort and sacrifices. By choosing to spend time in the teacher's company we prioritize the spiritual quest and our desire for enlightenment.

THE PHASE OF INSTRUCTION

Part of the teacher's role is to explain things to us, introducing us to a doctrine or spiritual teaching. Each aspirant needs clarification of some details of meditation practice or spiritual philosophy, or of the dynamics of the mind. Providing these explanations may or may not be the teacher's strong suit. Some teachers hardly speak at all. Others chat with students informally or answer simple questions but rarely give elaborate discourses. Others lecture skillfully. At this stage a student attends darshan or study groups or contemplates written texts and sacred scriptures.

In the teacher's company, we can have our questions answered directly so that we understand how to work with ourselves to evolve spiritually. The teacher's skillful instruction alleviates doubts and deepens our confidence in the path we're following. We start to feel the uplifting effects of purifying our bodies, our minds, and our atmosphere.

ESTABLISHING A SPIRITUAL PRACTICE

The stage of discipleship is the time to establish a discipline that leads to a state of freedom. For example, this might entail practicing meditation, prayer, yoga asanas and pranayama, mantras, or visualizations, following the breath, cultivating mental concentration and tranquility, and meeting challenges with calm equanimity. The practices of meditation, yoga, and Self-inquiry lead directly to a state of clear and peaceful awareness.

At first we learn a set of methods or techniques within one particular tradition. Later most people develop a regimen of their own that blends elements of several disciplines or traditions. For example, my own practice combines meditation, hatha yoga, dreamwork, astrology, and music. What's most important is to find a sadhana that's in alignment with our own personalities and inclinations. I'm not inclined to do many devotional practices, but I'm quite drawn to the fortifying rigors of hatha yoga. We must find our own way.

This stage also involves learning what conditions are most conducive to practice. I like to practice hatha yoga before sunrise and meditation near sunset. I especially enjoy practicing yoga while listening to music; I meditate while soaking in baths and hot springs or sitting somewhere quietly under a tree. Gardening is another activity that is conducive to breath meditation, mindful awareness, japa yoga (silent mantra repetition), and quiet remembrance of teachings. I know other people who get the most out of formal practices in front of an altar.

Certain sound and spatial environments support and enhance a vibrant inner life, and creating these conditions becomes an enjoyable part of the new self-discipline. It's also important to identify which influences in our lifestyle, workplace, and household disturb our peace of mind and create obstacles and distraction, hindering meditation. In the home and workplace, we can utilize the presence of beauty and the power of music, tone, and silence to create a meditative atmosphere.

During the stage of discipleship we practice a yoga or discipline that works for us so that we feel radiant and joyous. One person may enjoy sitting zazen or in contemplative prayer, while others practice martial arts or ecstatic dancing or Sufi *zhikr* (remembrance of God). Hazrat Inayat Khan said, "The way you choose is the way for you."[4] When you find the right practice or combination of practices, you will know it because it will feel good; it will feel integrative. It will take you to a place you want to return to again and again, even if it involves some arduous effort.

OBSTACLES AND PITFALLS

Many obstacles arise as we attempt to establish a spiritual discipline. Our busy lifestyles can make if difficult to find time to practice. There are innumerable distractions, and we may feel uncertain of whether we can sit quietly and meditate when we have responsibilities and there are so many entertaining and stimulating movies and websites and TV shows that are grabbing for our attention. Or when we do practice, sometimes we resist and get bored. Addictions, excessive drinking, fixations, and frustration about unfulfilled desires can all divert us from sadhana. We have to make the decision that we'll feel better if we make a little space in our life to sit on a cushion, take a few breaths, and get more deeply centered. This is a stage when we rouse the will to overcome all obstacles so that we can pursue our practices.

One potential pitfall at this stage of establishing a spiritual discipline or yogic lifestyle is a feeling of superiority over others. We may even become fanatical or try to convert others to our path. Our friends, neighbors, and family members might not share our excitement about our fascinating teacher or lineage, and this can cause feelings of alienation.

Another pitfall is imbalance, for example, becoming too intense or overzealous about our spiritual practices. A man named Roger gave this account:

> My teacher had spoken a lot about the importance of physical purification, and I became totally obsessive about fasting and detoxing. I'd go on weeklong fasts on water and do all kinds of bizarre enemas, like prune juice, and drinking all this psyllium seed. I was meditating for hours every day and hardly sleeping. At one point I went to see my parents for a month and I found a place where I could go get colonics. So for that month I was working as a grill cook in a greasy Italian restaurant cooking veal cattiotore while I was fasting and doing a monthlong program of daily colonics while visiting my parents. It was totally out of hand. My parents were so glad when I left! Finally, when I went back home and saw my teacher, he said, "You're taking all of this a little too far, aren't you?" I saw that I'd gotten way out of balance with all the practices I was doing. It just wasn't appropriate to my environment.

LEARNING ONE THING WELL

In discipleship one central task is to master specific instructions or techniques that the teacher imparts. Part of the teacher's role is to introduce us to some basic practices that we can do consistently. In 1979 my hatha yoga teacher, Allan Bateman, taught me a series of sixteen yoga postures, three breathing exercises, and relaxation. As I explored other systems of yoga over the years, I noticed that many of them were more complex and exhaustive than Allan's method. I was always curious to learn new exercises, so I once asked Allan to teach me new poses and yogic techniques. To my surprise he declined, asking, "Have you mastered everything I've shown you?" I had to admit that I hadn't and that I could still learn to do the basic poses with greater effortlessness and precision. Thus, over the years I keep going back to the basics, rather than worrying about whether I've achieved the most advanced and difficult poses. The basic practices are always abundantly nourishing. Periodically I branch out and learn other methods and new postures, but I always come back to the sequence I learned from Allan. This discipline has been deeply transformative for me over a period of decades.

I believe it's better to find one method and to work with it deeply rather than learning many different techniques that we'll never practice on a regular basis. Such dilettantism is useless window-shopping. Some spiritual teachers emphasize methods that are too complicated, too demanding, and too time consuming for the average person to undertake regularly. A wise teacher passes on a manageable, useable set of methods that students can take home and practice consistently.

Developing a daily practice tends to bring about immediate changes, such as reducing one's intake of cigarettes, alcohol or drugs; greater care and refinement of diet; and voluntarily waking up early to stretch, breathe, chant, and meditate, to rouse the fires of conscious life. These changes usually result in peace and mindfulness as well as gratitude and expansion of consciousness.

MY EARLY EXPERIENCES OF MEDITATION

For several years I spent summers with my teacher, Swami Muktananda, and then practiced meditation while studying and working.

After the Arcata retreat I had flown home to the East Coast and begun my freshman year at Wesleyan University in Connecticut. I installed myself in my dormitory room and unpacked my yoga books, a meditation blanket, and pictures of my teacher, creating a makeshift altar inside a small closet that would serve as my yogi's cave. This was where my meditative journey was launched. I spent hours meditating in this small, consecrated space, especially in the early morning between four and six a.m., before anyone else was awake. I put my legs into the lotus position and turned deeply inward, sometimes entering a quiet, breathless samadhi. For a while I had a recurrence of an intense state of consciousness I remembered from childhood: I felt myself entering a nonphysical realm of pure geometry and magnetically charged archetypal forms, where I perceived conical, cylindrical, and pyramidal shapes that had a palpable density and energy mass. I came out of these meditations in a somewhat spacy mood, feeling as if I'd just visited another world. I reflected on the fact that I had already perceived this inner world when I was four or five years old.

At that time I was gripped by the living energy I felt in the practices of hatha yoga and meditation. I was something of a loner and always scouted out the quietest places I could find on campus—chapels, forests, cemeteries. I had one girlfriend in high school, briefly, and was not very comfortable or interested in dating or relationships. When I arrived at college, I avoided partying and abstained from alcohol. While my neighbors in the dorm blasted their stereos and did their share of drugs and carousing, I was trying to meditate. I just wasn't in the mood to get loaded; I'd already done plenty of partying in high school. I'd been zonked on acid and smoked plenty of weed. I went to my first Grateful Dead concert at age eleven with my sister Michele, and heard some fantastic concerts at the Garden and the Fillmore East. I'd seen Jimi Hendrix, Rolling Stones, Tina Turner, Frank Zappa, and the New Riders of the Purple Sage in concert, and saw The Who perform their rock opera *Tommy*. Now I faced a similar kind of environment at college. People in the dorm were drinking and partying; that's what college students do. Yet this was a moment when I had an intense longing to know God, the universal consciousness, the all-pervasive Spirit. I was more drawn to Ramakrishna and Meister Eckhart than to Bruce Springsteen and *The Rocky Horror Picture Show*. I was more interested in books on yoga philosophy than guzzling beer at keg parties. I assume that most people viewed me as a total bore. But I didn't feel naive, prudish, or judgmental. I didn't mind that other people wanted to do drugs and get wasted—it simply wasn't what I wanted to do at that point. I was focused on the spiritual path. The lack of support and the difficulties I faced trying to meditate in that environment only made my commitment grow stronger.

Sometimes we have to persevere in following a spiritual teaching or way of life when no one else around us is doing so. Our faith and one-pointedness is thoroughly tested in such circumstances. Sometimes interpersonal crises cause us to feel ostracized, ridiculed, or shunned for pursuing an unconventional lifestyle. Occasionally there are irrevocable endings and changes in our social contacts as we intensify an inner quest.

A spiritual apprentice learns the importance of keeping the right company, spending time with other seekers or staying alone, quietly keeping one's own company in meditation. Gradually one learns to sustain a feeling of inner peace amidst any company and under all conditions. But there are stages where it's desirable to establish a protected place of meditation. This is why some aspirants enter monasteries, ashrams, and communities where they can dedicate themselves to contemplative practice in a quiet, supportive environment.

I was filled with the urge to meditate intensely, three times a day. I woke up early and went to sleep early. I did my hatha yoga postures and breathing exercises. When I wasn't in class I spent my time reading books on yoga, mysticism, Jung and depth psychology, anthropology, mythology, and world religions. I was absorbed in these fascinating studies and kept mostly to myself.

With each successive session of meditation, I plunged deeper within. When I locked my legs into lotus posture, my breath immediately became very soft, very shallow, until it was barely flickering, and I found myself resting in a place between the in-breath and the out-breath. My mind became focused in mantra repetition. When my breathing slowed down, I perceived a vast inner space. Sometimes my breathing seemed to stop altogether, and in the space between breaths, an intense *prana* was generated as my mind became absorbed in meditation. As the ripples of breath and thought subsided, my mind became completely still. At first I only sustained this briefly, but gradually, as my concentration grew stronger, I entered states of breathless awe, and my solid physical boundaries dissolved into a sea of pure consciousness. I experienced that *I am that consciousness.*

I melted my mind into the sound of the mantra Guru Om, *Guuuuurrrrrrrrruuuuuu Ooooooooooooommmmmmmmm.* This mantra was alive with shakti. I intonated each sound so it vibrated in my body. Other thoughts dispersed as the mantra imprinted its vibrations into my awareness. The sounds merged into infinity. Several times my awareness floated up above my body, and from an elevated vantage point I looked down on myself. Every cell of my body was alive with consciousness. I perceived strange liquid forms around me and saw mysterious shapes, lights, and images with my eyelids closed. But more important than any visions was the perception of a vast energy pulsating with intensity in all dimensions.

In deep meditation the mind becomes as calm and clear as an alpine lake. In this tranquil state, the individual mind becomes entrained to the mind of the universe, the infinite consciousness that pervades everything. And so I began to explore the inner world.

Sometimes I felt my body become as small as a grain of sand. At other times I expanded and felt all-pervasive, without boundaries or limits. I perceived that I'm not just this physical body, this personality, these thoughts, feelings, and desires. I am the Self, a field of vast awareness. These meditations left an indelible imprint on my mind and body, and after I ended each session and had finished massaging my feet (which often fell asleep), I tried to remember what I'd perceived and felt. My teacher's instruction and energetic influence propelled me into an accelerated period of inner growth and inspired me to undertake practices that gave me direct experiences of awakening. These experiences became the foundation of my spiritual life and shaped the person I would become and the work I would later undertake as a student of comparative religions, a psychotherapist and spiritual counselor, a yoga teacher, and a university educator.

LIFE GUIDANCE

The teacher not only initiates the process of spiritual unfoldment, he or she also guides it toward completion. This can include supervision of the aspirant's practices and guidance of the student's worldly life and personal development. Ideally the teacher is attuned to the student to assure that an initial transmission is being well integrated. For example, the teacher can advise the student if shaktipat has caused an awakening of kundalini that is intense and frightening. Some students receive individualized instruction regarding their spiritual practice. One practitioner said:

> My teacher told me I was meditating too much and that I needed to stop and eat more and work outdoors and use my body. Once I was more grounded he suggested I start meditating more intensely again. The timing seemed much better and my meditations had better results. I had better concentration, less strain, and I felt more clarity and peace and happiness, rather than feeling spacy and disconnected and burned-out like I did before.

A teacher can serve as a source of practical guidance through some of life's most important transitions and decisions. The stature of teachers can be ascertained by examining how effectively they guide their students' lives. A teacher's influence either leads students to change themselves and their lives in positive ways or it doesn't. Our trust in the wisdom of teachers deepens through seeing the results of following their recommendations. For example, Loretta was grateful to her teacher for advising her to go to medical school, even though he taught an intensive form of meditation practice and often advised students to minimize their worldly ambitions and pursuits. She said:

Many of his students were having a hard time making it in the world. A lot of them didn't have any money and people were more into hanging out and meditating than going out and getting a job. It was pretty striking when I started doing this intense school thing. Years later, when I was a practicing physician, he said to me, "Lots of people can sit and meditate a lot, but not many can live an enlightened life while remaining active in the world. The measure of your spiritual advancement is your ability to do this work with a cheerful dedication to service always in your heart." He taught me that my work in the world is my spiritual practice.

Once I wrote a letter to Muktananda saying I wanted to quit college so I could go to India and devote myself to meditation. I thought that becoming a yogi meant deemphasizing the intellect. He replied that I *must* finish college and that I wasn't under any circumstances to quit school. He said, "Nurture your interests in your studies like a small, fragile flame, until it grows into a blaze." There was no room for hesitation. I trusted his guidance, and to this day I feel that he directed me responsibly. He correctly perceived that continuing education and intellectual development were quite necessary for my personal evolution.

Of course, sometimes the best teachers are the ones who don't tell us what to do at all. Ultimately, we have to develop discernment and the ability to make our own decisions. But at this stage we're willingly influenced by a teacher and acknowledge the blessing of being guided by someone who knows our character and needs so well.

PERSONAL CONTACT WITH THE TEACHER

As we begin to do some intensive spiritual practices, we have an even greater need for the teacher's company to deepen our understanding and to guard us from pitfalls such as laziness, discouragement, or inflation. One sign that our path is being properly guided is that we feel our teacher's willingness to engage in open communication. There's little point in having a teacher if he or she won't relate to you as a person. What good is a teacher who's never available to talk to you or answer your questions? A teacher shouldn't act like you're asking a big favor because you request guidance about a matter of personal importance.

I once counseled a man named Doug, who was a close student of a Tibetan Buddhist teacher whom I'll call Lama Z. Doug's girlfriend became pregnant and he decided to marry her. His new responsibilities began to cut into the long hours he'd been dedicating to working for a business owned and operated by the lama's spiritual community. After he'd heard the news, Lama Z's only comment to Doug was, "Too bad about the girl." Doug was hurt by this statement, which implied strong disapproval of this turn of events. The implication was that Doug would no longer be able to do his spiritual practices because he'd be tied down by his family responsibilities. Another student, his supervisor at the business, said, "You're compromising your position with Lama Z." Doug felt misunderstood and perplexed by their statements and their negative attitude toward his marriage.

I asked Doug if he felt there was anything nonspiritual about marriage and childrearing. Couldn't these activities and commitments, like any other endeavors, be fields or vehicles for the practice of the dharma, the path to enlightenment? Maybe the lama and his other student were falling into the dualistic trap of making a distinction between dharma practice and worldly life. Doug agreed. His next impulse was to leave Lama Z immediately. I asked Doug if it had occurred to him to talk to his teacher about his concerns and to ask him directly if there was some reason why his teacher should disapprove of him becoming a householder. I told him, "If the lama is unwilling to speak to you about your questions and address them in a personal way, then perhaps he isn't really your teacher. If he makes you feel bad about your choices, if he makes you doubt the positive value of your human commitments and responsibilities, then perhaps you should question whether he's the right teacher for you."

Doug gathered up his courage to speak to Lama Z, who, when he better understood how his words had affected Doug, graciously apologized and gave Doug his blessing to marry. Doug has continued to have a long and fruitful discipleship under Lama Z's guidance, and this episode was a critical turning point in their relationship. Both Doug and Lama Z learned important lessons, illustrating how student and teacher can learn from each other. Students have a responsibility to speak their minds to teachers and to not submit unquestioningly. And teachers have a responsibility to listen to students and to not be inflexible or claim to be infallible. We'll return to these themes throughout the book.

Through face-to-face contact, we establish a personal relationship with the teacher. Once I left the ashram's morning chanting program early to go to work. I was kneeling down to tie my shoes when suddenly Muktananda appeared and started walking toward me. He stopped and stood right in front of me so I could touch his feet. He placed his hand on my head. As I looked up into his eyes, I saw infinite space and the stars and a man drunk with inner ecstasy. For an instant I glimpsed his state of consciousness. As he walked away I was reminded of the ancient Buddhist mantra *Gate gate paragate parasamgate bodhi swaha* (Gone, gone, gone beyond, gone completely beyond, awakened, so be it). After this experience I felt more connected to my teacher, more reverent, more respectful of his greatness.

My friend Stuart Sovatsky gave this account of his personal contact with a great yogic practitioner:

In 1983 I got introduced to Swami Kripalu's sole remaining renunciate disciple living in America, Swami Vinit-Muni, who lived in Canada. He was taking on no new students. He had only two students living with him in a secluded place. I wrote a letter, hoping he'd let me come visit. He'd turned several of my friends away. To my surprise he told me I could come and visit him. Vinit did ten hours of sadhana a day, from 4 or 5 a.m. until noon and then again in the afternoon. That was all he ever did for the last thirty years. He lived in a tiny shack. Very simple. Humble. Cooked for me. Wouldn't take any money from me. Put me up for two or three weeks at a time. Taught me on a one-to-one basis for six to eight hours at a time, reading the Hatha Yoga Pradipika, translating it and going over it line by line. It was like a father-son relationship in addition to the teaching. Then, during that first retreat, either he gave me an experience or I had it through the intensity of the practice: I did the *simhasana* (lion pose) with my tongue sticking out for two or three minutes. And when my tongue came back into my mouth it was exactly like peaking on LSD. I had a sense of infinity, and any thought I had was amplified greatly. If I had a thought that was self-deprecating I felt like I was in hell. If I had the thought of recognizing the vastness of everything it was utterly inspiring and silencing with awe. That went on all night. Anything I worried about would be very exaggerated. Anything I was happy about would be just wonderful. The next day I saw Vinit. I'd been doing sadhana in this little building separate from where he lived and I was in there with the windows completely blocked off with blankets. Vinit said, "Last night you had an experience. But then some thoughts from your life came in and the experience ended." I then learned that he had some kind of psychic ability.

GREAT ANSWERS TO DEEP QUESTIONS

Evolved teachers address our deepest questions in unexpected ways. Once, in 1979, I asked the Zen master Joshu Sazaki Roshi a question. He'd been sitting completely still for two hours and hadn't moved at all except to take a few sips of tea. My question, asked with some degree of urgency and overseriousness, was: "Roshi, what Zen discipline do you recommend for Western students?" His reply: "The highest discipline of Zen is to manifest silence when you meet others." He certainly lived what he taught. This was a great response because it undercut my urgent question about formal practices and showed that Zen was a way of being, not a set of techniques that one applies to oneself.

Someone once asked Tarthang Tulku Rinpoche his views about sexual morality and conduct. He said, "The best sexual morality is complete relaxation."[5] This response was disarmingly simple and helpful. Similarly, someone once asked Kalu Rinpoche, the venerable Tibetan Buddhist yogi, a question about sex and how it could be utilized as a vehicle for inner transformation. Some members of the audience were appalled that such a question was posed of the elderly monk, who presumably had little experience of sexuality in his own life, which had been dedicated to intensive spiritual practice. To everyone's surprise Kalu Rinpoche responded, "When you reach the moment of truth, tell yourself, 'Now I have finally arrived!'"

A teacher may also uproot all of our questions. I experienced this in the presence the Vedanta teacher Jean Klein. He seated himself in front of his audience and sat for half an hour without uttering a word. He silently conveyed Self-knowledge, Self-realization. After that half hour of sitting, I had no questions at all. He quietly conveyed the peace, presence, and awareness that is in itself the highest teaching and transmission, the answer to all questions. It's contentless and has no beginning or end. No technique is needed to realize it. We only need to merge our consciousness back into its source.

SILENT TRANSMISSION

Some great teachers communicate the enlightened state not by lecturing, but through a wordless transmission of Being. The illumined teacher spreads the enlightened state simply by *being* it, by abiding in that state of consciousness. We've seen that sometimes teachers instruct us in techniques such as meditation, prayer, or visualization. They explain complex philosophical doctrines, teachings of the masters of the lineage, or the meaning of mystical texts. A teacher may prescribe a set of practices for the student, such as a certain number of mantra repetitions or breaths to count, or a course of yoga postures. But the most profound instruction may occur when teachers convey peace and expanded awareness through their silent presence.

Once as a teenager I meditated with the great yogi Dr. Ramamurti Mishra. I felt and observed that the moment he closed his eyes, his senses were drawn deeply inward and he was absorbed immediately in a state of samadhi. Following his example I felt my awareness drawn magnetically into a deep inner space. In Patanjali's classic *ashtanga,* or eight-limbed yoga, *pratyahara,* turning the senses inward, opens the door to meditation and to abiding in Self-realization. The power of this practice was viscerally communicated to me, without words or explanation. Meeting Dr. Mishra once and meditating with him for fifteen minutes made an impression on me that has lasted my entire life.

One teacher famous for the power of his silent transmission was Bhagavan Ramana Maharshi. Annamalai Swami, a contemporary teacher in the lineage of Ramana Maharshi, has stated:

If you enter a dark place with a lamp, light falls on everyone who is near you. You don't have to tell people, "I have a light" because they will all be aware of its presence. In the presence of a *jnani* like Bhagavan, the spiritual darkness of devotees is put to flight by the radiant light of *jnana.* In Bhagavan's case this light cleaned and calmed the minds of all who were near him. When mature devotees basked in this light they sometimes had an experience of the Self. The radiation of this spiritual power was Bhagavan's *mauna diksha* [initiation through silence]. He radiated this power quite effortlessly. It was not done by an act of volition, it was a natural consequence of his realization. Bhagavan didn't need to speak about the Self. He *was* the Self, and he radiated its power all the time. Those who were receptive to this power needed no verbal explanations from Bhagavan. The spoken teachings were only for those who were not able to tune into his silent radiation.[6]

Ramana Maharshi himself explained:

The highest form of Grace is silence (*mouna*). Guru's silence is the loudest *upadesa* (spiritual instruction). It is also Grace in its highest form. All other initiations are derived from *mouna* (silence). They are therefore secondary. *Mouna* is the primary form. If the Guru is silent the seeker's mind gets purified by itself. . . . The books say that there are so many kinds of *diksha* (initiations). They also say that the Guru makes some rites with fire, water, *japa*, *mantras*, etc., and call such fantastic performances *dikshas*, as if the disciple (*sishya*) becomes ripe only after such processes are gone through by the Guru. . . . Such is the Guru. Such is Dakshinamurti [a legendary yogi of antiquity]. What did he do? He was silent; the disciples appeared before him. He maintained silence, the doubts of the disciples were dispelled, which means that they lost their individual identities. That is *jnana* and not all the verbiage usually associated with it. Silence is the most potent form of work. However vast and emphatic the *sastras* may be, they fail in their effect. The Guru is quiet and peace prevails in all. His silence is more vast and more emphatic than all the *sastras* put together.[7]

DARSHAN

One of the joyous and transformative aspects of the student-teacher relationship is having the opportunity to see illumined teachers in person, to have their darshan. Darshan literally means a gaze or a look—having a look at the teacher. It's also the time when the teacher has a look at you and when you may receive the teacher's glance—which can be a conduit for transmission of the teacher's love, power, and awakened consciousness.

It's said that one can receive the grace of great beings through even a moment's contact. In 1996, while traveling on a tour through Southern India with my father, we arrived one day at Srinageri, site of an ancient Shaivite temple and home of one of the four Shankaracaryas, among the most powerful and widely respected Hindu spiritual leaders. A yogi only rises to the rank of a Shankaracarya after a lifetime of sadhana and demonstrated spiritual attainments. We learned from other visitors that we'd just missed darshan but that the Shankaracarya would soon pass by where we were standing. My father had never seen a *sadhu,* a holy man, of this stature before, but he instinctively assumed a respectful stance, with his hands placed in the yogic gesture of namaste. The Shankaracarya stepped outside and started walking past us. He looked at us for only a moment, but I felt the power of his glance. He had tremendous shakti. He was observing a day of silence so no words were spoken, but everyone was much moved by his presence. He had a wild, fierce expression, as well as a look of supreme detachment. It was a marvelous darshan, a glimpse of an awakened being. This turned out to be a fortuitous event, as the Shankaracarya died about a month later, thus we had a rare opportunity to see him.

My friend Rick Amaro told me this story:

After I had stayed with Neem Karoli Baba for some time at Kainchi, I asked him to bless me and my girlfriend, as we were going to depart. From inside his darshan room he stood up and looked into me, silently, for a long time. I felt a tremendous expansion of my perceptual space. He stood there gazing at me like that for three or four minutes. I felt my breath going in and in, and the air became rarified. I felt like I was expanding into infinity, like I was going out on LSD. I was in that state as we left to continue our journey. Someone next to me said, "I've never seen him do that before!" That blessing and transmission of his presence has always stayed with me.

If we're fortunate enough to meet a truly great teacher, we find that simply being in his or her awakened presence and having a look at him or her can inspire and intensify our striving for Self-realization. Being with such a teacher activates a pure, unconditioned awareness and confronts us with everything within ourselves that creates limitation. A man named Robyn recounted this remarkable darshan experience:

My father, Leo Bogart, at Chennakesava Temple, Belur, Karnataka.

Father and son enjoying companionship as pilgrims at the threshold in Belur.

Years ago I went on a pilgrimage to India with my teacher at the time, Pir Vilayat Inayat Khan. We had the opportunity to have the darshan of a very powerful and very elderly saint in Delhi named Baba Sita Ramdas Onkarnath. My teacher told those of us present, "If you go in there and look this being in the eye and ask for something, then afterward you have to be willing to not carry grudges, to not tell lies, to live in truth." There was a tremendous commotion at the back of the tent as the saint's followers arrived and they all began to go nuts with devotion toward this guy. Finally the sadhu comes into the tent, held up on one side by Pir Vilayat and by a man named General Uban Singh on the other side. The old Baba was nothing but skin draped over bones. He could barely sit up, he was so old. We were told that he could barely hear because there was so much cosmic sound in his ears, and that he could barely see because the divine light was so pervasive in his awareness. We were told that darshan would now begin, and immediately there was a stampede of Indian devotees. Big mobs started rushing up to the front. General Uban told everybody to calm down and said that they were going to separate men and women on different sides of the room. Things began to quiet down a bit as soon as they divided the sexes. So all the women go up first for darshan and this takes a long time, and I'm sitting there raking myself over the coals. Everyone was taking from this guy, mentally asking him for this or that, and I don't know if I can do what Pir Vilayat said—if I can be truthful and let go of all my grudges. And I don't know if I can ask him for anything. Finally the men start going up and eventually I'm about third from the front of the line. Then suddenly all of these people rush up in front of me and I'm pushed way to the back by a swelling wave of lunatic Indian devotees. This gives me more time to think about what I'd like to ask this guy for. All of this took a really long time so I ended up being one of the last few people to go up for darshan.

When I finally get up there I kneel down. All this time, Baba has not spoken to anyone. General Uban is in a trance now, and

Baba is speaking through General Uban. People come up and ask the guy for different things, like enlightenment or healing for themselves or some family member. Baba responds to these people through General Uban. My turn comes and I go up and kneel down at his feet. I'm really afraid. I can't bring myself to look up into his eyes at all. I was in a place of really low self-esteem because I was in India with people who were all having all these high mystical experiences and I wasn't having any. I reached over and touched his feet with a garland of flowers each of us had been given. And inside, at the deepest level of myself where no one could hear, silently I said, "Look, I don't know what to ask you for. I see everyone taking from you. So if you can see anything in me that is worthy as a gift to you, please take it." Right then I looked up at him and he started to open his eyes. And I was so scared I looked away. And then General Uban spoke and said, "He wants you to know that he accepts your gift." I just shattered. I started to weep uncontrollably. In this place where no one else could hear or know, he knew what was in my heart.

Darshan can be quite informal or highly formal. It's an occasion to offer flowers, pieces of fruit, or other gifts to the teacher as an expression of our gratitude and our sincere interest in receiving transmission. Students may bow before the teacher or greet the teacher in some other way. The teacher may sit quietly or may openly greet students and engage in conversation.

It's often only in the setting of formal darshan that students of renowned teachers with many followers are able to establish a personal relationship with the teacher. In this setting students' questions are addressed, their inner needs are met with a loving response by the teacher, and their faith is awakened and renewed. In the presence of an enlightened teacher a variety of responses can be elicited, such as feeling very peaceful or becoming very emotional for no apparent reason. Tears well up, or we feel an inexplicable ecstasy. We feel inner heat, or pressure in the head, or energy moving through the chakras. Some will experience *kriyas,* spontaneous physical movements initiated by the awakening kundalini; or we enter meditation effortlessly. Our deepest fears and insecurities are often stirred up and brought out into the open through contact with the teacher, and sometimes a deep-seated neurosis can become activated in the teacher's presence.

During my ashram days, complex feelings came up for me during nightly darshans, where anyone who wished to could approach Muktananda. He greeted each person with a quick brush or tap with a large wand of peacock feathers, which he wielded like a royal scepter. My experience was that he always reflected my own inner state. When I was angry he seemed peeved. If I wasn't doing my practices, he ignored me. When I was in a serene, loving, and centered state of consciousness, he greeted me with love and respect. When I was very emotional and uncertain, he responded with compassion, concern, and a reassuring gaze. When I made sincere efforts to meditate, I felt that he knew it.

As an example of the internal dramas elicited by darshan, here are some brief selections from my journal that record several months of nightly darshans with Muktananda in 1976, when I was eighteen years old:

3/28/76: Had his darshan, gave him bananas. Received one hit with the peacock feathers.

4/1/76: Baba stormed around the ashram furiously turning off lights and thermostats. Everyone knows he's been angry all day. At evening darshan he came in and said, "You're all fools! Why should I talk to you?" Everyone cowered! Then he said, "Don't you remember what day it is? April Fools!" Everyone was in hysterics laughing at this little prank!

4/3/76: During afternoon meditation Baba walked around the room and gave everyone the touch. Nothing much happened in meditation and with my eyes closed I asked him silently for some experience that would strengthen my faith in our connection. A few minutes later Baba walked all the way back across the room, came up behind me and touched my lower back with his big toe. I felt a spark of electricity that jolted my body forward.

4/6/76: For the past few days, the shakti has been working in the top of my head. I feel pressure in the crown of my head, and my body is heating up during meditation.

4/15/76: I inwardly offered Baba my self-pity when I bowed to him during darshan. He gave me two bops with the peacock feathers.

4/20/76: I went up for darshan angry with Baba. He completely ignored me. No bops.

4/23/76: I feel senselessly content and happy. There's nowhere else I'd like to be.

4/24/76: I hate all this chanting and bowing. I've got to get out of this place.

4/26/76: I'm having big problems with Mom and Dad. They were very upset when I told them I wanted to drop out of school and go to India. Tonight Baba said, "You shouldn't get fed up with this world. You will never find God if you run away from your affairs."

4/27/76: As I approached Baba for darshan, I inwardly surrendered to the divine will, to universal consciousness. I let go to whatever will happen. He tapped me twice with the feathers. I looked up at him, he looked at me, then he tapped me again.

5/6/76: Many subtle kriyas, energy in my third chakra. My body is burning with intense heat.

5/29/76: Very calm meditation tonight with very light, subtle breathing, prana steady.

6/11/76: I told Baba on darshan line that I'm still doubting the connection between us and whether he's really guiding me. He assured me there's a strong connection between us and that I'll understand it more over the course of time. When I returned to my seat I felt an intense throbbing and twitching of kundalini energy at the base of my spine. Baba, in midsentence, raised up his sunglasses, looked at me grinning with luminous eyes, and pointed right at me.

At first we offer gifts to the teacher: flowers, fruit, pictures we've painted. All of these are offerings of love, gestures of respect, and expressions of gratitude. But gradually we offer something more subtle: ourselves. And we offer the joy that is generated through daily meditation.

TAPASYA

During the phase of discipleship, the aspirant listens to a teacher's instructions, practices the recommended techniques, has opportunities to ask questions, and is inspired by the teacher's presence. At this stage one also learns that to achieve a transformed condition requires active purification to consume inner limitations. In yoga philosophy this is the principle of *tapas,* which means "heat" or "burning." The practitioner performs *tapasya*—vigorous practices such as asanas, chanting, mental concentration exercises, or physical cleansing regimens that eliminate impurities of body and mind and prepare the body and psyche to hold the energies of intensive meditation. The aspirant gradually becomes on fire with a longing for enlightenment, for union with God, for absorption in the One. Ramakrishna is perhaps the best example of a teacher who demonstrated this burning desire for a state of spiritual union.[8] The fire of practice generates constancy of awareness.

In many schools of mysticism, it's taught that before experiencing illumination, an aspirant must engage in a lengthy process of purgation

Yogi practicing tapas under the tutelage of Lord Shiva. Mahabalipuram.

through penances and austerities. In the words of F. C. Happold, a British schoolmaster and author who wrote about history, religion, and philosophy:

> The Mystic Way is usually . . . divided into three stages: the Way of Purgation, the Way of Illumination, or the Illuminative Life . . . , and the Way of Union, or the unitive life. . . . The Indian philosopher Radhakrishnan uses a somewhat different scheme to describe this path to perfection. The three stages of the way of perfection he calls Purification, Concentration, and Identification. . . . He who would tread the Mystic Way is bidden not only painfully to learn to annihilate the selfhood but also to turn his attention more and more from the multiplicity of the phenomenal world, with its classifying and image-making, its logical reasoning and discursive thinking, so as to attain that "simple seeing" of which the mystics speak; for not until the eye has become single can the whole body be filled with light.[9]

During this phase of purgation or purification, teachers may inspire us to attempt intensive practices that we might not have undertaken otherwise, for example, a yoga retreat or a Zen *sesshin,* a period of intensive meditation involving many hours of practice each day. Sufi practitioners may do a forty-day retreat. All Jesuits go through the strenuous Exercises of St. Ignatius. It's also possible to create our own rigorous program for self-transformation.

THE DARK NIGHT

Those embracing a life of spiritual discipline may experience a dark night of the soul, described by the Spanish mystic St. John of the Cross as a time of inner desolation, a desert of the heart, an extended period of dryness, depression, and inner emptiness.[10] His treatise "The Dark Night of the Soul" narrates the soul's journey through various hardships and difficulties encountered in the process of detaching from the world and seeking union with the Creator. The poem describes the ordeals people endure on the path, including purification of the senses and purification of the spirit.[11] Former interests and sensual pleasures no longer bring joy, and there's a heightened awareness of their ultimately unsatisfying nature. Only enlightenment and Self-realization will quench our thirst for peace and inner freedom. Desires, worldly interests, and ambitions dry up, yet we're hardly in a state of bliss; the divine presence withdraws from our awareness. This is a time of testing, and we need to bravely continue our practices through this difficult period.

In the book *Pilgrims of the Stars,* mystic and singer Dilip Kumar Roy describes the torments he experienced after coming into contact with Sri Aurobindo, the great mystic sage and guru.[12] Roy's career as a musical performer began to feel totally empty, yet it took a long time before he could let go of the fame, adulation, and aesthetic pleasure his career brought him so he could dedicate himself to the interior journey at his teacher's ashram in Pondicherry. The dark night may be a time of inner despair and desolation on the spiritual path. During such a phase, we're often beset by doubts about the path we've chosen.

During my college years, I experienced such a dark night, losing interest in music, which had been my strongest interest, as well as in sports, movies, novels, and other pastimes. My attention was turned inward, and I spent much of my time meditating when I might have been developing a social life. I met from time to time with Charles Gonzalez, a gentle Jesuit priest who taught at Wesleyan, discussing issues that arise for mystics such as conflicts about desire and renunciation and the loneliness one can experience on the path. Father Gonzalez was a radiant man who exuded love, purity, and a spirit of service. I was fortunate to have such a spiritual friend during that desolate period.

The spiritual apprentice inevitably suffers to some degree while passing through stages of purgation, as old attachments are released and our worldly desires and ambitions may seem empty and unreal. Hazrat Inayat Khan once said, "The bringers of joy have always been the children of sorrow."[13] Yet our wise teacher's words and kind presence give us renewed hope, courage, and enthusiasm.

GRATITUDE AND DEVOTION

[The guru is like] a wish-fulfilling tree granting all the qualities of realization, a father and a mother giving their love equally to all sentient beings, a great river of compassion, a mountain rising above worldly concerns unshaken by the winds of emotion, and a great cloud filled with rain to soothe the torments of the passions. In brief, he is the equal of all the Buddhas. . . . To have full confidence in him is the sure way to progress toward enlightenment. . . . Whether or not we achieve realization depends entirely upon our devotion to the guru.

DILGO KHYENTSE RINPOCHE,
THE WISH-FULFILLING JEWEL

A great teacher's guidance and blessings may evoke in us a deepening devotion, which can be expressed through reverence or bowing to the teacher, through inward remembrance, and through a willingness to serve and actively practice the teachings. Devotion can also emerge through an internal healing event in the teacher's presence that generates love and gratitude.

Once, while I was on retreat at my teacher's ashram in Ganeshpuri, India, I became very discouraged. I didn't feel that my spiritual practice was proceeding well or bearing fruit. My health was bad, and my energy was low. My meditations were barren. I was lost and didn't know what direction my life was taking. I had doubts about finding a job and a career. At one point a week-long chant of the mantra *Om Namah Shivaya* was held in the ashram. On the final morning, Muktananda was expected to arrive in the temple to celebrate the conclusion of the chant. I stayed up all night so I would get a good seat up front, near his throne. I sang and meditated through the dark hours of the night. At sunrise the temple filled up with devotees, until the place was packed. Right before Baba arrived, one of his assistants came over to me and told me I had to move so that some very important honcho could sit up front; he pointed me toward a seat much farther back in the room. I was crushed and became absorbed in feelings of disappointment. I'd waited all night so I could sit close to my teacher, and now this unjust, arbitrary pandering to ashram VIPs had snatched this opportunity away from me.

Then I got absorbed in the chanting. I closed my eyes and dissolved into the sounds of the mantras. I spoke to my teacher inwardly, saying, "Baba, I don't know who I am, or where I'm going in life, or what I'm supposed to do next. All I know is that I honor you, I trust you, and I love you."

I opened my eyes and Baba was looking right at me. His gaze was full of love, concern, and compassion. I looked down for a moment, but he didn't avert his eyes. He kept looking right at me so I knew that he knew what was happening inside me. I experienced an instantaneous recognition of what physicist and mystic Victor Mansfield calls the "telepathic link" between the student and the guide.[14]

I felt a profound sense of relief. A few minutes earlier I'd been in a miserable state; now I was happy just seeing him. Now I remembered why I was sitting here in a crowded marble temple in monsoon-drenched India staring at a seventy-year-old Indian man in a saffron silk *lungi*. Now I realized my teacher's stature and his ability to guide me from within, at any distance. Physical distance did not matter. And even though some part of me was still skeptical about the whole idea of having a guru, I could never deny what just happened. As I joined in the rousing finale of the chant, I felt waves of gratitude and devotion to the all-pervasive consciousness connecting all of us as one.

Some people have reservations about the idea of devotion because it encourages us to view the spiritual teacher through the lens of idealizing projections and makes us vulnerable to exploitation and an unwillingness to look realistically at the teacher's human faults. David Frawley comments:

> Many of our problems with gurus come from our misunderstanding of guru worship. We create a personality cult around the guru, rather than using the guru as a vehicle for worshipping the divine. When gurus are worshipped, it is not their human side that should be honored but the Divinity working through them, the Divine guru. Guru worship can be one path of spiritual growth, but it is not the only path. In knowledge approaches (*jnana yoga*), the guru has the role of an instructor. In devotional lines (*bhakti yoga*), the guru is usually subordinate to the chosen form of God for worship. While for some great gurus, like Ramana, Maharshi, or Anandamayi Ma, guru worship appears appropriate, few gurus are of this stature.[15]

True devotion is directed not just to a teacher but to the Self, the god that dwells within us. This is the nondual understanding of devotion. Yet there are stages when it serves our transformation to maintain

*Seekers can find refuge wherever people congregate to meditate
and to be in sacred space. Srinageri.*

the dualistic attitude of a lover in devotion to the beloved. Ram Dass
used to cite a teaching of the great mystic Ramakrishna, who said, "I
don't want to become sugar, I want to *taste* sugar." Devotion is a sweet
and blissful state that lifts our spirit and instills trust that a mystery is
unfolding and guiding us. And sometimes it feels better to pursue the
practices and also enjoy the happiness of devotion and inner contentment in communion with others on the same or a similar path.

FINDING A COMMUNITY OF PRACTITIONERS

As I mentioned earlier, sometimes during the transformational process we have to leave behind elements of our past, including past relationships, and occasionally we part ways with many of our former

companions. Some period of feeling completely alone seems to be a typical divine test. Fortunately, new friends eventually appear, those who share our interests and commitments. Many seekers find that it's both inspiring and reassuring to meet with other people for meditation, chanting, study of mystical biographies and texts, or discussion of our experiences on the path. Sometimes this leads to a more formal involvement with a spiritual group or community, which can be very joyous. There's an undeniable power in chanting, meditating, or practicing yoga with other people in a group. And living in community with others can have its memorable as well as its comical moments. Roger (cited earlier) reports:

> I was the head cook at the Maharishi University during the first "7000 Course," when seven thousand people meditated together twice a day for three weeks. I was the guy who got to cook breakfast and lunch for all those people. For one meal I cooked one ton of broccoli! The first day of the course a storm blew through town with the darkest clouds. It felt incredibly ominous, as if the evil gods were out to destroy us. The water line to the kitchen broke. I had to organize a big water brigade to ferry water into the kitchen. This huge obstacle came up, but we got through it. I had this great crew of people. After that, for the next three weeks it was blissful. We'd met the initial resistance. Everything flowed. Everything worked. It was a marvelous experience of living and working in community.

POSSIBLE RISKS OF INVOLVEMENT

The personal accounts in this book attest to my belief that involvement with a spiritual teacher's group or community can be life-transforming, but to be fair it's important to acknowledge that involvement can also pose some dangers. One could fall under the influence of a charismatic but psychologically imbalanced person or become involved in a movement that ends in disaster. The stories of leaders such as Jim Jones,

David Koresh, and Marshall Applewhite, who prodded their followers into group suicide or confrontations with civil or military authorities, should caution us to carefully consider the implications of involvement with a group. It's important to look closely at the environment that's growing around the teacher. Is there a prevalent atmosphere of paranoia within the group? Are visitors greeted with warmth and welcomed without being subjected to an aggressive sales pitch? Be especially cautious whenever attendance at a meeting, a retreat, or a seminar is coerced, or if you feel that recruiters are too actively courting your participation.

You should feel free to come or go from a group at any time. Many years ago, a friend of mine was involved with the Hare Krishna movement. For some time he enjoyed the austere life and the daily *kirtan,* or chanting of divine names, on city street corners. Then he became a personal attendant to one of the head swamis of the movement, who used to beat him frequently. Many years later this same swami was convicted of murder. He was clearly a violent and abusive man not worthy of the rank of spiritual leader. Once my friend figured out that he no longer loved or trusted his teacher and announced that he was considering leaving, he was given the silent treatment by members of his community. For weeks he was constantly followed around so that he was never left alone. He wasn't permitted to use the telephone or to speak with anyone outside the group. Eventually he escaped by punching his kirtan group leader in the nose and making a run for it. My friend is a brilliant and creative person, and his real life began once he busted out of this cult's oppressive shell.

ANOTHER FALSE MESSIAH

Lest anyone minimize how destructive it can be to participate in a group led by a deluded, false teacher, consider the example of Shoko Asahara, leader of the Japanese cult Aum Shinrikyo (The True Teaching of Aum), the group responsible for poisoning thousands of people in a nerve gas attack on the Japanese subway system in March 1995. Asahara claimed to have achieved enlightenment during his travels in India and became a proponent of yoga and meditation. Most of his followers only saw Asahara on TV or video. Those who tried to leave Aum were told they would burn in a Buddhist hell. Members were subjected to severe privations, torture, and near starvation. Some were kidnapped or murdered. Members were encouraged to seek ordination, take vows of chastity, cut all ties with the world, renounce their families, and sign over all worldly possessions and property to Asahara. The group also coerced members into turning over the assets of other family members. In 1995 the group's assets were estimated at more than a billion dollars.

Asahara believed that the whole world would proclaim him the Future Buddha and the savior of humanity. He began preaching Judaeo-Christian themes of the approaching Armageddon and that World War Three was imminent. To survive he believed Aum needed to be armed for self-defense, and thus the cult began buying weapons of mass destruction to wage war against Japan, the United States, and the rest of humanity. This war, he said, would end in victory for Aum. He predicted earthquakes, volcanoes, and chemical and nuclear war. Driven by these paranoid delusions, Aum began developing chemical and biological weapons, including strains of the deadly Ebola virus collected in Zaire by Aum scientists. In short Asahara was a megalomaniac predicting war, with limitless funds to buy weapons and deadly chemicals. When Asahara was finally tracked down by police after the sarin attack in the subway system, he was found in a crawl space less than three feet tall, holding the equivalent of $100,000 in cash.[16]

SIGNS OF MIND CONTROL

The sobering reality is that many charismatic teachers prove to be charlatans, and quite a few religious and spiritual groups turn out to be destructive and dangerous cults.[17] It can be a nightmare to discover that the community we're affiliated with is utilizing elaborate strategies to keep us bound to the group and serving its interests, which aren't always in our own best interests. Effective means of controlling thought and behavior have been developed to dominate individuals and groups, and these methods are routinely employed within some groups ostensibly dedicated to spiritual awakening.[18] Thus, any seeker considering involvement with a community should be familiar with the signs of manipulation or coercion.

In his book *Combatting Cult Mind Control,* counselor and former cult member Steven Hassan describes the components of mind control, "a system of influences that disrupt an individual's identity . . . and replaces it with a new identity."[19] He says mind control is a social process

> achieved by immersing a person in a social environment where, in order to function, he must shed his old identity and adhere to the new identity desired by the group. . . . The person usually shows a radical personality change and a drastic interruption of his life course. [Mind control refers to] those systems that seek to undermine an individual's integrity in making his own decisions. The essence of mind control is that it encourages dependency and conformity, and discourages autonomy and individuality.[20]

According to Hassan there are four main components of mind control often seen in cults: control of behavior, control of thoughts, control of emotions, and control of information. *Behavior control* is control of the group members' environment, where they live, what they wear, what they eat, the amount of sleep they get, and the jobs they have. Rigid schedules are maintained, with free time greatly restricted. People work, eat, and live together, and any form of individualism is discouraged. All are subjected to an authoritarian chain of command.

Thought control refers to "indoctrinating members so thoroughly that they internalize the group doctrine, incorporate a new language system, and use thought-stopping techniques to keep their mind 'centered.' In order to be a good member, a person must learn to manipulate his own thought processes. . . . [Cult] ideology is internalized as 'the Truth,' the only map of reality."[21] The group doctrine filters all incoming information and determines how information can be thought about. Thinking becomes black versus white, us versus them. Good is equated with the leader and the group, and bad with everything outside the group. It's claimed that the group's doctrine is scientifically proven and provides answers to all problems. Students learn to block out criticism of the group, and to defend their new identity as group members against their former identities. Denial, rationalization, justification, and wishful thinking prevail.

> If information transmitted to a cult member is perceived as an attack on either the leader, the doctrine, or the group, a hostile wall goes up. Members are trained to disbelieve any criticism. . . . Paradoxically, criticism of the group confirms that the cult's view of the world is correct. The information presented does not register properly.[22]

Group members are taught to use thought-stopping practices to counteract "bad" thoughts, to drown out the negativity. Thought-stopping short-circuits a person's ability to test reality, so the person can think only positive thoughts about involvement with the group.

Emotional control means manipulating and narrowing the range of a person's feelings. Guilt and fear are used to keep members under control, often by creating an outside enemy believed to be persecuting the group, for example, Satan, the FBI, psychiatrists, family, rival sects, deprogrammers. Within such a group, loyalty and devotion are the most valued emotions. Members aren't allowed to express any negative feelings, except toward outsiders. Members are taught never to complain or to criticize a group leader, only themselves.[23] Interpersonal relationships are strictly controlled and members constrained as to whom they can marry, go to bed with, or spend time with. Members are kept off balance, receiving praise one minute, castigation the next. Feelings of dependency and helplessness are fostered through forced confession of past "sins." These confessions are often used against members later on to keep them in line. Participants are also subjected to phobia indoctrination so that they have panic reactions (sweating, rapid heartbeat, feeling lost and defenseless) at the thought of leaving the group. They're told that if they leave they'll die, burn in hell, go insane, or commit suicide. Members are made to feel that security is possible only within the group.[24]

Information control is the process of denying people the information they need to make sound judgments, so they become incapable of doing so. Members of such groups have no access to newspapers, TV, radio, magazines, or books. They have no free time and read only material disseminated by the group. They aren't allowed to discuss anything critical of the leader, doctrine, or organization. Members spy on one another and report improper activities or comments to leaders. New converts aren't permitted to talk to one another without an older member present to chaperone them. Most importantly, people are told to avoid contact with ex-members or critics.[25] Group leaders screen members' letters and phone calls, while members know nothing about scandals, lawsuits, or internal disputes occurring within the group.

Those who have been subjected to mind control often experience considerable conflict and difficulties in trying to sever their connection with such a group. Often they need assistance in the form of exit counseling to free themselves from a coercive group and its insidious mental, emotional, and behavioral programming. I refer the reader to Steven Hassan's book for further information.

Note that some degree of behavioral control is to be expected in any spiritual community, including healthy groups. Regular scheduling of work, study, and other activities can free the mind so that members can focus on intensive spiritual practice. In traditional Buddhist monasteries, no food is taken after noon for precisely this reason, and during meditation retreats silence is often observed. When we detect behavioral control within a group, we can ask ourselves several questions:

Have we consciously chosen austere living conditions (such as practicing meditation in silence for long periods of time, limiting food intake, or accepting a period of celibacy) because these disciplines support us in one-pointed pursuit of enlightenment? Having lived within these behavioral strictures for some time, do they still serve our spiritual growth? Or do they weaken us physically and emotionally? And is the group flexible enough to allow us to find our own discipline and daily rhythm of activities, including both a reasonable amount of work and enough quiet time for sleep, meditation, and personal care? Or are we pushed to the point of exhaustion by a dehumanizing schedule of grueling labor? Is every moment's activity rigidly prescribed? Is there room for us to be ourselves, or do we have to suppress our true feelings, thoughts, or personalities or else face group censure? Our answers can help us decide for ourselves whether or not we're involved with a healthy community. A life of hard work and intensive pursuit of expanded consciousness through contemplative discipline is one thing. To have every aspect of our existence dictated by others so that we have no free will is another matter entirely. Such an atmosphere stifles all creativity and prevents students from growing. It's a wholly unsuitable atmosphere for higher evolution.

Regarding thought control, it's normal for a spiritual group to teach its doctrine and for members to be enthusiastic about these teachings. The question is, are other views considered and discussed? Are questioning and open inquiry welcomed and accepted, or does an oppressive atmosphere prevail? Are members punished for holding a different opinion or viewpoint? Does a hostile and defensive atmosphere prevail, rather than a joyous and accepting one? These are important questions, as we'll note again in stage seven, when we discuss the need for open and honest discussion within spiritual communities.

Where emotional manipulation is present, a dangerous atmosphere may exist within a group. The practices of phobia indoctrination are especially destructive and crazy-making. A woman I knew had just left a community and was panic-stricken because the group had indoctrinated her to believe that those who left the group would be cursed in all undertakings. Whenever she faced any difficulties, she attributed it to "the guru's curse." In contrast a healthy community uses no coercion to establish commitment. Moreover, a healthy spiritual community provides some support for a person's emotional response, in contrast to groups where all individuality is submerged to the group will. Looking, acting, and thinking like a clone isn't conducive to spiritual growth, notwithstanding the ways this might help us "transcend ego."

While not all spiritual groups exhibit these forms of mind control, we should be cautious about deeper involvement if we become aware that they're being employed. Equipped with knowledge of some of the danger signals, we can proceed into deeper involvement with a teacher or community. Another thing to keep in mind is that groups change over time. A community that started out innocent, joyous, and free can later become rigid, controlling, and oppressive. We need to continue to monitor our feelings about the teacher and the group throughout our time of involvement.

❧

If we're students of an ordinary teacher or helpful guide, stage three, discipleship, may be as far as we proceed on this path. We may receive instruction in a technique and then go our own way. We may experiment with participation in a spiritual group but decide at some point that it doesn't suit us. Or we may proceed into deeper transformation by undergoing a process of testing that allows us to receive a teacher's most transformative influence.

STAGE FOUR

꙳

Testing

Trust, Surrender,
and Refinement of the Personality

The master who had to teach the method and the exercises
had first to test the [student] to determine whether he was
willing and able to undergo the hardships that awaited
him on the Path. The newcomer was sometimes made to
wait for days at the Sheikh's door, and sometimes as a
first test was treated very rudely. Usually three years of
service were required before the [student] could be formally
accepted in a master's group.

ANNEMARIE SCHIMMEL,
MYSTICAL DIMENSIONS OF ISLAM

Once the student has become committed to discipleship and is pursuing
a spiritual practice, a period of testing ensues. There are two main types
of tests: tests of the student's faith in the teacher and commitment to
the spiritual path, and tests of the student's character.

THE SHEIKH AND THE LAMB'S BLADDER

My friend and teacher Sangye Drolma told me this story:

A man went to a sheikh for teaching. The sheikh was very simple and austere, sitting by himself in a mosque in a state of high meditation. He had only this one student, no others. After visiting the sheikh for several months, the student thought, *How great it would be if my teacher had more disciples to receive his teachings.* The following day the student arrived at the mosque and found that the teacher was now surrounded by a huge entourage of followers. Each day thereafter large crowds came to the mosque for his blessings and discourses. The media was there with microphones and cameras. The sheikh had been discovered. But now the student could barely see his teacher, much less have personal conversations with him.

After several weeks the student became sad and discouraged and thought, *I miss the old days when it was just me and the sheikh, when I could have close personal contact with him every day. I wish all these people would just go away.*

The next day, when the student went to the mosque, he noticed something strange. Every time the sheikh moved he made disgusting farting noises and people in the audience were holding their noses and complaining that the sheikh exuded nauseating odors. The crowd started yelling and cursing the sheikh, calling him a fake and a charlatan and throwing tomatoes and pieces of fruit at him. The student sat watching this in amazement. People started storming out of the mosque angrily, and in a short period of time the room had cleared out completely. Suddenly the student was the only person left in the room with the sheikh.

When they were alone together, the teacher pulled up his robe and revealed that he was holding a lamb's bladder under his arm, next to his body. When the sheikh rubbed it or moved his body, the bladder made a revolting farting sound. It stank abominably. The sheikh said, "I heard your request and granted your wish. Everyone else thought I was disgusting and began to doubt and denounce me. But you sat here and never wavered. You didn't lose faith in me despite my strange actions. That's how I know you're worthy to be my student."

TESTS OF FAITH IN THE TEACHER

Sometimes teachers behave in a strange manner to instill doubt about their sanity, integrity, or good intentions. Indeed, some teachers explain that their bizarre or inexplicable behavior is actually a means of testing their disciples. One man reported that he was working at his job as a housepainter in a town near his teacher's ashram:

I was painting away and I looked up and there was Swamiji. He looked so happy. He smiled and asked me to join him for a walk. I said of course. After we had walked for a few minutes, Swamiji pulled a cigarette out of his pocket. He lit it and began to puff on it. Immediately all my judgments came up about smoking—it's not healthy, it's not spiritual, a yogi would never do it. He smoked that whole cigarette and kept looking me straight in the eye. After that, for the next few days I became filled with doubt. Could it be that Swami X was a fraud, that I'd been deceived, that he wasn't enlightened? I felt that he was a hypocrite, telling us to live these pure lives, but here he was polluting his body. I started to think about leaving Swami X. But then I realized that Swami X's strange behavior didn't change how I felt about him. The core of his presence was unchanging. He was serene, loving, and filled with inner dignity and power. These were the qualities that I loved and admired. I didn't care if he smoked.

Sometimes the scalpel of the guru's surgery on the student's ego is very painful. A teacher may make an outrageous demand, ask us for a large sum of money, yell at us, or even strike us physically. Consider this story of the Tibetan Buddhist yogi Nāropa and his teacher, Tilopa:

> When Nāropa made his mandala and venerated him with folded hands, Tilopa glanced once at him. Nāropa prayed and asked for instruction. "If you want instruction, give me your girl." When Nāropa did so, the girl turned her back to Tilopa, looked at Nāropa, smiled and cast sidelong glances at him. Tilopa beat her and said: "You do not care for me, you only care for Nāropa." Nāropa did not lose faith in the propriety of his Guru's actions, and when he sat there happily without the girl, Tilopa asked him: "Are you happy, Nāropa?" And Nāropa answered: "Bliss is to offer the mudra as fee to the Guru who is Buddha himself, unhesitatingly."[1]

How many students would remain contented and devoted if a guru demanded a spouse or partner as "payment" and then beat her or him in front of us? Probably most of us would flee. Such a test would deeply challenge our Western standards of ethics. I have heard stories of a teacher who tested the faith of two of his close, longtime students very fiercely. He stabbed one of them, his personal attendant, with a fork. The disciple received this without complaint and his devotion to his teacher remained constant. The other student got burned profoundly in the fires of testing when the teacher made sexual advances toward the student's teenage daughter. The outraged student left the teacher immediately. There are some tests that are just too painful for even the most committed devotee to submit to with absolute faith. Just the thought of these awful tests can feel like a face-to-face encounter with the mysterious Tilopa, or with Bhairava, the fierce and terrible, ego-destroying aspect of Shiva.

In the stage of testing, we're confronted with attachments and asked to make an offering of our fears. Some teachers deliberately sow the seeds of doubt in our minds to determine our level of trust. But if we've come this far with a teacher and feel significant changes inside us flowing from our spiritual practices, then our trust will not be easily shaken. That trust opens the channels for a stream of transmission, which is ultimately the transmission of our own being.

Another test of faith occurs when the teacher completely ignores the student for some period of time, sometimes causing the student to feel completely rejected. At this juncture a student who is wavering or incapable of trusting the teacher may flee, while one who understands the teacher's instructions will be undeterred and continue to practice meditation and self-inquiry. Such a student demonstrates commitment not only to the teacher but also to the discipline and inner mastery that discipleship entails.

FIERCE TEACHERS

There are teachers who deliberately and effectively use their intensity as a means of transforming and liberating students. Such teachers bring us face to face with our fears and expose our weaknesses—our lack of courage, our wounded pride, our insufferable arrogance, our desire to be rescued by others. Shedding light on these areas can make us stronger. In hatha yoga we practice *virasana,* the hero pose, or pose of the brave. A spiritual apprentice needs bravery and courage to outgrow being weak, fearful, and contracted. A longtime student of kundalini yoga told me,

> I'm one of the lucky ones who got to be in Yogi Bhajan's presence, to receive his ray and feel his intensity. He was a very directive and forceful teacher, not just some calm yogi. He told us exactly what he wanted us to do. And we were young; we needed that to pull ourselves together. Some people didn't like that, didn't want someone telling them what to do. And so they left. Their loss.

If we're bold and trust the teacher, we can be transformed by fiery teachings. One man gave this account of a lesson from a hatha yoga master:

I went to Hawaii for a weeklong retreat with a very intense yogi. He annihilated me completely. He kept us moving all the time, and my body started to get burning hot. I felt weak and uneasy, and he kept pressing me to my limits in every exercise. After the first day I was exhausted. By the second and third day, I was mentally and emotionally drained and defeated. He was so strong and powerful and demanded so much of us that I became frightened that something terrible was going to happen to me. A few times he yelled at me for being so afraid. I kept saying, "I can't do it." And he looked me firmly in the eye and he kept saying, "You can. Come on. Do it." We did so many handstands and so many back bends. After a while I just let go to it and my body stretched to its limits, which were beyond what I'd thought my limits were. That was amazing to me. By the fourth and fifth days, I had faced a lot of my fear and gone beyond it. His fiery teaching liberated me by forcing me to go beyond my limits. I felt more powerful and confident than I ever had.

Some intense and fiery teachers behave in ways that on the surface might seem arrogant, grandiose, and inflated. Take a teacher like Bikram Choudhury, a man with a very strong personality who once said, "I have balls like atom bombs, two of them, 100 megatons each. Nobody fucks with me." But his students find his self-confidence infectious and say it inspires them to work extremely hard at their yoga to rouse a similar poise, strength, self-mastery, and belief in themselves. For that reason some consider him to be a very great teacher. And so what seems like arrogance to one person can be a living flame of inspiration to another. For this reason it's up to each one of us to discern whether a teacher is someone to place one's trust in. I was given a helpful teaching on this by my friend Nur Richard Gale:

In the Eastern Christian (Greek and Russian Orthodox, Syrian, and Coptic) traditions, they have always emphasized the doctrine of humility. The disciple is always cautioned against "vainglory" in a teacher, which means deceit, or pride in self and raising oneself above others. This is the most dangerous sign in a teacher. Humility is always said to be the antidote to vainglory. And the way to discern if a teacher is lost in vainglory is to observe his or her state of humility.

To be an effective means of instruction, the teacher's fierceness should *feel* compassionate. We can receive and benefit from fierce instruction if we sense that we're truly loved by our teacher. When we lose all sense of the teacher's compassion and love for us, trust is shaken and we inwardly revolt. At this juncture some students proceed directly to the stage of separating from the spiritual teacher.

CRAZY WISDOM OR ABUSIVE CONDUCT?

Sometimes the process of testing causes us to resist the teacher or to want to escape from his or her presence as soon as possible, feeling that we need to protect ourselves. It can be uncomfortable to bear the feelings evoked by intense spiritual discipline and the teacher's exposure of our fears. At this phase we must choose whether or not to submit to the guru's testing.

Some adepts are forceful slayers of the ego, impersonal and sometimes cruel. Association with such a teacher can light a fire under us that can either destroy or purify. Whether this proves to be a cleansing fire or a destructive one depends on both the integrity of the teacher and the courage of the student to consciously live through an exposure of the ego that can be quite unsettling. The mystic guide's job is to liberate us, and to accomplish this goal spiritual shock therapy may be necessary.

There's a long tradition of crazy-wisdom teachers who make outrageous demands of students or engage in actions that seem strange or inexplicable. Georg Feuerstein describes crazy wisdom as the world-wide tradition of spiritual adepts whose behavior and teaching prove shocking to ordinary moral sensibilities and challenge widely held norms of thought and conduct. These are the crazy adepts of Tibetan Buddhism, the eccentric teachers of Ch'an (Zen), the holy fools of Christianity and Islam, the *avadhutas* and *bauls* of Hinduism, and the tricksters and religious clowns of tribal traditions. In order to teach spiritual truths, these masters often adopt quite unconventional means—certainly means that are not ordinarily associated with holy folk. They resort to alcohol and other drugs, and they use sexuality for instructional purposes. . . . Their generally outrageous behavior does not at all conform to our cherished ideas of religiosity, morality, and sanctity. . . . Their seemingly crazy deeds have the express purpose of topsy-turvying consensus reality in order to lead to spiritual breakthroughs. . . . The crazy-wise teachers are eccentrics who use their eccentricity to communicate an alternative vision to that which governs ordinary life. They are masters of inversion, proficient breakers of taboos, and lovers of surprise, contradiction, and ambiguity. . . . That which tricksters, clowns, mad lamas, Zen masters, holy fools, rascal gurus, and crazy-wise adepts have in common is active rejection of consensual reality. They behave in ways that outwardly manifest the reversal of values and attitudes intrinsic to all genuine spirituality.[2]

The idea of fierce, crazy wisdom has strong roots in Tibetan Buddhism, with its magnificent, ego-slaying demon-deity Mahakala. There is nothing gentle about the training of Tibetan Buddhist monks and yogic aspirants. We see this in the stories of the Kagyu yogis Tilopa, Nāropa, Marpa, and Milarepa, who passed through arduous, harrowing tests and became intense gurus whose behaviors could be fiery and perplexing. A descendant of these practitioners, the Vidyadhara, Chögyam Trungpa Rinpoche was definitely a fierce teacher. One of his longtime students told me the following:

I loved Trungpa very much, but he wasn't always a nice person. He wasn't very kind; he had a kind of ruthless compassion. Most of his students were terrified of him. He experienced trauma in his life. In childhood he was displaced and exiled from Tibet. He was separated from his mother at age two because of being recognized as a tulku, so he didn't grow up with many small acts of kindness. People were traumatized around him right and left. That wasn't his concern. He was constantly a vehicle for dharma transmission. When you were around him, you could feel it vibrating like an intense electrical force.

An example of Trungpa's wild and inscrutable behavior was a widely publicized incident at a Halloween party during a 1975 Vajrayana retreat, where the inebriated guru decided to have the assembled party-goers strip off their clothing. Two of the guests, the poet W. S. Merwin and his girlfriend, decided to hide in their room. Apparently Trungpa had become annoyed at them for questioning the bloody war imagery used in some of the Tibetan Buddhist chants. Trungpa didn't believe a trainee should talk back to a guru, even if the trainee was a famous writer. Merwin was a visiting poet who'd requested permission to attend the retreat even though he hadn't done the arduous preliminary practices and wasn't familiar with the guru's unpredictable personality and unconventional methods. Trungpa sent for Merwin and his friend, but they refused to return to the party. Trungpa then sent a larger contingent to retrieve them, this time ordering them to join the party. When Merwin resisted Trungpa told his attendants to use whatever means were necessary. A group forced their way into the poet's room by smashing down the door, and after a bloody scuffle in which Merwin tried to defend himself using the jagged end of a broken bottle, he and his girlfriend were dragged screaming and crying into the party, where Trungpa yelled at them and other people stripped off their clothing. Following this incident the poet Allen Ginsberg, a committed student of Trungpa's who hadn't been at the party, was among those asked to condemn Trungpa's behavior and was left in an uncomfortable position as he didn't wish to denounce his teacher publicly. This posed a very great test of faith in his teacher, just as it tested the trust of all those present and of almost everyone who has heard about this incident.[3]

Hearing this story not only do our jaws practically hit the ground in shock, we're also left wondering if there was truly any wisdom in this craziness. It sounds to me as if, in a very intoxicated condition, Trungpa was reckless and impulsive, not considering that his actions could ignite such a berserk and violent episode. I imagine that his intention may have been to shine a light on the students' unwillingness to unmask themselves in deep humility. I can imagine an alternative scenario that might have ensued had Merwin and his girlfriend agreed to pack up their minds and bravely obey the order to take off their clothes, just because the guru said so. Yet I don't think it's hard for anyone to empathize with Merwin and his friend for defending themselves against a marauding mob, which must have been a traumatic experience. We're left questioning whether this was truly "skillful means" in spiritual guidance or simply abuse. Yet Trungpa was an undeniable force as a teacher. Paradoxes abound.

In a case like this, where a teacher makes strange demands, we're left to consider whether these outrageous behaviors are truly expressions of crazy wisdom, intended as tests for students, or is this abusive conduct? For example, suppose a teacher demands more and more money from us and then claims that this is to free us from our attachment and clinging. Is this exploitation or a crazy-wisdom teaching? One determining factor is the closeness and longevity of the relationship between student and teacher. I might allow a teacher I know well to wield a scalpel to my ego. In such a context I might be able to trust the process. I might be able to unmask and emotionally disrobe; there's a container in place. In this case Merwin and Trungpa barely knew each other, so it was very hard to trust the teacher's motives. Someone else commanded by the guru to disrobe might have seen some humor in the situation and accepted it in a good-natured way, without fighting it.

One of Trungpa's students told me that Trungpa later expressed regret about the incident, but also regret that he'd agreed to allow Merwin to attend the retreat in the first place, given that he wasn't a committed practitioner and didn't have a context for understanding a request for surrender to a vajra master's command. Merwin was placed in a predicament he wasn't prepared to understand, and the situation didn't serve him well at all. Apparently this whole episode was a humbling learning experience for the guru himself. But some of his crazy-wisdom teachings were more effective; we'll see this later.

In creating challenging tests, some teachers shine a spotlight on our fears; on our attachments to public image, name, reputation, and possessions; or on our cravings for drugs or alcohol. Sometimes teachers confront us head-on and arouse our defenses and suspicions. Their unpredictable actions can be unsettling and provocative. At this stage we either flee or we confront our doubts and sharpen our commitments. We may come to feel grateful to the teacher for revealing our attachments, rigidity, and self-righteousness.

TESTS OF THE STUDENT'S CHARACTER

The human heart must first be melted, like metal,
before it can be molded into a desirable character.

HAZRAT INAYAT KHAN, *COMPLETE SAYINGS*

Spiritual teachers test our character, maturity, and understanding. Discipleship is a path of purification that shows us what we're made of. In making a commitment to enlightenment through spiritual apprenticeship, we implicitly agree to a process that will reveal neuroses, fixations, and imperfections. This is a process that at times can be intensely uncomfortable.

According to P. D. Ouspensky, the mystic Gurdjieff once recounted a story about an esoteric school he visited during his travels. This school practiced an exercise in which students were instructed to freeze in the exact physical position in which they found themselves at the moment of a designated stop signal. Students were taken by surprise and didn't have time to compose themselves; they just needed to stop everything and freeze. In the Gurdjieff teachings, the purpose of this stop exercise is to create favorable circumstances for self-observation by freezing a random moment, a practice that can lead to a satori, a spontaneous moment of awakening and enlightenment that marks an abrupt shift from our daily cognitive and emotional state. On one occasion a student of the esoteric school faithfully obeyed his teacher's instruction to freeze while he was standing in the rising waters of an irrigation canal. The water nearly drowned the man as he courageously obeyed the instructions and stood immobile. He barely escaped with his life, but the man was transformed by having the courage to face trepidation and the possibility of death.[4] This story illustrates the radical commitment to self-observation sometimes needed on the spiritual path. We may be pressed in various ways to unconditionally trust and let go, beyond ego, beyond fear.

Testing may involve specific instructions that are difficult for the student to carry out. The teacher may ask the student to give up sex, drugs, a career, or a relationship, or to commit to a particular job, diet, marriage, or spiritual practice. A student who loves to meditate but isn't very grounded or practical may be asked to work long hours at a job so there's no time for meditation.

One man who'd been very promiscuous in his young adulthood and confessed to having sexually exploited many women was requested by his teacher to marry a woman whom at first he found unattractive. After struggling with this instruction, he befriended this woman and eventually chose to marry her. He told me that this marriage helped his evolution on the spiritual path. He perceived his wife as a goddess and dedicated himself to her service. His teacher asked him to master the difficult test of learning to love another human being. His heart changed; a sex-obsessed person preoccupied with lust and the strategies of seduction became a devotee of the divine feminine and a being full of love.

Sometimes testing reveals and affirms the maturity and integrity a student already possesses. One teacher arranged to have someone offer a bribe to a disciple who was a police officer; he refused the bribe, and his good character was demonstrated. Another teacher spread rumors about a student to see if he'd get angry. The student remained silent while other people gossiped about him. He remained steady and continued meditating without being distracted by other people's opinions and criticisms.

Some tests challenge us to exceed our limitations. A woman named Jessica reported:

My teacher sent me away to start a human-service project where we set up kitchen facilities and shelters for indigent children and adults in northern India. We clothed and fed people and made sure they got some kind of medical care. At first I was put off by this assignment. I thought when I finally found a teacher that I'd do intense meditation practices in a retreat somewhere. Instead, I got thrown right into the thick of life in an enormous overcrowded city with many social problems. I learned so much from that experience. I grew as a human being. I discovered what compassion means. I learned courage, especially as I watched these people coping with so many adversities. And I learned to instill courage in others, to strengthen them to carry on. I'm so grateful for the test that my teacher set for me.

RESTING THE EGO AND ABIDING IN THE SELF

To awaken spiritually we need to overcome the misperception that our identity is solely tied to our physical appearance, our rational mind, our opinions, and our social status. Certainly it's important for all of us to be concerned in an appropriate way about our social personas and to achieve a healthy feeling about our bodies. But we can become preoccupied with projecting a particular image or fixated on body dissatisfaction or negative body image, to the degree that we become totally identified with the body. Intellectual development is also important, but if we get too wrapped up in our thoughts, fantasies, memories, and intellectual constructs, we become identified with the contents of the mind. So, too, we identify with our feelings—our resentments, fears, cravings, and aversions. Patanjali, author of the Yoga Sutras, calls this *asmita,* false identification with the instruments and vehicles of consciousness—body, mind, and feelings—rather than with consciousness itself, the indwelling spiritual essence.[5] Asmita is identifying with the ego instead of with the Self, the *Purusha,* the inner seer who is none other than the inner guide. Yoga is the practice of serenely abiding in this deeper, more vast and silent consciousness. The fierce testing by a teacher and the tests of life expose obstacles to Self-awareness. According to advaita vedanta philosophy, when the false is removed, what remains is Reality, or Brahman. This is knowledge. The great guru Shankara wrote:

O prudent one, lose all sense of separation and enter into silence. Realize that you are one with the self-luminous Brahman, the ground of all existence. . . . The Atman is the reality. It is your true, primal self. It is pure consciousness, the one without a second, absolute bliss. It is beyond form and action. Realize your identity with it. Stop identifying yourself with the coverings of ignorance, which are like the masks assumed by an actor.[6]

To liberate us, great teachers create tests that expose our false identification with the ego and root out impurities such as imperious, self-important attitudes, rigidity, oversensitivity, slothfulness, and feelings of superiority—or inferiority. The process of testing teaches us to let go of our lesser identities in order to awaken to our greater identity.

A figure capturing the nature of this phase of the path is the Hindu tantric goddess known as Chinnamasta Mahavidya, a name that translates as "the seduction and destruction of illusion."[7] The image on page 126 depicts illusion as a decapitated woman standing on a lotus with

Chinnamasta Mahavidya.

streams of blood pouring out of her neck, holding her own head in her hand. Like Chinnamasta, the guru's job is to hand us our egos on a platter. If you don't want to get burned, then don't stand near the fire. If you don't want your illusions and limitations to get chopped, then stay away from the guillotine. In her other hand Chinnamasta carries a sword or scimitar, showing that she's self-decapitated, a symbol of self-surrender and self-sacrifice. It reflects the way we enter a situation in which we are likely to be deftly "beheaded" when we submit to the teacher's fiery training. A fierce tantric deity wearing a garland of skulls (representing myriad rebirths), the decapitated goddess represents overcoming ego-centeredness, experiencing defeats and exposure of the ego, and discovering the openness of nonegoic consciousness. When you offer yourself fully and appear to be "headless," you begin to live from a place beyond the mind, with intensified feeling and desire. Cobras wrapped around her body signify that serpentine energies move through her. She represents the blissful, throbbing aspect of divine consciousness, or *citi*. Chinnamasta stands upon the naked bodies of the lovers Radha and Krishna, drawing their energy through her feet, signifying the sparking, transmutation, and circulation of sexual energies, the awakening of kundalini, and the overcoming of duality, unifying the opposites of asceticism and eroticism. The blossoming petals of the lotus flower signify the unfolding of our potential and are symbolic of divine purity and serenity.[8]

Chinnamasta is a symbol representing this stage of testing as a process that cuts through our illusions, fears, and negativity. Most of us still have a lot of work to do on our character development, and a spiritual teacher who carefully studies us will often make us conscious of all our shadows and rough edges. If a student is overly weak, depressed, or vulnerable, the teacher may pose a challenge that encourages the person to grow stronger and more assertive. When the student is a very difficult, hostile, arrogant, or hard-headed person with personality flaws that are evident to everyone but himself or herself, the teacher may be quite forceful in revealing these qualities. I once saw Muktananda give a thorough tongue-lashing to a man who'd been observed many times breaking ashram rules. Afterward, the man was humbled and remorseful, and his behavior and demeanor seemed to change. But challenging the student's ego isn't the same as abject humiliation, where the student is seriously traumatized and emotionally damaged by the experience.

Later we will discuss how in some cases the line between humbling and humiliation is rather blurry.

Swami Muktananda began exposing my ego from the very beginning. The first time I ever spoke to Baba in 1974, when I was sixteen, I asked him a question about spiritual pride. I'd been reading Chögyam Trungpa's book *Cutting through Spiritual Materialism,* which was relevant to me because at the time I was feeling slightly superior to some of my high school classmates who hadn't discovered the wonders of yoga and the spiritual path. In response Baba said, "There was once a young boy who was a great yogi. He was such a great yogi that he developed *siddhis,* powers. One of his siddhis was that he could say a mantra over a bowl of oatmeal and make it expand so much that it covered the entire surface of the Earth. Do you have any such powers?" When I nodded no, he said, "Well, wait until something happens. Then you can get conceited about it." His response deftly deflated me. I felt like a complete fool, but afterward I had a good laugh at myself.

My big ego was also exposed through some lessons in the area of work. For a long time I was condescending and had a negative attitude about my assigned jobs in the ashram. I used to get steamed up over being asked to clean toilets, vacuum hallways, and mop floors. I did my jobs quietly and without complaint, but inwardly I was huffy and disdainful. I often wondered why I couldn't be assigned to work in the library or do editing work for ashram publications or anything more interesting than these menial tasks. I particularly disliked jobs that felt as if they were made up just to keep us ashram residents occupied.

Once I spent over a month engaged in an absurd work project. I was part of a crew charged with the task of using buckets to transport an enormous pile of rocks from a parking lot to the basement of a building, which had a very low ceiling. I kept dropping the rocks and bumping my head on the low ceiling, and the heavy buckets were throwing my spine out of alignment. I began to get really tired and bored. Then I became intensely angry about all the time I was wasting on this task. I began to plan how I'd escape from this ashram gulag.

This job often made me think about a story epitomizing the phase of testing in spiritual apprenticeship, the story of Milarepa, the Tibetan yogi whose teacher, Marpa, made him spend twelve years building numerous stone edifices, tearing each of them down and then rebuilding them. Years of backbreaking labor brought Milarepa to the brink of absolute despair, extreme physical exhaustion and pain, and the loss of all hope that he would attain enlightenment in his lifetime. Later Milarepa came to understand why he'd been tested so severely: It turns out that prior to seeking instruction from Marpa, Milarepa had been involved in black magic. He'd learned to cast spells to seek revenge against an evil uncle who'd stolen Milarepa's father's property and deprived the rest of the family of its rightful inheritance. Milarepa was informed that it was because of the negative karma he'd accrued through these violent, destructive magical acts that Marpa needed to test him so ruthlessly, to purify him fully. Only then was he fit for instruction and initiation.[9]

Reflecting on this story, I became absorbed in the fantasy that I was being tested like Milarepa and purified through my arduous labors of all my past karma. After a while, however, I began to realize that perhaps it was no great spiritual test. At that point I returned to the ordinariness of the task, the naked sensation of the weight of the rocks, their density and smoothness, the sensations of my tired, aching muscles carrying the buckets.

For a while I made quite a show of how hard I was working. When people passed by, I'd let out grunts and moans so everyone would see how difficult my job was. I made a point of appearing strong and energetic and showing off how muscular I was. I was lost in the drama of it all, the sheer heroism of being out there in the sweltering heat working like a prisoner on a chain gang. Then I realized that nobody gave a damn what I was doing. I was just a skinny, long-haired teenager puffing out his scrawny chest, doing some stupid job. This realization struck a blow to my sense of specialness.

I'd been doing this job for so long, yet the task was nowhere near complete. The pile of stones was enormous. There was no clear reason why we were being asked to move them. Yet there was nothing else to do. And so I surrendered to my assigned task. I tried to do it better. I began to grow more mindful, ducking carefully to avoid beheading myself. I began to feel invisible and merged into the activity of doing the job. I wasn't invested in the outcome. I became the work, practicing meditation in motion. The job was doing itself; I was just the instrument. I felt a sensation of emptiness and impersonality, but also peacefulness in doing the work in this manner. Soon thereafter I was assigned another job.

I gained tremendously from this experience. I burned out a lot of egotism, a feeling of being above doing ordinary labor. I came to respect the value of every task and occupation and learned to do daily labor with love. I came to feel joy in doing simple jobs thoroughly and well. One day I was sent off to sweep a remote pathway in a corner of the ashram grounds. I did the sweeping very carefully and mindfully, and as I did so I felt that I was sweeping the leaves from my mind as well as from the footpath. I was very peaceful as I did this. As I swept leaves that afternoon, I told myself that I would sweep the path so well that Baba himself would be pleased to walk on it. To my amazement, just as I was finishing my day's work, Baba showed up and walked down the path, followed by a trail of people. He stopped and looked at me and whispered, "Bahut accha," very good.

SELF-SURRENDER

Austerity, self-study and resignation to Isvara constitute preliminary yoga.

PATAÑJALI, *YOGA SUTRAS*

One day in Ganeshpuri, Baba was sitting quietly in his courtyard surrounded by people enjoying his darshan. The atmosphere was supremely tranquil. Gripped by some spontaneous impulse, I walked over to him, bowed down, and laid my head at his feet. Inwardly I felt myself let go completely. I surrendered to the divine will, to whatever was going to happen in my life. In that moment I let go of the desire for amazing meditation experiences. I let go of the desire for special recognition. I let go. When I looked up at him, he was very loving and compassionate. This was one of the most significant events of my life, this moment of self-offering. When I surrender I'm at peace. I experience blessings even in the midst of difficulties because I trust that what's happening is a lesson intended for me. As Hazrat Inayat Khan said, "No one will experience in life what is not meant for him. . . . There is nothing that is accidental; all situations in life work toward some definite end."[10]

We become true disciples when we surrender. Then our lives are in the hands of a greater intelligence, enfolded by its design. We trust the forces of guidance to lead us to our destination. To surrender is to experience serenity. Our hearts reach out to meet our source and origin, saying: "All that I am, all that I do is for you, Spirit. I leave the results in your hands, as I don't know what's best for me and for the good of all beings. I leave all that for you to decide. Please guide me so I'll know and do what I'm supposed to do. Act through me so your intentions are fulfilled. Let me know what you want for me, even if it's not always what I want for myself."

Meister Eckhart, the Catholic mystic sage, said:

In general it is the will of God that we surrender our wills. . . . Apart from complete surrender of the will, there is no traffic with God. . . . Yield completely to God and then be satisfied, whatever he does with his own. The only true and perfect will is the one that has been merged with the will of God, so that the man has no will of his own. . . . Relax and let God operate you and do what he will with you. The deed is his; the word is his; this birth is his; and all you are is his, for you have surrendered self to him, with all your soul's agents and their function and even your personal nature. Then at once, God comes into your being and faculties. . . . For this birth in the soul God will and must have a pure, free, and unencumbered soul, in which there is nothing but him alone, a soul that waits for nothing and nobody but him. . . . When he finds you ready he must act, and pour into you, just as when the air is clear and pure the sun must pour into it, and may not hold back. . . . You need not look either here or there. He is no farther away than the door of the heart. He stands there, lingering, waiting for us to be ready and open the door and let him in. You need not call to him as if he were far away, for he waits more urgently than you for the door to be opened. You are a thousand times more necessary to him than he is to you. The opening of the door and his entry are simultaneous.[11]

SURRENDER, NOT SUBMISSION

Some people mistrust the idea of self-surrender, seeing it as a naive response that invites exploitation. But inward surrender doesn't always mean that we submit to whatever the teacher asks us to do. If doubts are stirred and we're feeling mistrustful, we have the right to ask a teacher why a particular test or acceding to a difficult request will serve our growth and well-being. Testing by a skillful teacher has only one goal: to free the student of ignorance, fear, unhealthy attachment, and areas of resistance to change. Where we sense teachers have other motivations, driven more by their own desires, then we may need to resist. Brenda, a longtime student of a teacher from India, gave the following account:

> Once I felt a very strong sexual energy emanating from my teacher toward me. It was intense. He didn't say anything, but intuitively I knew that he wanted to have sex with me, and he was checking out whether I was interested or not. I totally ignored it. I wasn't interested at all. I was a yogini, a meditator, not one of his *gopis,* worshipping him. That wasn't my path at all. He never bothered me again after that.

In some situations we have to refuse to comply with a teacher's command or reject unwanted advances. And all children need to be taught to say no to any older person who touches them inappropriately or asks them to take their clothes off, even if it's in Swami's room. Respect, gratitude, and devotion toward a teacher don't have to entail mindless acquiescence to any request a teacher may make of us. Here the advice of Swami Radha, a highly accomplished female spiritual teacher, is pertinent:

> Disciples should not do anything that goes against their conscience. They need to use discrimination, and for female disciples that is often a stumbling block. Women have learned to listen to their fathers, their male teachers, their professors, their male doctors, and they do not use enough discrimination. Aspirants should study and find out what is involved in spiritual life and not just race ahead looking for acceptance by a male as if the guru by virtue of his title will automatically make them spiritual.[12]

A woman named Sara told me, "I concluded that my studying with him and receiving his blessing didn't require that I become his consort. I fulfill my sexual needs elsewhere, and I expect him to do so too, with someone appropriate. I just wish he could openly adopt one woman into this role instead of being sneaky and surreptitious about it." Unquestioning submission to emotional, sexual, or financial exploitation will not bring accelerated spiritual growth. We need to assess whether our experience makes us more liberated, joyous, or enlightened. We needn't be powerless victims.

John Welwood distinguishes between submission and surrender:

> To understand the value of commitment to a genuine master, we need to distinguish between mindful surrender, which can be enlivening, and mindless submission, which is a deadening flight from freedom. . . . For many people today, the idea of surrender implies losing intelligence or individuality to another person and

taking a weak, submissive, "one down" position. True surrender, however, is never enslaving, but rather is a genuine step toward empowerment, the discovery of one's own most genuine power. . . . The recent critics of narcissism in our society tend to see all involvement with spiritual masters in this light, failing to distinguish between submission as a developmentally regressive retreat from maturity, and genuine surrender, which allows people to move beyond egocentricity to a fuller realization of their being. . . . With a genuine spiritual master, surrendering means presenting oneself in a completely honest, naked way, without trying to hold anything back or maintain any facade. . . . Being in the presence of a true master is a rare opportunity to let down all one's pretence, to unmask and simply be as one is.[13]

In a story that encapsulates the transformative potential of testing, a man named Karl described a test that led to self-examination and unmasking in his teacher's presence:

Darshan with my teacher was intense because he was so unpredictable. One day I approached him and he began yelling and cursing at me, accusing me of doing all these things I hadn't done. I said, "Guruji, no, I didn't do these things." He slapped me a couple of times hard on my back and told me to go away and come see him tomorrow. I went back to my room frightened that I'd committed some terrible act, but I couldn't figure out what it was. I was very upset because I didn't know why he'd turned on me suddenly. I had no idea what I'd done wrong. I searched myself and thought, "I know I didn't do these things he accused me of, but have I done anything else that might have hurt anyone?" I'd done a thorough moral inventory through my involvement with Alcoholics Anonymous, but now I mentally reviewed different periods of my life and I saw various instances of discord with others. I could think of a number of people I still had issues with. Later on that evening I called up some of them and talked for a long time. I felt really sorry about the thoughtless, insensitive things I'd done. But I also felt compassion for myself. I saw how I'd been motivated by fear and ignorance, lust and jealousy. And I felt tremendous love for everyone. By the time I was finished that night, I felt peaceful because my conscience was clear, and I felt more self-love. And that feeling continued the next day when I went back for darshan. I was very open and sensitive because so many of my imperfections had been brought into the open. I knew my teacher might still be mad at me and start yelling again. I understood that I had many impurities I knew he was aware of. But I loved him, and I loved myself. In that frame of mind, I came before him. He got up out of his seat and rose to embrace me. We hugged for a long time. He whispered in my ear, "Your essence is completely pure." He smiled at me with a golden warmth. And that was the last time he ever spoke to me.

❧

Surrender is the awareness that we can't always control the course of events or other people's actions and that we have to trust the plan that life has for us, even when it doesn't match our ideas or our concepts. When we surrender in a state of calm acceptance we become less defensive and more available to Spirit and an intelligence greater than ourselves. With this attitude the spiritual apprentice endures the purifying fires of testing and thus becomes receptive to the greatest gift the guru has to offer: the mystery of grace.

STAGE FIVE

❧

Grace and Guru Yoga

Receiving the Teacher's Spacious Gaze

The void Mind-Essence is my Guru's body;
My Guru is Dorje Chang, with the Wisdom-Body;
My Guru is Tilopa, with the Six Miraculous Powers;
My Guru is Nāropa, with the Net of Myriad Spells;
My Guru is Marpa, to whom I owe the greatest debt.
They sit ever upon my head as my glory;
If you have a pair of clear and sincere eyes
You will see them as real Buddhas.
If with sincerity and faith you pray to them,
The rain of grace will ever fall upon you,
If you offer practice and devotion,
The treasury of Accomplishments will be opened to you.

THE HUNDRED THOUSAND SONGS OF MILAREPA

At certain stages the meeting of minds that occurs between student and teacher ceases to feel like a relationship between two separate individuals. Through conscious attunement and merger with the teacher's presence and through clear awareness, the student can have experiences that are profoundly peaceful, holy, or numinous, bestowing tangible and mysterious blessings. Now the living Spirit is transmitted and revealed through the teacher's contagious influence. Georg Feuerstein writes:

> The enlightened teacher communicates Shiva-Shakti, or Consciousness-Power, by his or her mere existence. He or she is in fact not different from that Reality because he or she no longer suffers from the presumption of being a finite being with a body and mind that is ultimately separate from other beings. An enlightened person lives as, and out of, the fullness of the single Reality. Therefore, his or her sheer presence has transformative power, which is of advantage to those who can attune themselves to it. . . . The teacher's communication of that which is Real has a purifying effect on the disciple who receives this spiritual transmission. And that is its whole purpose. The teacher's transmission can have very different effects in the disciple. It can lead to utterly blissful states or violent emotional reactivity, feelings of well-being or episodes of illness. Regardless of the effects, the primary function of spiritual transmission is to intensify the disciple's whole life.[1]

It's because of this transformative influence that all schools of yoga in India recommend that a spiritual aspirant seek out the company, or *satsang*, of an illumined being who resides constantly in an expanded state of consciousness.

> In the company of the God-realized master, the practitioner is continuously exposed to the realizer's spiritualized body-mind, and by way of "contagion" his own physical and psychical being is gradually transformed. . . . For this spontaneous process to be truly effective, the disciple must consciously cooperate with his guru. He accomplishes this by making the teacher his focus of attention. This is the great principle of sat-sanga. The word means literally "company of the True" or "relationship to the Real." Sat-sanga is the supreme

means of liberation in guru-yoga. And since the guru has from ancient times been deemed essential to yogic practice, sat-sanga is at the core of all schools of Yoga. It would not be wrong to say that all Yoga is guru-yoga.[2]

GIFTS OF SPIRIT

Through contact with a teacher, one may experience a descent of peace or an infusion of spiritual power. As a practitioner's tranquility deepens through meditation, the *guru tattva,* the principle of revelation of grace, begins to operate with greater intensity, bestowing uplifting gifts of Spirit. These experiences inspire us, increase devotion to the teacher, and strengthen our commitment to our practices. Such experiences are more likely to occur for those under the influence of a great teacher, not an ordinary one. An awakened teacher serves as a conduit of grace and a lightning rod of Spirit, through whom inner guidance and tangible blessings are conveyed to others.

With the cosmic serpent at his feet, blissful face radiating grace, hands raised in blessing and transmission, dancing Shiva embodies divine energy in motion and activates a living spiritual fire within us. Darshan of Shiva Nataraj, Tanjore.

We now find ourselves inside the inner temple, at the center of the guru's mandala, where we encounter the secret teaching at the heart of yoga lineages and many mystical and esoteric schools. This isn't a philosophy or doctrine but a direct spiritual transmission. This is the reason we've endured hardships and been ridiculed by worldly people: to place ourselves within this teacher's sphere of influence. We've been tested and provoked but have persevered, and now the visible teacher in physical form transforms into a larger presence and agency of something transcendent that suddenly bursts into flame in our awareness. The true nature of the guru is revealed to us suddenly, and we discover it is something greater than any individual. Our sustained effort to realize the state of pure consciousness, through meditation and devotion, draws to us Spirit's answer to our longing.

UNFATHOMABLE GRACE

In India there's an annual celebration called Guru Purnima, which is traditionally a day of celebration akin to our Mother's Day except that its purpose is to honor the guru. It's said that on Guru Purnima the guru showers blessings on all devotees. In the summer of 1976, I took a long bus ride to visit my teacher for this occasion. However, that day I had a very unpleasant reaction to the ashram and the thousand or so other people who were present. I was preoccupied with various personal problems and wanted some attention from my teacher. Instead, Muktananda was surrounded by a throng of devotees and I felt completely invisible. Discouraged, I wondered why I'd even bothered to come.

Later that evening I returned home to Manhattan. I went to bed, sadly bemoaning that no blessings had been showered on me. I slept soundly for several hours. Then at about three a.m. I awoke suddenly, sensing a presence hovering above me that felt like a cloud of bliss. An intense current of energy descended into my body, electrifying every cell. For perhaps twenty seconds, I was bathed in ecstasy. I lovingly received this visitation of the sacred, numinous Spirit, completely in awe. Then the energy vanished.

Over the next few weeks, I pondered this experience constantly, trying to figure out what had happened, as well as how to bring it back. Finally, I traveled to visit my teacher again. The day I arrived, he strode into a room where hundreds of students were seated. He sat down, looked straight at me, and said, "The grace of the guru is truly unfathomable!" He lifted up his sunglasses so his eyes were visible like bright suns and looked directly at me for several long moments. His statement had deep significance. I realized I could never intellectually fathom the mysterious energy that had visited and filled me that memorable night. And I realized that the appropriate response to receiving a gift of grace is to remain in a state of active receptivity and meditative constancy. Rather than trying to explain this experience with my rational mind, I was being instructed to live in devotion—not to a person, but to the divine Shakti that I now knew dwelled within me. So the next task was to make myself and my life a vessel capable of holding more infusions of that blissful cosmic energy.

Since the sumer of 1976, when I had this experience, I've been profoundly moved and filled with gratitude. My teacher revealed to me the mystery of the invisible Beloved. This was my personal Burning Bush episode, and it had absolutely nothing to do with my volition or will. There's a stage of spiritual life when you feel yourself existing in relationship to a transcendent Other that's infinite and undefinable.

When this experience of grace occurred, I'd just finished a religious studies course in which I read Rudolph Otto's book *The Idea of the Holy*. Contemplating my experience I realized that I'd encountered what Otto called the holy, the numinous:

The numinous is . . . felt as objective and outside the self. . . . [To describe the numinous] there is only one appropriate expression, *mysterium tremendum*. The feeling of it may at times come sweeping like a gentle tide, pervading the mind with a tranquil mood of deepest worship. It may pass over into a more set and lasting attitude of the soul, continuing, as it were, thrillingly vibrant and resonant, until at last it dies away and the soul resumes its "profane," non-religious mood of everday experience. It may burst in sudden eruption up from the depths of the soul with spasms and convulsions, or lead to the strangest excitements, to intoxicated frenzy, to transport, and to ecstasy. . . . It may become the hushed, trembling, and speechless humility of the creature in the presence of—whom or what? In the presence of that which is a *mystery* inexpressible and above all creatures. . . . Conceptually, *mysterium* denotes merely that which is hidden and esoteric, that which is beyond conception or understanding, extraordinary and unfamiliar.[3]

In its appearance as *tremendum,* the numinous has the characteristics of awefulness, overpoweringness, and urgency. The experience of the divine presence induces both awe and fear. And it's overpowering, having the qualities of "might, power, absolute overpoweringness. . . . [T]here is the feeling of one's own submergence, of being but 'dust and ashes' and nothingness. And this forms the numinous raw material for the feeling of religious humility."[4] As *mysterium,* the numinous is felt to be wholly Other, inducing "blank wonder, an astonishment that strikes us dumb, amazement absolute."[5] The mysterium also has the quality of fascination, entrancing us and transporting us into "dizzy intoxication."[6]

Otto says that the experience of the numinous also has the qualities of energy, vitality, passion, will, force, movement, excitement, activity, and impetus. The sudden infusion of numinous power into our bodies ignites internal sparks of life force, the heat of the awakening kundalini, the heaving and writhing internal serpentine movements of self-liberating consciousness, bursting our small vessels and returning to its inevitable freedom. The aspirant who receives this infusion of the light is visibly affected, becoming filled with awe and gratitude and alive with the reverberations of this spiritual visitation.

GRACE AND SELF-EFFORT

Experiencing the bestowal of grace and the presence of numinous spiritual energies, we may wonder about the relationship between grace and self-effort in contemplative practice. Is the experience of receiving such grace a result of our effort, or is it totally a gift, completely independent of our effort and striving? Did my longing for contact with the maha shakti have any causal relationship to its occurence? Sociologist of religion Dick Anthony identifies two major approaches to spiritual growth. The first is a charismatic approach, in which the teacher is viewed as a source of power, wisdom, or grace that can be transmitted to the student, who only needs to be open to receive it; the second approach is a technical orientation to inner growth, in which practicing contemplative techniques leads directly to illumination and enlightenment, without requiring a teacher's grace or subtle influence.[7] In a technical approach, the teacher's job is to instruct the student in such methods as prayer, meditation, or asanas and pranayama. After that it's up to the student to practice these techniques with discipline and intensity.

Those who favor a charismatic approach contend that no genuine spiritual advancement is possible through a purely technical approach, that spiritual practices are only effective when an enlightened teacher initiates the student and potentiates the mantra, the meditation technique. Those favoring a technical approach contend that a charismatic emphasis gives the teacher too much power and responsibility for our growth and also makes the student vulnerable to flaws in the teacher's character. If the teacher is the necessary agent of transformation, then a spiritual apprentice's progress could be hindered if the teacher proves to be an impure or imperfect vehicle for transmission of truth.[8] In a technical approach, progress is solely dependent on the student's effort in practicing techniques of self-transformation such as meditation or breathwork. There's no external agency that assists.

The technical approach to spiritual growth is rooted in awareness that the teacher's blessings won't do it all. To grow spiritually takes sustained effort as well as grace. We need both surrender and self-effort in our quest for inner freedom. One-pointed meditation focuses the mind and helps us relax into our real nature, the spacious, silent witnessing Self, which is the field of consciousness itself; inwardly we feel it as a sense of bliss and vastness. Self-realization is recognition that our own mind isn't separate from all-pervasive consciousness. A teacher can show us the way, teach us the doctrine, and embody the enlightened state, but we have to stabilize ourselves in this state through effort and disciplined practice. Some gentle tapasya and active sadhana burns away our laziness, fans the solar plexus fire, and activates our prana and vitality.

According to Swami Lakshmanjoo, a great teacher of Kashmir Shaivism, liberation comes when "the grace of Lord Shiva is showered on you, or when your God consciousness is liberated by the vibrating force of the teachings of your master." However, Swami Lakshmanjoo adds that the deeper stages of meditation "can only be accomplished through one's will and concentration."

> Even the Guru's grace will not help a seeker unless he is determined and fully devoted to maintaining awareness and concentration. . . . The spiritual aspirant who waivers and becomes disturbed gains nothing. . . . In the *Tantraloka* it states that if the master is elevated, and if the disciple is endowed with complete qualifications, then the master can assist his disciple. But on the other hand, if the disciple is not really qualified, then the master cannot properly help or elevate him.[9]

The teacher is a catalyst for the student's accelerated spiritual evolution and is to be honored for revealing a path to truth. But the teacher's assistance will be of no benefit if we don't strive intensely to practice meditation, yoga, and other disciplines, to experience our inner light, our buddha nature. Active self-purification centers us and refines our awareness so we become receptive to mysterious internal blessings and movements of energy. The more sincere effort we make, the more grace flows toward us, not only from our own teacher, but from all the saints and buddhas and siddhas. Self-effort and receptivity to grace are eternally wedded on the path of the spiritual apprentice.

Dedication to spiritual practice is like a magnet that draws the enlightening influence of a great teacher and the revealed presence of Spirit. Becoming established in the discipline of abiding as the Self, or unconditioned awareness, an invisible conduit opens to a universal power. One-pointed meditation and Self-inquiry, coupled with internal receptivity, elicits the bestowal of grace.

Traditions vary in the degree of emphasis placed on the two poles of self-effort and grace. Some lineages, such as Zen Buddhism, downplay the idea of receiving grace and blessings from above. It's understood that the teacher can show us a path, but we travel this path through our own effort, by actively purifying the mind through sitting meditation and refining our actions by following the precepts or making an intense effort to grasp the meaning of a koan. Zen isn't a particularly devotional path and features no deities; self-effort is essential to progress.

In contrast the mystery of grace is a central feature of the Christian faith. Catholics believe that the spirit of Christ flows down through the Pope to the cardinals, bishops, and priests, and that this grace is dispensed down to the faithful through the sacraments, especially Baptism and Holy Communion. The symbolism of these rites was explained by historian of religions Mircea Eliade:

> [T]he Eucharist is reminiscent of the cult agapes practiced in Mediterranean antiquity, especially in the Mystery religions. Their goal was the consecration, and hence the salvation, of the participants through communion with a divinity. . . . The convergence with the Christian rite is significant; it illustrates the hope . . . of a mystical identification with the divinity. . . . Every believer accomplishes mystical union with Christ through the sacrament of baptism. . . . Baptism not only insures the new life of the believer but accomplishes his transformation into a member of the mystical body of Christ.[10]

The language of these rites is filled with themes of incorporation: in Baptism the individual is absorbed into the body of the church, while through Holy Communion the person symbolically takes Christ, in the form of the Eucharist, into his or her own body. The passage just cited evokes themes that are pertinent to seekers and followers of every religious and spiritual tradition: the longing to merge with, or experience identification with, a spiritual teacher, to take the teacher inside, to absorb the teacher, and to make oneself like the teacher. We long to experience oneness with a great being who is a conduit for grace. We want to awaken in ourselves the same radiance, refined character, and serene wisdom. In this stage we experience mystical identity with the teacher, who embodies the enlightened state and who is literally the way to liberation.

THE GURU IS ONE'S OWN MIND

As the psychic tie between teacher and disciple grows stronger, we sense that the teacher knows us fully and inwardly witnesses us. We sense that our spiritual teacher is very close to us, recognizes our soul, and is familiar with our inner thoughts and feelings. Recall the story "The Sheikh and the Lamb's Bladder," recounted in stage four, in which the teacher responds to the student's innermost thoughts and longings. The ability of the spiritual teacher to examine the essential character of the aspirant is described in Sufi texts: "[T]hey tell about the *firasa,* 'cardiognosia' (soul-reading), of a master. 'Beware of the *firasa* [discernment] of the faithful,' it was said, 'for he sees by God's light.' Innumerable stories are told about a sheikh's insight into a disciple's heart; he was able to tell his secret wishes, hopes, and dislikes, to understand signs of spiritual pride or hypocrisy the very moment the [student] entered his presence."[11]

Swami Muktananda showed me many times that he could access my innermost thoughts and emotions. In 1976 I spent several months living in his ashram in South Fallsburg, New York. One day I had an argument with my parents on the telephone. They thought I'd been brainwashed and abducted into a dangerous cult and insisted that I leave the ashram and return home. I refused adamantly. I told no one about this incident. Later that afternoon Baba entered a room where over 800 people were seated. I was sitting a good distance from him and off to his side, well out of his immediate line of sight. He sat down and began to speak, saying, "There was once a young man who loved to meditate. His parents were scientists and skeptics and told him that he was a fool to waste his time meditating. But the young man was very intelligent and handled the situation very well, not like these young men these days, who when they get to be eighteen years old start telling their parents to shut up and go away and not bother them!" Then my fierce teacher turned in his seat and gave me a stone-faced, Shiva-like stare. He was very intense!

Two years later I spent the summer in his ashram in Ganeshpuri. After several years of austerity and a pure lifestyle, I began to experience a resurgence of old desires. One afternoon I lay on my bed in the dormitory fantasizing about smoking pot with a woman I was attracted to back home. The following day I got on the queue to ask Baba a question about an unrelated matter. There was a man in front of me on the line who was visibly dazed and disoriented. It turned out that he was a diabetic who wasn't taking his insulin shots, which accounted for his strange demeanor. But before this fact was discovered, Baba asked him repeatedly if he'd been taking any drugs. "Did you smoke hashish or take *bhang* in town?" he asked the man. Then Baba looked at me and told me to look through the man's shoulder bag. "See if there are any drugs in there," he said. I didn't find anything. A few minutes later, after he'd answered my other question, Baba pointed his finger at me and said, "And don't chase drugs!" There was no place to hide from him; he could inwardly see me and know what was happening inside me.

Swami Muktananda had reached a level of consciousness where he was one with my own mind. He was established in the jewel-like awareness of the Self, which is the root of every mind, the universal consciousness from which our individual consciousness springs. I realized that I'm always seen by the guru, who is none other than the God within me. As Ramana Maharshi used to say, "Guru, God, and Self are one." Having my teacher demonstrate knowledge of my inner life showed me that I'm always seen in the eyes of Spirit. Moreover, realizing the oneness of the guru with my inner Self supersedes the fact that the teacher's personality may exhibit imperfections.

PSYCHIC ATTUNEMENT
OF TEACHER AND STUDENT

Spiritual apprenticeship engages us in a relationship not just with a person who instructs us, but with a presence that transforms us. The guru isn't just a teacher, because that implies someone separate from ourselves teaching us something that we don't know. Through deep meditation, the spiritual apprentice forges an inner link with the teacher. Boundaries between the two now become more fluid.

In the Sufi tradition of spiritual instruction, it's recognized that spiritual guidance is an alchemical process that occurs through a blending or interpenetration of psychic boundaries. The consciousness of the student and teacher meet in inner space, where ultimately there's no separation. In the early stages of Sufi training, the student listens to the teacher's words, reflects on them, recognizes their truth, and practices these teachings. Later, the student experiences *fana fi' sheikh*, "annihilation in the master," a state of transcendence of the ego and merger with the consciousness of the teacher. Sheikh Nur Richard Gale explains:

The real point here, more than a sense of union with the teacher, is to experience the *stage* of the teacher. You don't deify the teacher. You're striving for the *maqam*, the station of a teacher, that level the teacher is stable in. There are states of consciousness that can be broader than our *maqam*, states of expansion, ecstasies of different levels. But the *maqam* is where the teacher is stabilized in awareness. We're concerned with that level the teacher is at, and what one is trying to do is to discover oneself in that station. So it's really annihilation in the station where the teacher is stabilized.[12]

In Sufism the teacher consciously attunes to the student in meditation to vibrationally uplift the aspirant on inner planes. Through these meditations the teacher becomes deeply familiar with the character and evolutionary stage of the student, prescribes practices to aid the student's unfolding, and closely supervises these practices. The teacher's attunement expresses a sense of solemn responsibility toward the student and a conscious effort to promote the student's evolution. Schimmel writes,

> The master watches every moment of the disciple's spiritual growth; he watches him particularly during the forty-day period of meditation that became, very early, a regular institution in the Sufi path. . . . The sheikh interprets the murid's dreams and visions, reads his thoughts, and thus follows every movement of his conscious and subconscious life. . . . The strong relationship between sheikh and murid is exemplified in the technique of *tawajjuh,* concentration upon the sheikh. . . . One speaks in Turkish of *rabita kurmak,* "to establish a tie" between master and disciple. The sheikh, too, would practice *tawajjuh* and thus "enter the door of the disciple's heart" to watch him and to guard him every moment.[13]

As the realization of this inner tie becomes more constant, as the psychic connection grows, our contemplation of the teacher becomes the foundation for a most transformative practice.

MEDITATION ON THE TEACHER'S FORM

Several mystical traditions recommend meditations involving visualization of the teacher and a feeling of inner union. According to the Yoga

Sutras (I.37), a yogi can attain steadiness of mind by fixing his or her attention on a being of purity who is free of attachment.[14]

> Because of his realization, the guru is considered to be an embodiment of the divine itself. This "deification" of the God-realized master must not be misunderstood. He is not God in any exclusive sense. He is, rather, thought to be coessential with the transcendental Reality. That is to say, he has abrogated the ordinary person's misidentification with a particular body-mind. He abides purely as the transcendental Identity of all beings and things.[15]

In his book *Play of Consciousness,* Swami Muktananda writes a detailed account of this practice.[16] He described how he focused all of his attention on his guru, Nityananda, mentally installing the guru inside his own body until he began to identify with him fully. Practicing this meditation on the guru's form and inner state, he began to act, feel, and perceive as his guru did. Through meditation on the teacher's expanded, joyful state, the disciple is uplifted into the same state of consciousness. The practitioner of guru yoga gazes at the teacher's physical form, meditates on a picture of the beloved spiritual master, or inwardly invokes mental images of the teacher, imagines seeing the world through the teacher's eyes, and meditates, as the teacher does, on the bliss of pure consciousness.

Some skeptics might view meditation on the guru as a dangerous exercise in disassociation, or regressive dependency on an idealized figure. Yet such practices are explicitly described in many spiritual traditions and prescribed as a means of awakening. For example, in Sufism students are transformed by learning to observe enlightened qualities like mercy, radiant joy, and patience in the teacher, and consciously absorbing these qualities into themselves. Sufi teacher Atum Kane writes:

> This stage is centered upon incorporating archetypes and qualities into one's personality. . . . [W]hile contemplating the power that

moves the universe, you awaken that same power in yourself. The use of mantras or *wazifa* promotes the embodiment of a quality in the personality by repeating the sounds which correspond with its vibrational frequency. Perhaps the most valuable meditation in this vein is that of entering into the consciousness of a great human being who manifests a particular quality to a high degree of perfection. The quality ceases to be an abstraction and one discovers how it can function in a person. The blending of two opposite qualities is very difficult, but can be experienced by meditating upon the sovereignty and humility found in Christ or the combination of detachment and compassion present in Buddha. Reflecting [on] the lives of such beings shows how these qualities functioned in very concrete situations, and can be related to the problems one faces. . . . The key meditation [at this stage] is that of the Ideal Being. Creative imagination inspired by one's longing for an ideal forms a being in whom one can discover one's vision of perfection in human form.[17]

Here, the path to enlightenment is to consciously identify with a person who has already attained that state—an awakened being who embodies and models enlightened qualities. If we aspire to become a great businessperson and closely observe the conduct, habits, and acumen of a successful businessperson, we're likely to become like this person. To become a great musician or tennis player, it's useful to fix our minds on those who have achieved greatness in these fields, closely observing their technique, then practicing and imitating as best we can. To become an enlightened, serene, awakened human being, we must find someone who has attained this stature, contemplate this person's freedom, luminosity, and joy, and strive to internalize them. Visualizing the state of the teacher, we become deeply focused in meditation, resting mind and body in the stillness, radiance, and clear light of our intrinsic awareness.

The practice of meditating on an enlightened teacher seems to magnetize the power of grace that flows through such a being so that it enters the student and transforms the student's consciousness. At this stage we perceive the guru not just as an individual person who is physically present, but as a powerful energy that lifts us up on inner wings so that our spirit takes flight. We realize that we're disciples of the divine grace–bestowing power; we're disciples of the inner light.

When I stayed at the Ganeshpuri Ashram in 1978, I followed the daily schedule of work periods, chanting, and meditation. This was a very focused environment in which to do intense sadhana. There was no other reason to be there. I was most interested in getting as near to my teacher as I could so I could study him closely. Muktananda often taught that as a student attunes to the guru's enlightened mind, grace begins to flow effortlessly to that student. Contemplating this truth I started to practice guru yoga, meditation on the guru's form. I mentally visualized my teacher, feeling that I was seeing through his eyes, walking in his body, laughing with his laughter. This practice was extremely potent for me. I walked around in quiet ecstasy, in love with the inner light in everyone.

At this time Baba was initiating people in an intense siddha meditation method, silently intoning the mantra *So'ham,* merging these sounds with the in-breath and out-breath. *So'ham* means "I am That, I am consciousness, I am pure awareness." Sometimes Baba taught us to reverse the sounds, forming the mantra *Hamsa.* They're one and the same, interchangeable. Through this method the meditator's in-breath and out-breath become subtle and refined, until the breath barely flickers, leading to a breathless state of awe and a deep space of meditation. Practicing this method I felt myself in an expansive state while walking, eating, working, talking, and meditating. During periods of meditation, my breathing slowed down, becoming very shallow, and my mind barely rippled; the waters became still. I was in a state that was thought-free, serene, and unwavering. This is the state of awareness becoming aware of itself, which Kashmir Shaivism calls *pratyabhijna,* the experience of Self-recognition. At every moment consciousness is pulsating everywhere, in everything. In Shaivism this is called *spanda,* the vibrant, throbbing, expansive quality of divine consciousness. Shiva's blissful self-reflective consciousness emanates beauty and radiance throughout all creation. And this is the state of the guru. *So'ham:* I am That. The experience was electrifying. I was in a protected environment where I could allow myself the freedom of letting go of the world and immersing in this adamantine Shiva state, where I was inwardly one with my teacher. I felt we were seeing through the same eyes. For several weeks I continued this practice of identification with the guru and absorption in the consciousness of the inner Self.

One day I sat in Baba's courtyard, gazing at him. He wasn't doing anything special, but his presence conveyed immense power. He sat reading the newspaper and chatting with various people. As devotees approached him, I watched him blissfully greet everyone as one and the same being, as vibrations of the divine presence. Then he sat silently in a timeless emptiness. I focused on him while recognizing him as my own Self. Suddenly, Muktananda looked me over and seemed to thoroughly examine my state of consciousness. His gaze was full of light. Our eyes met in silent recognition of our oneness. My heart expanded outward to be one with him. All of this happened in an instant. He was very loving, waggled his head several times, and said, "Bahut achha" (very good). Afterward, I was quietly exuberant as I recalled this meeting of minds with my teacher.

PERILS AND PROMISE OF GURU YOGA

Some will say that it's courting disaster to imagine ourselves merging as we gaze into some exalted guru's eyes. Frankly, I believe one of the reasons practices such as this were traditionally kept secret is so that other people wouldn't spoil the experience by telling practitioners that they were crazy for doing this. Nonetheless, the skeptics have a point: the practice of merging inwardly with a teacher can make us vulnerable to exploitation or loss of boundaries and discrimination. Merging with the teacher can take unhealthy forms, as we'll see. Guru yoga can be a problematic practice for those without an adequately differentiated sense of self, who may be receptive to a teacher's magnetism yet may become overly dependent or unable to perceive the teacher's imperfections of character. But inward merger with a teacher's enlightened mind doesn't mean that we should naively invite the teacher to violate our boundaries.

In this level of practice, we retain our identity as individuals, yet we're consciously striving to realize a state beyond the ego, through meditation on a being who lives in that state. By now we've observed the teacher's character and developed trust in the teacher's motives and intention. Thus we allow ourselves to identify with the teacher's awakened state, to see the light in the teacher's eyes, and to gratefully receive it without paranoia or fear of exploitation. With this attitude we reverently observe the teacher. I know this language may sound flowery to people who haven't had the experience, but those who have had the good fortune to meet a siddha guru such as Swami Kripalu or the Sixteenth Gyalwang Karmapa will attest that these teachers have a captivating presence.

To deepen our understanding of guru yoga, it's helpful to consider the distinction, articulated by Lama Govinda, between the Hindu concept of *shakti* (power) and the Buddhist concept of *prajna* (wisdom):

> The concept of *Sakti,* of divine power, of the creative female aspect of the highest God (*Siva*) or his emanations does not play any role in Buddhism. While in the Hindu Tantras the concept of power (*sakti*) forms the focus of interest, the central idea of Tantric Buddhism is *prajna*: knowledge, wisdom. To the Buddhist, *sakti* is *maya,* the very power that creates illusion, from which only *prajna* can liberate us. It is therefore not the aim of the Buddhist to acquire power, or to join himself to the powers of the universe, either to become their instrument or to become their master, but, on the contrary, he tries to free himself from those powers, which since aeons kept him a prisoner of *samsara*. . . . The attitude of the Hindu Tantras is quite different. . . . "United with the *Sakti,* be full of power," says the *Kulacudamani-Tantra*. "From the union of *Siva* and *Sakti* the world is created." The Buddhist, however, does not want the creation and unfoldment of the world, but the coming back to the uncreated, unformed state of *sunyata,* from which all creation proceeds. . . . The becoming

conscious of this *sunyata* is *prajna:* highest knowledge. The realization of this highest knowledge in life is enlightenment, i.e., if *prajna* (or *sunyata*), the passive, all-embracing female principle, from which everything proceeds and into which everything recedes, is united with the dynamic male principle of active universal love and compassion, . . . then perfect Buddhahood is attained.[18]

In Hindu yoga meditation on an enlightened guru sometimes turns into an attempt to absorb shakti from the teacher, who is seen as emanating "rays" of power. The student can become addicted to the teacher's shakti and feel weak and diminished without periodic infusions of this power. In this way dependency on the magnetic power of the master may be created. In contrast, in Buddhism, prajna is emphasized; thus, the Buddhist approach to guru yoga stresses the practitioner's identifying with the teacher's wisdom mind. It's not a question of absorbing shakti from the teacher. We aren't seeking power through our practices; we seek wisdom and compassion. These qualities awaken in us as we contemplate the mind of the enlightened ones.

TIBETAN GURU YOGA

Meditating on an enlightened being is strongly emphasized in Tibetan Buddhism, where guru yoga is considered an essential practice that leads to inner awakening, a potent means of transformation. Here the aspirant invokes, supplicates, and meditates on the illumined buddha Padmasambhava, known as Guru Rinpoche, the eighth-century yogi and teacher who established Buddhism in Tibet, the buddha whom Guatama Buddha had predicted would be even greater than himself. As the great Dzogchen Buddhist master Dilgo Khyentse Rinpoche says, "Guru Rinpoche is the lord or protector of all sentient beings because all turn to him for refuge. . . . Beings afflicted by poisonous emotions and accumulated karma who turn their minds toward him will receive his compassion and his blessings.[19]

Meeting the enlightened mind of Guru Rinpoche.
Thangka from author's collection.

In perhaps the clearest discourse on guru yoga ever written, *The Wish-Fulfilling Jewel,* Khyentse Rinpoche states:

> Guru yoga, the union with the nature of the guru, forms the foundation for all practices, and there are many different techniques for its practice. . . . There are outer, inner, secret, and most secret methods. . . . The outer method . . . is to visualize the guru dwelling above our head and to pray to him ardently with fierce devotion. The inner method is to realize . . . that our own body, speech, and mind are inseparable from the wisdom body, speech, and mind of the guru. . . . The secret method is to meditate upon the guru in his *sambhogakaya* form, the body of divine enjoyment. The most secret method introduces us to the natural state of awareness. . . . On the absolute level, the teacher is one with the very nature of our own mind, which is itself the essence of Buddhahood.[20]

Khyentse Rinpoche explains the stages of guru yoga as follows: We begin with visualizations of a pure buddhafield and of a vast assembly of yogis and buddhas, with Guru Rinpoche above our heads, dressed in elaborate garb, wearing a lotus crown. We visualize ourselves as his consort, Yeshe Tsogyal, fully devoted to Guru Rinpoche and able to receive his teachings and his stream of blessings. Then we offer the supplication and Seven-Branch Prayer, including (1) *prostration* to Guru Rinpoche, the antidote to pride; (2) *physical offering* of water bowls, flowers, incense, lamps, and food, as an antidote to greed and miserliness, and mental offerings of whatever we cherish most, including our own body, spouse, property, and money; (3) *confession of all negative actions* of body (killing, stealing, sexual misconduct), speech (lies, gossip, slandering others, angry and hurtful words), and mind (envy, wish to harm others, adherence to false views) that hinder progress toward enlightenment; (4) *rejoicing in virtue,* finding joy in the accumulation of merit by others, without envy or attachment, the antidote for jealousy and hatred; the practitioner cultivates positive actions (through prostrations, circumam-

bulations of sacred sites, and offerings to the community of practitioners) and samadhi, one-pointed awareness of the absolute; (5) *requesting
the turning of the wheel of dharma,* the antidote for ignorance; the aspirant requests teachings and rejoices when the teacher gives them; one's
own teacher is identified with Guru Rinpoche; (6) *requesting the teacher
to stay in this world* until all sentient beings have been rescued from the
wheel of samsaric existence; and (7) *dedicating the merit of the practice*
to the benefit of all sentient beings, that they might attain liberation.

At the subtlest level of guru yoga practice, the practitioner visualizes
himself or herself as a *yidam,* an enlightened being or chosen deity who
is the focus of meditation, realizing that "one's body, speech, and mind
have always been inseparable from the body, speech, and mind of Guru
Rinpoche."[21] The essence of the practice is to generate oneself as a deity
so that Guru Rinpoche's mind is recognized to be "undifferentiable
from your own."[22] Rick Amaro, a Buddhist scholar-practitioner and a
student of Chögyam Trungpa and Lama Tarchen Rinpoche, explained
the significance of this practice to me as follows:

> In guru yoga you're generating devotion to the teacher's mind as phe-
> nomenal reality, the world of appearance. The Buddhist Mahamudra
> or Dzogchen level of understanding is that the world as it appears
> is the teacher, and is your own mind, inseparable. There's not one
> hair's breadth difference between the phenomenal world and my
> mind. The awareness dawns that I am the phenomenal field of pres-
> ence, beneath the appearance-awareness distinction. Buddhists say
> that awareness is inseparable from appearance, and vice versa. As
> Padmasambhava himself said, "As a thing is viewed, so it appears."
> But beneath the distinction between appearance and awareness is
> the field of presence. Guru Rinpoche *is* the field of presence, which
> is also one's own buddha nature. We supplicate him in the practice
> of guru yoga to inhabit this field of presence fully, so we can wel-
> come the world as our own mind and relate to it with friendliness
> and compassion without distinction. Then we leap into space fully

and overcome the primordial fear of space that inhibits us from opening to the world. We become more fearless with space and recognize that our own mind is inseparable from space. Furthermore, we recognize that space is luminous. Recognizing this luminosity of space-awareness awakens in us openness, clarity, and wonder. So by supplicating Guru Rinpoche, we supplicate our own dharmakaya mind, our original, primordially pure awareness.[23]

The significance of the figure of Guru Rinpoche deepens with further contemplation. According to Chögyam Trungpa, Padmasambhava, who first appeared as a child on a lotus in the center of a lake, represents our "primordial innocence," a "fresh and sparkling" quality of awakeness in which there's no duality. He's the personification of a playful, exploratory approach to life that's open to miraculous events, including a sudden flash of enlightenment.[24] Padmasambhava represents "complete and total openness that makes us able to transcend hope and fear. With this openness we relate to things as they are rather than as we'd like them to be. That basic sanity, that approach transcending hope and fear, is the attitude of enlightenment."[25]

Trungpa Rinpoche finds rich symbolism in Padmasambhava's efforts to introduce highly complex Indian Buddhist doctrines to the somewhat simpler, agrarian population of Tibet in the eighth century. The perspective of Padmasambhava "is not the point of view of sentient beings trying to attain enlightenment, but the point of view of an enlightened person trying to relate with sentient beings. . . . The approach here is to recognize oneself as being a Buddha already."[26]

In guru yoga we view the figure of our own beloved teacher as a living buddha, the embodiment of fully expanded consciousness. Contemplating the qualities and the awareness of such a being, we ourselves become a buddha, an awakened being. By attuning to the teacher's wisdom mind, the meditator finds a doorway to inner freedom and reaches out to merge into the heart of the infinite.

༄༅

At the Threshold
of Awakening

Glimpses of the Goal

Through unmistakable learning and contemplation, he should enter the gate of Mahayana and Vajrayana, and practice them diligently with great determination; then finally, he can please his guru with his real experiences of Enlightenment, which are produced step by step through his devotion.

THE HUNDRED THOUSAND SONGS OF MILAREPA

There are many signs that an aspirant is advancing toward buddhahood or the state of Self-knowledge, the elevation of consciousness into Spirit. One is the emergence of positive virtues: patience, kindness, desire to serve other beings; quieting of obsessive desires; absorption in meditation; serenity and equanimity; and abiding in the unchanging light of consciousness.

A key sign of progress is that our daily lives become filled with tranquility and mindfulness, and we learn to maintain peace of mind and an uplifted attitude in a variety of circumstances. Lonnie, a longtime Buddhist meditator, told me this story:

> Late one night in New York a very large black man approached me near the Bowery and demanded money. His breath reeked of booze and his eyes were bloodshot. His shoes were torn and his clothes were ragged. He was easily six foot five and I was scared of him. He stared at me with menacing eyes. I could've walked away quickly but I felt a composure in my body that I remembered from the practice of meditation. I took a breath and for a brief moment I saw in his eyes the eyes of Mahakala, the Tibetan deity of time, usually depicted as a wild demon—a ferocious black deity that helps bring us to enlightenment. I felt compassion for this suffering sentient being. I gave him two dollars and looked him in the eye and I noted how cold it was and asked him if he had a place to stay indoors for the night. The man's demeanor softened. He looked sad for a moment, then said it had been a long time since anyone had expressed concern. He was genuinely grateful for the money. At that moment I felt that my spiritual practices were actually worthwhile because I was seeing real changes in my actions. In the past I would have been too scared and shut down to speak to someone in this way.

EQUALITY VISION AND CONTENTMENT

The spiritual apprentice develops equality vision, seeing the same pure light or Buddha nature in everyone. A story is told about the great Advaita Vedanta philosopher Shankara:

> One morning, when he was on his way to bathe in the Ganges, he met a *Chandala,* a member of the lowest caste, the untouchables. . . . For a moment inborn caste-prejudice asserted itself. Shankara, the Brahmin, ordered the Chandala out of his way. But the *Chandala* answered: "If there is only one God, how can there be many kinds of

men?" Shankara was filled with shame and reverence. He prostrated himself before the Chandala.[1]

I learned a similar lesson once. I was at a party where a man named Don talked to me incessantly and began to annoy me so much that after a while I began to deliberately ignore him. Then, a rather prominent and popular man named Steve arrived, and I rushed over to speak with him. Steve didn't remember me at all, and while polite, he wasn't at all interested in talking to me. I was brushed off exactly as I'd brushed off Don. Later I saw Don again and spoke with him at length, seeing his luminous essence. We became fine friends.

Related to equality vision is acceptance and detachment. We learn to accept whatever comes in life with the detachment of Lord Shiva, the great ascetic, who receives whatever is placed in his begging bowl—sometimes sumptuous feasts, sometimes scraps of rotting fruit.

But this doesn't mean that we're completely passive and resigned. On the contrary those who are accomplished exercise will and self-determination, applying the law of karma—the awareness that we form our future through every action and through our daily habits. We accept responsibility for what we've created in our lives and strive, through each act, to create a better future for ourselves and others.

MOMENTS IN THE LIGHT

The potent methods learned from our guides help us focus so we reach an expanded state. Meditation polishes the mirror of the mind so we can perceive the clear, reflective space of that mirror, as well as the ever-changing images reflected in it. Hatha yogis tune up the body and subtle nervous system so that every cell and muscle fiber awakens and becomes more perceptive and intelligent. These kinds of spiritual practices help us shed layers of bodily and emotional armor and transcend our usual cognitive conditioning. Neurophysiologist Arthur Deikman called this effect the *deautomatization of consciousness*—a dishabituation of attention that shifts us into a perceptual mode that's more vivid, sensuous, and animated. Spiritual practices are methods of deconditioning, making us receptive to new modes of perceiving, knowing, and feeling. That's the function of yoga, meditation, breathwork, fasting, chanting, drumming, or ecstatic dance. According to Deikman mystical experience involves perceptual expansion and opening to new dimensions of the total stimulus array, so that aspects of reality previously unavailable enter our awareness.[2] Thereafter in daily life we grow more conscious, mindful, and appreciative of each moment's richness and beauty. And occasionally we break through to a moment of unexpected lucidity, a condition of heightened wakefulness, shifting into the perspective of pure, unconditioned awareness. The mystic practitioner reaches infinitely varied illuminated states. The great American psychologist William James wrote:

> I remember the night, and almost the very spot on the hillside, where my soul opened out, as it were, into the Infinite, and there was a rushing together of the two worlds, the inner and the outer. It was deep calling unto deep—the deep that my own struggle had opened up within being answered by the unfathomable deep without, reaching beyond the stars. I stood alone with Him who had made me, and all the beauty of the world, and love, and sorrow, and even temptation. I did not seek Him, but felt the perfect union of my spirit with His. The ordinary sense of things around me faded. For the moment nothing but an ineffable joy and exaltation remained. It is impossible to fully describe the experience. . . . I have stood upon the Mount of Vision since, and felt the Eternal round about me.[3]

At this stage seekers devoted to spiritual practice experience their own moments of enlightenment. Michele, a long-time meditator, said:

> I had a vision of white light in meditation one day. It was staggering. Then I realized I could see that light everywhere around me with

my eyes wide open. It was my own emanation. A few days later I saw my teacher. She smiled at me and said, "It's beautiful, isn't it? White light everywhere!" And she laughed.

In the *Crest Jewel of Discrimination,* Shankara says:

Now I shall tell you the nature of the Atman. If you realize it, you will be freed from the bonds of ignorance, and attain liberation. There is a self-existent Reality, which is the basis of our consciousness of ego. That Reality is the witness of the three states of our consciousness, and is distinct from the five bodily coverings. That Reality is the knower in all states of consciousness—waking, dreaming, and dreamless sleep. That Reality sees everything by its own light. No one sees it. That Reality pervades the universe. It alone shines. The universe shines with its reflected light. . . . Its nature is eternal consciousness. . . . It is the knower of pleasure and pain and of the sense-objects. . . . This is the Atman, the Supreme being, the ancient. It never ceases to experience infinite joy. It is always the same. It is consciousness itself.

With a controlled mind and an intellect which is made pure and tranquil, you must realize the Atman directly, within yourself. Know the Atman as the real I. Thus you cross the shoreless ocean of worldliness, whose waves are birth and death. The Atman is indivisible, eternal, one without a second. . . . Its glories are infinite. . . . It is the witness of the mind. . . . It is the inner Being, the uttermost, everlasting joy.[4]

The experience of enlightenment is lucidly described by groundbreaking author and consciousness researcher, John White:

The perennial wisdom is unchanging; truth is one. That is agreed on by the sages of all major religions and sacred traditions, all hermetic philosophies, genuine mystery schools and higher occult paths.

Enlightenment is the core truth of them all. Even more broadly, it is the essence of life—the goal of all growth, development, evolution. It is the discovery of what we ultimately are, the answer to the questions: Who am I? Why am I here? Where am I going? What is life all about? . . . . Paradoxically, the answer we seek is none other than what we *already are* in essence—Being, the ultimate wholeness that is the source and ground of all Becoming. *Enlightenment is realization of the truth of Being.* Our native condition, our true self, is Being, traditionally called God, the Cosmic Person, the Supreme Being, the One-in-all. . . . We are manifestations of Being, but like the cosmos itself, we are also in the process of Becoming—always changing, developing, growing, evolving to higher and higher states that ever more beautifully express the perfection of the source of existence. . . .

The truth of all existence and all experience, then, is none other than the seamless here-and-now, the already present, the prior nature of that which seeks and strives and asks: Being. *The spiritual journey is the process of discovering and living that truth.* It amounts to the eye seeing itself—or rather, the I seeing its Self. In philosophical terms, enlightenment is comprehending the unity of all dualities, the harmonious composite of all opposites, the oneness of endless multiplicity and diversity. In psychological terms, it is transcendence of all sense of limitation and otherness. In humanistic terms, it is understanding that the journey is the teaching, that the path and the destination are ultimately one. In theological terms, it is comprehending the union of God and humanity. In ontological terms, it is the State of all states, the Condition of all conditions that transcends the entire cosmos yet is also everyday reality, since nothing is apart from it or ever can be.

When we finally understand that Great Mystery, we discover our true nature, the Supreme Identity, the Self of all. That direct perception of our oneness with the infinite, that noctic realization of our identity with the divine is the source of all happiness, all goodness, all beauty, all truth.[5]

Spiritual training is dedicated to attaining these kinds of realizations. The guru, murshid, or sage is a vehicle for our awakening. Now we see with our own eyes, know and experience with our own body, our own heightened feelings; we have our own "noetic realization of our identity with the divine."

In Chinese Ch'an Buddhism, enlightenment is said to occur suddenly. Edward Conze, an Anglo-German scholar and translator of Buddhist texts, explains:

> Enlightenment according to Hui-Neng and his successors is not a gradual, but an instantaneous process. . . . The Ch'an masters did not intend to say that no preparation was necessary, and that enlightenment was won in a very short time. They just laid stress on the common mystical truth that enlightenment takes place in a "timeless moment," i.e., outside time, in eternity. It is an act of the Absolute itself, not our own doing. One cannot do anything at all to become enlightened. To expect austerities or meditation to bring forth salvation is like "rubbing a brick to make it into a mirror." Enlightenment just happens without the mediacy of any finite condition or influence. . . . It is not the gradual accumulation of merit which causes enlightenment, but a sudden act of recognition.[6]

Ramana Maharshi is an example of someone who experienced sudden enlightenment. At age sixteen Ramana was gripped by a fear of death and began diving inward to inquire into his true nature, asking himself *Who am I?* He soon passed into a state of permanent Self-abiding:

> When I lay down with limbs outstretched and mentally enacted the death scene and realized that the body would be taken and cremated and yet I would live, some force, call it *atmic* power. . . . rose within me and took possession of me. With that, I was reborn and I became a new man. . . . Our real nature is *mukti* [liberation]. But we are

imagining we are bound and are making various, strenuous attempts to become free, while we are all the while free. . . . We will be surprised that we were frantically trying to attain something which we have always been and are. . . . It is false to speak of Realisation. What is there to realise? The real is as it is, ever. . . . We are not creating anything new or achieving something we did not have before. . . . There is nothing to attain and no time within which to attain. You are always that. You have not got to attain anything. You have only to give up thinking you are limited, to give up thinking you are this body. The state we call realisation is simply being oneself, not knowing anything or becoming anything. If one has realised, he is that which alone is and which alone has always been. He cannot describe that state. He can only be that.[7]

In a letter to Ramana Maharshi, his disciple Paul Brunton wrote:

I remain perfectly calm and fully aware of who I am and what is occurring. Self still exists, but it is a changed, radiant Self. Something that is far superior to my unimportant personality rises into consciousness and becomes me. I am in the midst of an ocean of blazing light. I sit in the lap of holy bliss.[8]

The parting of the clouds leading to an expanded state can occur quite unexpectedly. Once I experienced a sudden illumination at Harbin Hot Springs, in northern California. One morning, after soaking for a long time in the hot, steamy pool, I proceeded to the freezing cold plunge. I was breathing deeply. As I sat in the cold pool, I assumed a meditative posture, gazed at the green beauty all around me, then closed my eyes and turned my attention inward. I began to practice guru yoga, intoning the mantra *Guru Om* while envisioning the radiant and blissfully serene form of Bhagavan Nityananda, who lived at a hot spring. In my inner eye, I saw his dark body absorbed in meditation. Imagining his silent, adamantine presence, I became very still. Suddenly, a powerful energy rushed up my spine and through the top of my head. My consciousness traveled up the ladder of Being into realms of light beyond form and material consciousness. I was in a state of awe. A few minutes later, I returned to body consciousness exhilarated, drenched in light, feeling the sensation of cold water on my skin. Opening my eyes the world had a heightened luminosity as I breathed in the forest smells and the effervescence of crystal-clear waters.

On another occasion a sudden illumination occurred at a low point, a moment of suffering, when I felt the solace of the invisible. One night I was upset about a loss and very bitter about my fate. As I sat in meditation, I realized that something had been taken from me and something else was being given in its place. I closed my eyes tightly in pain and thought silently, *So, is that what you have in mind? You want me to let go of what I want so you can give me what? Your presence? Is that the bargain?* As these words arose, my eyes flooded with tears and there was a surge in the crown of my head. My whole body was blanketed by peace and a sudden wave of shakti ran through my body. And at that moment, a voice within me said, *Exactly.*

I asked several longtime yogis, yoginis, and meditators about their own experiences of blessings, awakenings, and mystical states of consciousness. A woman named Phyllis gave this account:

I lived with my teacher for several years in a community. I rarely left the grounds. I was focused solely on the final adventure of consciousness—the quest for Self-realization. I meditated four or five hours a day, did my job, and rested quietly. That was my existence. I spoke very little. As I got more and more absorbed in meditation, my teacher showed greater interest in me. He'd look at me from time to time and I knew he was monitoring my progress. One day I saw a beautiful beam of golden light project from his eyes into mine. Afterward, I went into a very deep meditation where I saw a tiny blue dot that scintillated with blue-white light. After that I meditated even more intensely. I had experiences of traveling to other planes of existence where I had visions of great masters like Ramakrishna, Shirdi Sai Baba, Jesus, and Shakyamuni Buddha. My teacher's energy and my daily meditation made my mind clear so I could perceive other dimensions.

Experiences of illumination generate a desire to strengthen our efforts to cleanse the body, mind, and heart. The aspirant breaks through into realms and perceptions that were previously hidden. We're released from self-preoccupation into the freedom of divine contemplation. We perceive the spiritual ground of existence and feel a greater determination to live that vision ceaselessly.

Some disciples reach a stage of maturity in which they're stabilized in an illumined state. Jill, who has meditated and lived by her guru's teachings faithfully since 1962, said:

I cannot say whether or not I've gone to the farthest stages of the Path, but I can say in truth that I see only God, all the time, shining in the face of every being, shimmering in every leaf and flower. My quest has been fulfilled. I think of my teacher with reverence and love, yet I'm not fixated on him. I learned from him to look within myself to find peace.

Here are two more accounts of awakenings. Joseph, a long-time practitioner of Transcendental Meditation, reported:

The first time I went on retreat, I became very emotional. Once I just burst into tears and I had no idea why. Then I experienced a settling down in the body and in the space of the mind. Thought became quieter and ceased to fill the mind. I'd meditate to a certain place and then stop. There was a feeling of an obstruction. Then one day, during meditation, it broke. It felt brittle, like ice or glass. When that inner obstruction broke, I fell through into infinite space. I felt like I was suspended above a body of water with no end.

The bliss and pleasure of this experience were indescribable. I felt a vibration moving up through my toes and through my whole body. Then I felt myself falling farther until there was nothing. Sheer vastness. Eventually I resurfaced. Some time had passed that I couldn't account for. I had experienced pure consciousness without an object of attention. Later on, during this same retreat, I found myself altered in my waking state. I wasn't in contact with things anymore. Everything seemed really far away from me. There was an unreality to things that previously had seemed real and tangible. I had a sense of empty, intangible, dreamlike phenomena that were taking place that I had no relationship to. I was the witness of all phenomena. My relationship to the mind and body had shifted so that it was no longer who I was. I rested in a very deep stillness. This persisted for several days.

Once at a retreat I became aware of someone making a loud moaning sound. I was somewhat annoyed by this and thought, *That person shouldn't be doing that.* But he or she persisted. I began to be really annoyed because I was having a deep meditation, and this noise was disturbing me. I didn't appreciate that. Then as I came out of meditation I realized that I was the one making this noise. I had no idea it was me! My body was moaning and moaning. I had lost body awareness. The bliss was almost unbearable. It was like an orgasm, only thousands of times more intense. And it was everywhere in the body, not localized in one place.

Joseph perceived the Atman, or Self, as witness and as consciousness without form. His experience of merging his awareness into the stillness of Being was immeasurably blissful. Similar themes appear in this account by my friend Stuart Sovatsky:

I met my teacher Swami Kripalu when he came to America in 1977. I saw golden light around him. I cried in his presence all the time. I had eye contact with him and received transmission. All my contact with him was inspiring. If I could find someone else more moving than he was, I'd follow that person. I've never found anyone else like him. I gave up my job to follow him across the country in 1977. I had shaktipat experiences that changed my consciousness and my body sensations for months. I had experiences I was graced with, that I didn't earn through meditative efforts of any kind. They were given. Ongoing states of bodily pleasure. Tingling, seething feelings throughout my body. A writhing sensation in the cells, in the base of the spine and the throat, and constant ecstatic quivering in the tongue that has never gone away for the past twenty-five years.

I did practices to cultivate these experiences. The most radical thing I did was to take vows of *brahmacharya*. I remained celibate for ten years. I got up at four or five in the morning and practiced hatha yoga, meditation, pranayama, and chanting before I went to work. During chanting I found myself crying a lot for no apparent reason. It felt good. For a two-month period, I got to the point where I didn't want to speak. I could have given up speaking. A lot of my experience has been in the throat and heart area. I was experiencing the *khechari mudra,* a yogic process in which the tongue reaches up inside the palate toward the brain. It brings about a transformation of the larynx and tongue. The tongue stretches back and up spontaneously. It would happen during chanting or meditation or while practicing asanas. I felt like Romeo stretching up to Juliet in the pineal gland; it had the feel of romantic ardor, longing.

My practice plateaued for a while. Only after I finished school did I have the time to practice intensely again. I did as much as I could. Then in 1984 or '85, I did a long yoga retreat with Baba Hari Dass. After that I experienced a nine-month period of enlightenment in which I just enjoyed being. Being was enjoyable. Vision was enjoyable. The sound of things was enjoyable. I thought, *I'm enjoying my Self.* Later, during a long period of fasting, physical purification, pranayama, japa, and hatha yoga, all of a sudden my body started to have a thrill. My whole body, every cell was thrilling, quivering with joy. It was extraordinary. That went on for about a day and a half. Then it filtered away, despite my efforts to keep it. I've had other subtle experiences involving the cranial vault. I close my eyes and feel this cathedral-like ascending space. I had a number of experiences of the hormones of the pineal gland scintillating in this spiraling, sparkling descent into the space of the closed-eye darkness. I was amazed by that radiance. I thought, *This is the glimmer of infinity.*

Such accounts describe peak moments of the spiritual path, turning points in our journey of evolving consciousness. They are to be savored, celebrated with gratitude, and integrated into our daily lives. Disciplined yoga and meditation practices can propel us into a wide range of expansive, enlightening experiences.

INTENSIFICATION OF PRACTICE

At this stage the spiritual aspirant attains consciousness of the Self, the radiant awareness that is the essence of who we really are. These experiences, brief moments in the beginning, may inspire us to realize the expanded state with greater constancy. John White writes, "Enlightenment . . . is an endless process—not simply a one-time event. True, there are quantum leaps in awareness that mark the spiritual path. . . , but one white-light experience does not a mystic make, nor a saint. Even the most spiritually elevated people have found there are states of being beyond their present level of development."[9]

The seasoned aspirant may feel an intensified desire to practice yoga and meditate to sharpen the state of mindfulness. There's a strong motivation to practice with energy and refinement, so the mind and heart become clear and jewel-like. With deeper commitment to this process, countless physical, emotional, attitudinal, and subtle energetic impurities and limitations are consumed on the ascent toward the summit of freedom.

At this point spiritual practice becomes a focal point of daily life, and the seeker will want to minimize distractions and frivolous activities and develop dispassion and detachment from desire. We aren't unfriendly toward pleasures and good times, but we recognize that ordinary fulfillments, such as heavy drinking and overeating, are fleeting and bring no lasting peace or satiation of desires. We practice and maintain a state of calm receptivity, with senses steady and a quiet mind, without needing to fill every moment with stimulation or conversation. Rooted in the Self, in mindful attention, the yogi is steady and serene.

With this awareness comes a spirit of renunciation. This has different meanings for different people. For most people renunciation doesn't mean turning away from the body, our loved ones, and the need to work and earn money. Occasionally a serious practitioner will choose to undergo formal rites of renunciation, even entering monastic orders as a commitment to their path. But in general, when I use this term, I'm not talking about the need for long retreats or strenuous asceticism. One may practice renunciation amidst our everyday activities by returning to the state of a detached, peaceful witness and relinquishing attachment to the transitory. For example, the great sage Nisargadatta Maharaj continued to run a business and raise a family while abiding in the state of Self-realization. Renunciation is the determined effort to cut through mental chatter, the speed and stress of daily life, and the desperate pursuit of elusive objects of desire. Renunciation means striving to grow more calm and spiritually centered within our present environment and circumstances. Someone at this stage of spiritual apprenticeship pierces the veil of maya and is determined to reach a more unified state of consciousness. Shankara says:

When renunciation and the longing for liberation are present to an intense degree within a man, then the practice of tranquility and the other virtues will bear fruit and lead to the goal. Of the first steps to liberation, the first is declared to be complete detachment from all things which are non-eternal. Then comes the practice of tranquility, self-control, and forbearance. And then the entire giving-up of all actions which are done from personal, selfish desire. Then the disciple must hear the truth of the Atman, and reflect on it, and meditate upon it constantly, without pause, for a long time. Thus the wise man reaches that highest state, in which consciousness of subject and object is dissolved away and the infinite unitary consciousness alone remains.[10]

THE GOAL IS ALREADY ATTAINED

Attachment to a method is important. Indeed, it accelerates our progress to engage in spiritual practices with discipline, whether it's sitting meditation, fasting, yogic breathing, or other methods. By fanning the flames of consciousness, we consume our limitations.

But sometimes we need to let go of techniques and allow our own inner wisdom and the intelligence of each moment to guide us. We seek that state beyond all methods, where our freedom isn't bound by a single practice or technique. The goal is recognition of our true nature, which is already liberated. This was the perspective of the great Advaita Vedanta philosophers. Vedanta scholar Lance Nelson explains:

> Liberation is not something that can be brought into existence, as if it were a product of action. Nor is it something that can be acquired. Rather the opposite is true: It has no beginning, and it is eternal. Being our very Self, it is eternally accomplished, eternally attained. Ontologically speaking, we are always liberated. . . . [T]here is no bondage, no seeker of liberation, and no one who is liberated. . . . Mukti [liberation] is in truth an atemporal state that has always been ours. . . . To speak of attaining liberation is therefore, figurative.[11]

In Vedanta the Self, the state of intrinsic awareness, is already attained. It's not some distant goal, but rather our eternal nature, the very ground of existence. As Annamalai Swami puts it:

Don't make the mistake of imagining that there is some goal to be reached or attained. If you start to think like this you will start looking for methods to practice and people to help you. This just perpetuates the problem you are trying to end. Instead, cultivate the awareness "I am the Self. I am That. I am *Brahman*. I am everything." You don't need any methods to get rid of the wrong ideas you have about yourself. All you have to do is stop believing them. . . . The Self is always attained, it is always realized; it is not something that you have to seek, reach, or discover.[12]

Although the goal is already fully present and realized, many seekers only come to understand this truth after following a compelling inner urge to go on journeys and pilgrimages to distant places seeking wisdom, teachers, and empowerments, trying to get themselves to the next level. To conclude this chapter, let's examine the fascinating story of a man whose path of discipleship and study took him on an epic quest in the Far East.

A PATH OF SPIRITUAL SCHOLARSHIP AND EROTIC MYSTICISM

Prolific author and esteemed professor Mircea Eliade (1907–1986) lived a fascinating life that included both intense self-discipline in pursuit of a scholarly vocation and an enlightening journey into the practice of tantric sexual yoga. Eliade was a very serious person. By the age of thirty, he had published fifteen books and achieved widespread recognition as an authority on world religions. This is the man who described the distinction between the sacred and the profane and who studied the hierophany, the divine self-disclosure, the manifestation of the sacred that is at the heart of myth and ritual, religion and mysticism. As a teenager in the 1920s, Eliade developed a strong interest in yoga and shamanism and became fascinated with India, soon exhausting all the resources available in his native Romania for continuing his studies of

Indian languages, philosophy, and culture. He got the idea of writing to an Indian maharajah he'd heard was a philanthropist. Eliade asked for aid in traveling to India to study philosophy and Sanskrit. The maharajah wrote back offering him a scholarship and introductions to some prominent people. Eliade's sojourn in India lasted three years, beginning in November 1928, when he was twenty-one years old.

Arriving in Calcutta he settled in at the home of the teacher the maharajah arranged for him to meet—Surendranath Dasgupta, the most esteemed scholar of religion and philosophy in modern India. He was a great pundit, the author of immensely learned books. Dasgupta was an imposing guru, an intellectual giant. Eliade began a program of study that involved twelve to sixteen hours a day of learning Sanskrit and translating scriptures and yogic texts. He steeped himself completely in the ancient culture, language, and philosophy from which the tree of yoga springs.

Complicating matters immensely, Eliade started to fall in love with Dasgupta's brilliant and beautiful daughter, Maitreyi, a poetess. They were attracted to each other but were never allowed to be alone together until they were assigned the task of working on the index for Dasgupta's *History of Indian Philosophy*. As Eliade recounts, "One day our hands met over the little box of cards and we could not unclasp them."[13] Soon, however, Maitreyi told Eliade that her father had found out and she'd confessed everything. Immediately, Dasgupta kicked Eliade out of his house and banished him forever. He was suddenly rejected by his guru and mentor.

I can only imagine the bewilderment Eliade must have felt—the whirlwind of his feelings for Maitreyi, their sudden, irrevocable separation, and the traumatic end of his discipleship with his philosopher-guru. He continued his journey, traveling to Hardwar and Rishikesh, seeking a hermitage where he could dedicate himself to yoga practices. He met Swami Shivananda and stayed in his ashram for some time. Then in December 1929, a woman named Jenny arrived at the ashram from South Africa. Jenny was dedicated to the austere yogic lifestyle practiced in this community and often came to Eliade seeking spiritual guidance.

Over the Christmas holiday, Shivananda left town for a speaking tour, and Jenny came to visit Eliade. They got involved in discussions of tantric yoga, the topic of texts he was currently reading and translating. Although he tried to avoid the subject, Jenny was insistent on finding out what he knew, and they soon began their own explorations of tantric sexual practices. This was strictly forbidden according to yogic tradition, for a guru was said to be necessary to pursue these methods safely. For several weeks Eliade visited Jenny frequently and they made love through most of the night. He wrote:

> From then on I came late, after midnight, and returned to my kuitar an hour before dawn. I succeeded in preserving my lucidity and my self-control, not only in the "preliminary rituals," but also in all that followed. Jenny was astonished, but I sensed that I was on the road to becoming another man. Sometimes I only slept two or three hours a night, yet I was never tired. I worked all the time, and I worked better than ever before. I understood then the basis of all that vainglorious beatitude that some ascetics, masters of Hatha-yoga proclaim. I understood, too, the reason why certain yogis considered themselves to be like the gods, if not even superior to them, and why they talk about the transmutation and even the immortality of the body.[14]

At that time Eliade lived in a hut next to another hut inhabited by a *naga* sadhu, an ascetic with matted hair.

> Upon returning to my hut one morning in March, I found my naga neighbor waiting for me in the doorway. "I know where you've been," he said as soon as we had entered the kuitar. "I believe you could be compared with Maha Bhairava! But do you have enough virya (energy) to proceed on this path? People of today are impure

and weak. Very soon you will feel a strong fever in the crown of your head. You will know then that you do not have much time. It is better that you stop before this happens."

He had spoken as clearly as he could, using whole clauses of Sanskrit so that I could understand him. I understood him.

"But what if I find a Guru?" I asked.

"You already have a Guru," he said smiling. Then he saluted me, bringing his palms together in front of his face and returned to his hut.[15]

Eliade's secret tantric love affair was an initiation into erotic mysticism leading to an elevated state. This incandescent relationship gave Eliade his most profound knowledge of yogic practices. For a brief moment, these two lovers touched eternal glory. His story reminds us that glimpses of enlightenment are often transient and evanescent experiences, and not always repeatable. Sometimes the right circumstances come along that allow a person to enter the temple of sacred sex with another person. It's a matter of karma and destiny, chemistry and feeling, and perhaps a momentary alignment of the planets. In the study of mysticism, we watch to see what happens next, in the aftermath of mystical moments, samadhis, and hierophanies, how the person's goals begin to change and the soul's priorities are clarified. Eliade's adventures in India were the inspiration and starting point for his remarkable career devoted to hermeneutics, the interpretation of myths, mystical texts, and world religions. On the basis of these milestone events in his path as a spiritual seeker, Eliade discovered his life's work: to describe the human encounter with the sacred, in monumental works such as *Yoga: Immortality and Freedom*, *Rites and Symbols of Initiation*, and *The Myth of the Eternal Return*.

I'm struck by how Eliade matured in the process of separating from his teacher, Dasgupta, as well as by breaking the traditional guideliness for secret practices, boldly pursuing the realization of tantric yoga and the discovery of his own *axis mundi*. This is a reminder that there's a phase of the disciple's journey when the student, the seeker of spiritual knowledge, seeks emancipation from teachers and is ready to individuate.

This is the crossroads where we feel an urge for greater independence and begin to think about departing from the guide who thus far has accompanied us. We may be keenly aware that a teacher was the match that lit our flame, and for this we'll be forever grateful. But we also feel a pressing need to be about our own business, to develop households and occupations, couples and families, and to unfold ourselves in works that express our inborn talents in whatever form suits us best, whether in writing and research, the arts, public speaking, business, gardening, medicine or healing arts, law, or some other form. We could follow a calling to work for social change or in a field of scientific research, or pursue esoteric studies. Each of us is called in different ways into the field of human and planetary service.[16]

❧

We're fortunate indeed if we ever get the chance in this lifetime to spend time in the presence of a teacher capable of leading us to an expanded state. That gracious being shows us glimpses of the goal and teaches methods that activate all of our potentials as yogis and meditators and also as maturing individuals. But that process may eventually necessitate a change in our commitments if we decide we need to set a different course that trails outside the teacher's orbit. The guide can point the way, but we have to find our own path home.

STAGE SEVEN

⌘

Separating from a Spiritual Teacher

Maturation and Autonomy

The one with clear eyes will tell you to align your sight, with his finger and the head of the crow seated on the tree. Then, look beyond the finger and the crow, the moon is sighted. But if you hold onto the finger or the head of the crow, can you see the moon? Most teachers keep their students holding the finger and thus both are satisfied. As ego becomes inflated, the finger is worshipped and the new moon is forgotten. Only the selfless one says to go beyond and declares himself a mere indicator, a humble messenger not to be held.

H. W. L. POONJA, *TRUTH IS*

Everything in life is cyclic. All things begin, develop, change, and eventually come to an end. We find a teacher, receive teachings, and eventually we need to move on and become more independent, even if we love that teacher deeply. Our needs in the life cycle change. There are times to be a disciple, devotee, or spiritual apprentice, and times to do something else with our lives. In many cases external training under the guidance of a spiritual teacher concludes. Either the teacher dies, or we lose interest and are ready to go in a different direction, or we leave in a state of fullness, having absorbed liberating knowledge, ready to establish our own life path.

A relationship with a spiritual teacher tends to become a focal point for some period of time. But we often try to freeze this experience into permanence, failing to recognize it as a phase. When we find an awakened teacher, we experience devotion and gratitude, surrendering from a place beyond the rational mind, feeling a cord of love connecting us. But sometimes we must part ways, even if we are profoundly grateful for the teacher's guidance and uplifting influence.

Some students never leave their teachers, remaining devoted for decades, even a lifetime. Even if a teacher engages in some controversial behavior, some disciples remain unshakably devoted. There are also instances where the student-teacher relationship runs astray, resulting in confusion, bitterness, or despair for the disciple. Many spiritual apprentices who've experienced surrender and devotion eventually feel a need to leave their teachers. I've found this to be true for many people who have had positive experiences, as well as for those who feel their teachers have disappointed, injured, or betrayed them.

Many difficulties and complications in student-teacher relationships arise or become evident at the moment when students attempt to individuate, to leave the teacher's immediate company to pursue their own life projects. While many traditions recommend a lengthy period of discipleship, there usually comes a time when students need to follow their own paths, whether it's because they've become disillusioned, feel they've learned all they can from the teacher, or have other responsibilities and interests to attend to. Some leave feeling the teacher's love, blessings, and continuing influence. In such cases the separation, whether permanent or temporary, can be undertaken amicably, with mutual goodwill, affection, and respect; they're separated physically but inwardly are one. Loretta, the woman whose teacher encouraged her to go to medical school, told me, "My teacher recognized that I needed to focus on my career and working, even though I had to move away and wasn't able to spend any more time with him. He told me I should go and not feel bad about it. It was time for me to fly on my own. It felt wonderful that I could leave knowing I had his full confidence."

However, in other cases the student's loving and devoted feelings toward the teacher begin to change, sometimes turning to mistrust, anger, or bitterness. I'm reminded of the story of Robert, a young man who spent eight years as a student of a guru who emphasized surrender and obedience. Robert became one of his teacher's personal attendants and felt privileged to serve him, feeling transformed by his close proximity with such a highly evolved being. However, he had left the community abruptly after the guru was confronted by others about financial and sexual misconduct. Robert sought counseling to work through his feelings of anger and betrayal and for help in adjusting to living on his own.

Several aspects of discipleship had become distressing to Robert even before the events that precipitated his departure. He had long dreamed about becoming a novelist and enjoyed trying to develop his stories. But Robert had abandoned his writing after the teacher spoke derisively of his ambitions, saying that Robert was entertaining fantasies of literary greatness to bolster his ego, as a defense against the teacher's fire of "ego-destroying grace." So he suppressed his creative interests, remaining a loyal and busy devotee. Now that he had decided to split from his teacher, he was angry and defiant, and felt like he'd been duped and lost out on several good years of his life. He was determined to succeed following his own path in the world, but he also felt afraid of the future, grappled with low self-esteem, and was troubled by guilt, the sense that he'd committed a terrible act and would possibly be punished.

Robert's story illustrates the rocky transition that some students face in leaving a spiritual teacher and reestablishing an independent life.

EMOTIONAL CONFLICTS IN SPIRITUAL APPRENTICESHIP

Developmental psychologist Daniel Levinson views the relationship between a mentor and a novice or apprentice as inherently conflictual because the novice simultaneously experiences both feelings of admiration and respect, and feelings of resentment, inferiority, and envy toward the mentor. In Levinson's view mentor-student relationships often end in conflict and bitterness because of the inherently ambiguous role of the mentor, who is a transitional figure, both parent and peer, who must eventually be left behind by the novice to fulfill the developmental task of "becoming one's own man."[1] Levinson writes, "The mentor who only yesterday was regarded as an enabling teacher and friend has become a tyrannical father or smothering mother. The mentor, for his part, finds the young [person] inexplicably touchy, unreceptive to even the best counsel, irrationally rebellious and ungrateful."[2]

We're especially prone to inner tension at this stage. We yearn for a good father or mother who will make us feel special, yet we may also perceive the mentor as a bad parental figure, a dictator, or a hostile judge. This split in our perception of teachers contributes to the conflict we experience when the time arrives to separate. Levinson describes the paradoxical nature of all mentoring relationships, which involve a temporary dependence of the novice on the teacher, with the novice to emerge transformed and independent. A similar insight was expressed by Ken Wilber in a discussion of relationships with spiritual teachers:

> Virtually all authentic Eastern or mystical traditions maintain that the guru is representative of one's own highest nature, and once that nature is realized, the guru's formal authority and function is ended. . . . Thus, once the student awakens to his or her own equally higher status as Buddha-Brahman, the function of the guru is ended and the authority of the guru evaporates. In Zen, for instance, once a person achieves major satori (causal insight), the relationship between

roshi and disciple changes from master and student to brother and brother (or sister-brother, or sister-sister)—and this is explicitly so stated. The guru, as authority, is phase temporary.[3]

While we may understand intellectually that discipleship is "phase temporary" (i.e., a developmental stage to be passed through), it can be emotionally stressful to actually go through the process of separation from a teacher.

THE CASE OF OTTO RANK

A relevant example of the complex dynamics of mentorship and apprenticeship is the relationship between the psychoanalyst Otto Rank and his teacher, Sigmund Freud, which led to a predicament Ira Progoff describes as "a disciple's dilemma."[4] Freud put Rank through college and graduate school, introduced him into the circle of his closest associates, and helped establish him in the psychoanalytic profession. But after years of receiving encouragement, guidance, praise, financial assistance, and professional favors from Freud, Rank needed to differentiate from his mentor. Matters came to a head in 1924 when Rank published *The Trauma of Birth,* where he first set forth his own theory. Progoff writes:

> Increasingly Rank found that it was his intellectual rather than his artistic energies that were being called into play, and a major part of his personality was thus left unfulfilled. . . . Nonetheless, his strong personal attachment to Freud—an attachment verging on dependence—and his sense of gratitude for favors received in the past prevented his breaking his connection in a deliberate or abrupt way. . . . But . . . the net effect of the book [*The Trauma of Birth*], and perhaps its unconscious intention, was to precipitate his separation from Freud. . . . Rank [later] made the acute observation that one of the aftermaths of a creative act is an attack

of guilt feelings, remorse, and anxiety. . . . In making this point, Rank may well have been describing his own experience, for we know that when *The Trauma of Birth* drew strong attacks from the Freudian circle Rank was on the verge of retracting his views. The thought of being cut off from Freud became exceedingly painful for him, for he feared the isolation and ostracism it might bring. . . . [The result of publishing this book] was to upset his accustomed position as the loyal disciple of a revered master. . . . Rank had much for which to be grateful, and his attachment to Freud was deep indeed. But how could he develop the artist in himself and fulfill his own need for creativity while remaining a loyal disciple? . . . His devotion to Freud . . . conflicted with the necessary unfoldment of his own individuality, and his act of self-liberation in writing *The Trauma of Birth* was followed by a sense of remorse that took many forms over the years and from which Rank never fully recovered. . . . [Although Rank moved away from Freud's circle in Vienna] it was much easier to separate himself from Freud geographically than psychologically. The man and his teachings remained at the center of a continuous struggle in which Rank was forced to engage within himself. . . . Freud, who had been his protector, was now his psychic adversary.[5]

This story illustrates the conflict we may face when standing at the crossroads between continuing allegiance to a mentor and the need to set forth on our own independent journey. This passage describes issues that are also pertinent to many guru-disciple relationships. Progoff notes that not only did Rank have a strong personal attachment to Freud, Freud was similarly attached to Rank and was eager to avoid defection by such a close and devoted disciple. This example demonstrates that to understand the problematic aspects of spiritual apprenticeship, we need to consider how the dynamics of transference and countertransference that occur in psychotherapy may also be present in student-mentor and guru-disciple relationships.

DEVELOPMENTAL ISSUES AND DISCIPLESHIP

Progoff describes a student's conflict between feeling unfulfilled as a disciple and feelings of gratitude, attachment, and dependency toward the mentor. Progoff also notes the fear of ostracism and the feelings of guilt and remorse often brought on by the student's need to separate and individuate. In addition there are several other issues that have a bearing on "the disciple's dilemma" in our current context.

Unresolved childhood issues with parents can contribute to complications regarding separation and individuation from mentors. Some people reenact early developmental problems in relationship to their spiritual guides, just as psychotherapy clients often do with their therapists. Disciples may remain too long in a state of unhealthy dependency; or they act out a lot of rage in a way that's similar to adolescents repudiating parents.

There are probably some followers of spiritual teachers who spend a lot of time in ashrams and retreat centers to avoid facing the challenging tasks of maturation in adulthood. Buddhist transpersonal psychologist Jack Engler notes that intensive spiritual practices, intended to lead beyond ego into transpersonal levels of development, can be contraindicated for those with many unresolved egoic issues, such as feelings of inner emptiness resulting from a lack of stable self-esteem or an inability to sustain interpersonal relationships.[6] In such cases intensive meditation often won't help us, and it can even be counterproductive.

Thus, at this stage we might benefit from attention to the basic tasks and challenges of ego development, such as achieving a positive feeling of self-worth and creating more nourishing emotional attachments. We need to achieve a degree of self-cohesion and self-awareness to thrive as individuals in this challenging world. In this phase we can strive for a deeper integration of personal and transpersonal development.[7] Where the primary focus of our affiliation with a spiritual teacher has been achieving higher evolution into transpersonal stages of consciousness, it's also important to do some work to resolve our neuroses and evolve the personality. This is a primary reason we may need to separate from a teacher.

In many respects discipleship and spiritual practices don't have the same goals, methods, or outcomes as psychotherapy.[8] Since many of us have unresolved issues about sex, money, work, self-esteem, and creativity that need attention, we need to recognize when these concerns can be better addressed in psychotherapy rather than through discipleship.

DISCIPLESHIP AND PSYCHOTHERAPY

Some confusion can result from not grasping the differences between psychotherapy and training under a spiritual guide. Some people hope or expect that their gurus will fulfill the role of a therapist. But a spiritual teacher generally isn't concerned with strengthening our sense of self, improving relationship skills, or working through difficult emotions, which are the traditional province of a therapist. A spiritual teacher's job is to reveal the Atman, the divine, pure consciousness beyond our individual identity, beyond the ego. If we approach spiritual teachers looking for the kind of supportive counseling a psychotherapist offers, we're setting ourselves up for disappointment and misunderstanding the role of spiritual teachers—that is, unless the teacher is also a trained psychotherapist.

And yet, particularly in the West, concepts derived from psychotherapy have influenced our attitudes toward the teacher-student, guru-disciple relationship. The field of psychology has seen widespread adoption of ethical codes for psychotherapists, which have impacted how contemporary Westerners assume spiritual teachers will behave. Some have come to expect spiritual teachers to abide by standards of ethics and behavior similar to those of other professionals such as doctors, psychologists, and counselors. This isn't always realistic, as many spiritual teachers aren't trained in these professions and committed to conform to their standards.

These issues have arisen in many situations where students have confronted spiritual teachers with purported abuses of their position. Some of these teachers have denied the charges outright, justified their actions as crazy-wisdom teachings, or contended that their students were acting like rebellious adolescents and treating them like a parental surrogate. Others have defended themselves on the grounds that their rebellious students failed to honor the sanctity of the spiritual teacher's position in traditional spiritual lineages, where trust in the teacher's methods and good intentions are assumed, and where the teacher's actions, motivations, or apparent abuses of power are rarely questioned. Recall the story of Milarepa and how he submitted with implicit trust to the apparently cruel and abusive treatment of his teacher, Marpa.

Nonetheless, the nature of spiritual teacher-student relationships may need to change as this tradition is revitalized in the West. While equality and a cooperative spirit weren't prevalent features of traditional discipleship, contemporary students of spiritual lineages expect a more democratic, less autocratic process of training. It's still an open question as to whether Americans steeped in democracy and individualism can, without considerable discomfort, hope to achieve spiritual liberation through nondemocratic forms of traditional discipleship that require unquestioning obedience and surrender.

I believe that the tradition of spiritual apprenticeship can be strengthened in our culture if spiritual teachers adapt to our present cultural context, by treating students with nonpossessive warmth, respecting their independence, showing a willingness to self-scrutinize and occasionally correcting their own behavior, and relinquishing demands for absolute surrender. They need ongoing work on their own personal emotional issues, their attachments and insecurities. This will help them avoid some of the pitfalls of many teachers. In short I'm suggesting that spiritual teachers need to be psychologically aware and mature, more like therapists doing ongoing inner work. This way the trust of students is earned and preserved. It's also worth noting the current emergence of a new wave of transpersonal psychotherapists who follow contemplative paths and are trained to serve as spiritual guides.

These practitioners can address personal, psychodynamic issues but can also aid clients experiencing awakenings and states of consciousness beyond the ego.[9]

Having briefly described the question of unresolved developmental issues, the blurring of distinctions between discipleship and psychotherapy, and some cultural assumptions regarding the authority of spiritual teachers, let's examine the transference dynamics that often affect the perceptions spiritual teachers and disciples have of one another.

TRANSFERENCE IN THE STUDENT-TEACHER RELATIONSHIP

In the phenomenon known as *transference,* our relationships with others are colored by feelings and perceptions derived from our earliest relationships with parents and other caregivers, which form a blueprint or internal working model of interaction with others. Transference is a part of all close human relationships. We rarely see others completely accurately because we view them through the filter of our fears and expectations, based on past experience of important people in our lives. According to Heinz Kohut, the psychoanalyst who developed the principles of *self psychology,* there are two main types of transference: mirroring and idealizing.[10] In mirroring transference we need others to mirror us, to acknowledge and validate us. We relate to people as sources of mirroring and validation for us, or we see them as withholding and failing to mirror us, which can enrage us. In idealization transference we're searching for someone to idealize and admire; we look for someone we perceive as perfect and worthy of our trust and esteem. When others disappoint us and fail to live up to our idealizations, we may feel angry and dissatisfied. Adequate satisfaction of our needs for mirroring and idealization is considered essential to healthy psychological development. To build self-esteem we need to be mirrored by others and reassured of our value; and to develop our personal goals and ambitions, we need idealized others whose qualities we can emulate.

Kohut also describes a third kind of transference, characterized by a desire to feel a sense of "twinship" or alikeness with another person. This alter-ego transference is relevant in cases where discipleship proceeds smoothly and the student develops an identification with the teacher. It may be one of the mechanisms operative in techniques in which the student meditates on the teacher. In the present context, I'll focus on mirroring and idealization transferences, since these commonly lead to complications.

MIRRORING TRANSFERENCE AND DISCIPLESHIP

In mirroring transference we seek empathic resonance from another person. By being consistently, accurately, and sensitively received by another person, we feel accepted and valuable to others and to ourselves. In mirroring relationships we don't perceive others in their actuality and otherness; they serve as what Kohut calls "self-objects," extensions of the self that we use to bolster our self-esteem and sense of specialness.

The spiritual teacher and the student mirror each other. The student receives mirroring if, as in Otto Rank's case, he or she becomes important and valuable to the teacher and receives attention, affirmation, and praise. Similarly, the spiritual guide may experience a mirroring transference with the disciple, basking in the novice's admiration, devotion, and love—although presumably there are teachers who've transcended such needs.

According to Jungian analyst Mario Jacoby, the person who serves as the mirroring self-object is greatly valued or even overvalued, as she or he becomes essential to our internal equilibrium and sense of self-worth. But when we perceive that such a self-object is failing to mirror or acknowledge us, we may angrily reject and devalue that person. In the absence of mirroring, we may also become depressed and susceptible to feelings of emptiness, confusion, or alienation.

For example, after leaving his spiritual teacher Robert (described earlier) was very angry but also felt disoriented and struggled with feelings of worthlessness and low self-esteem. For years he'd been preoccupied with winning the teacher's interest and approval and thus had, in a sense, been overvaluing the guru as a self-object. It was devastating to realize that his teacher wasn't very interested in him and failed to really see him or value him as an individual. It was also difficult to accept that his teacher had other favorite disciples, and that he didn't enjoy the teacher's exclusive love. These realizations enraged Robert, who sometimes sarcastically criticized and devalued his former teacher.

These dynamics can also be transposed. Teachers may be subject to overvaluing the mirroring self-object, so that the love and attention of students becomes essential to their self-esteem. Consequently, a teacher may angrily devalue a student who exhibits less devotion or has competing allegiances to other teachers or loved ones. This could account for the way some spiritual teachers expect and demand exclusive devotion. Even evolved teachers receive narcissistic gratification from their relationships with students—from being gazed at, adored, and listened to with rapt attention. The psychological immaturity of some teachers and unawareness of their own emotional needs for validation can contribute to difficulties and complications in the student-teacher relationship. Spiritual teachers need to examine their desire for mirroring, admiration, and idealization, so that they're gracious and compassionate if students reach the stage when they need to separate and individuate. This self-examination is important for anyone assuming the role of a spiritual teacher.

IDEALIZATION AND
THE SHADOW IN DISCIPLESHIP

According to Mario Jacoby, in idealization transferences one person projects archetypal images of perfection, omnipotence, and omniscience on the other person, whose perfection is equated with one's own perfection through a process called *intrapsychic fusion*.[11] We feel exhiliration when we feel we're connected to an idealized person. In childhood idealization is a precursor to the development of one's own goals and ambitions, as the idealized self-object becomes the foundation for imagining one's own aspirations or ideal self. Similarly, a disciple's devotion and tendency to view a spiritual teacher as a perfect, all-knowing being may be founded partially on idealization transference. Kohut and his coauthor, Ernest Wolf, write:

> Ideal-hungry personalities are forever in search of others whom they can admire for their prestige, power, beauty, intelligence or moral stature. They can experience themselves as worthwhile only so long as they can relate to selfobjects to whom they can look up. In most cases . . . the inner void cannot forever be filled by these means. The ideal-hungry feels the persistence of the structural deficit and . . . begins to look for—and of course he inevitably finds—some realistic defects in his God. The search for new idealizable selfobjects is then continued, always with the hope that the next great figure to whom the ideal-hungry attaches himself will not disappoint him.[12]

Through gradual disappointments—similar to those by which a child's idealizations of a parent are outgrown—we learn to perceive others more realistically; instead of viewing people as either all good or all bad, we realize that everyone possesses a mix of good and bad qualities. Only when we realize that we're idealizing others can we modify our own grandiose self-image, achieving a more realistic assessment of our talents and strengths. It's healthy for us to recognize our idealizations and disappointments in relationships and learn to accept other people, including our beloved teachers, as human beings, who have a mixture of good and bad characteristics. Then we can develop enduring relationships with others and stop constantly expecting them to be perfect and all good.

In some cases a disciple will engage in negative idealization, viewing

Ardhanarishvara, the symbol of the inseparable union of Shiva and Shakti, male and female, destructive and creative energies, and the path of achieving wholeness through transcending dualism and uniting opposites. Tanjore.

the teacher as the embodiment of absolute evil. Jungian psychiatrist Donald Sandner discusses this phenomenon, observing the tendency to project both positive and negative characteristics of our own bipolar shadow.[13] The unconscious, unintegrated, positive characteristics of the self "tend to be represented by superior, noble, heroic, spiritual or religious figures."[14] These figures become the objects of our idealizations. Conversely, the negative pole of the shadow complex, containing culturally undesirable qualities and personal characteristics that we reject or repress, tends to be projected so that we perceive others as evil, aggressive, or malevolent.

This perspective explains how Robert's idealization of his spiritual teacher turned into an angry, devaluing attitude toward a figure he now perceived as all bad—cruel, greedy, dishonest, authoritarian, and manipulative. This also helps clarify Otto Rank's predicament. As Progoff put it, "Freud, who had been his protector, was now his psychic adversary."[15] Dramatic reversal of a disciple's affection may occur when one accurately perceives a teacher's shortcomings; or it may reflect the student's unconscious projections onto the teacher.

AN ARCHETYPAL PERSPECTIVE ON SPIRITUAL APPRENTICESHIP

In addition to featuring some elements of transference, spiritual apprenticeship also has an archetypal basis. We gain an illuminating perspective on the student-teacher relationship from Jungian psychologist James Hillman's ideas about the archetypes of youth and maturity, respectively the *puer* and the *senex*.[16] In Hillman's view the messiah aspect of the puer is an aspect of the self that feels a sense of infinite possibilities and personal mission and is subject to psychic inflation. This constellates the complementary archetypal figure of the Wise Old Man or Wise Old Woman, who symbolizes perfection, psychic wholeness, and internal guidance of the self, from which the puer-messiah derives a sense of stability, power, and recognition. In the course of maturation, the puer-messiah is transformed through emergence of the puer-hero, the archetype of the youth heroically actualizing the puer-messiah's visions, goals, and sense of mission. However, the puer-hero corresponds internally not to the beneficent Wise Old Man, or senex, who guides and befriends the puer-messiah, but to the archetypal figure of the Old King of Power, symbol of power and social authority. The Old King of Power is a psychic image of both external and internalized social forces that stand in the way and thwart the puer-hero's ambitions. It's a symbol of the reality principle, the disapproving father and the society that doesn't immediately welcome and applaud the puer-hero's potentials and achievements. Thus, the puer-hero must fight to overcome the Old King in order to emerge as a person of power and achievement.

These archetypal themes illuminate a paradox in the internal world of the puer-disciple. The student-puer derives inspiration, strength, and comfort by associating with the senex-mentor when the latter appears to be a beneficent, helpful, wise figure. But the puer-novice attempting to actualize personal goals and possibilities also tends to perceive the senex-teacher as the embodiment or extension of all the social norms and institutions that obstruct the puer-novice's self-actualization. Thus, the puer-disciple will often come to struggle against a teacher who represents the old king of power.

In Otto Rank's case, these dynamics were evident in his increasing boredom in his position as Freud's follower. As Progoff writes, "A major part of his personality was thus left unfulfilled." Rank yearned for freedom and new channels of self-expression. As disciples something within us knows that further growth may not be possible while remaining in a position of deference or servitude with respect to a mentor or spiritual guide. Individuation often forces separation from the teacher and relinquishing the role of the loyal disciple. This process is considerably easier if the teacher can tolerate and celebrate the student's autonomy and need for independence to pursue a personal calling.[17] A teacher's wisdom and sincerity is evident in the way he or she accepts and encourages the student's natural need to graduate from tutelage.

SEPARATION, GUILT, AND SELF-APPOINTMENT

We may experience an identity crisis and a sense of loss when contemplating separating from a teacher. Letting go of one's identity as the loyal follower or disciple often evokes a frightening sense of being betwixt and between, in a undefined state of transition. This is more likely when the separation is frought with angry feelings toward the teacher. However, even when we know the time has come to pursue an independent path, we may experience considerable guilt and remorse regarding separation. It's like changing or terminating any important emotional attachment; the process generates anxiety.

Otto Rank noted that our instinct to separate, to individuate, and to create is always attended by feelings of guilt, which derive from the fear of injuring or abandoning a parental figure.[18] Recall how Rank's feelings of gratitude toward Freud and his fear of ostracism and isolation caused him to wish to remain in his disciple role. But the heroic personality, which in Rank's writings is often termed the artist, struggles against this guilt and wills himself or herself into existence as a creative individual. And just as modern artists must appoint themselves artists in the face of social disapproval, ridicule, or indifference, so too the growth of the creative personality almost inevitably requires severing symbiotic ties in an act of "self-appointment."[19] Similarly, spiritual apprentices need to overcome the guilt of separation and learn that it's okay to be independent, even if they continue to recognize a spiritual teacher's influence.

Teachers may exacerbate students' feelings of guilt by their actions or statements. For their own conscious or unconscious reasons, they may seek to keep a student within the fold, within the community of devotees. Thus we need to consider the emotional motivations of teachers as well as students to understand the complex dynamics of their relationship at this crucial stage.

One man I worked with was affiliated with an extraordinarily narcissistic teacher. Dale wrote his teacher a letter questioning his teacher's affairs with two students, his arrogance toward students during classes, and lies he'd told Dale directly. The teacher's response was full of scorn, condescension, and seething anger. He belittled Dale, saying, "You never were much of a student. I don't know why I invested so much of myself in someone so unworthy. If you want to learn anything from me, you must never question me or my actions." This so-called teacher actually wrote this disdainful message to his student.

Teachers have their own needs for power, admiration, fellowship, mirroring, as well as financial and organizational needs, all of which may become motivating factors in their efforts to prevent departures of their students. While some teachers may be free of such self-centered motivations, we shouldn't assume that all are. Most spiritual teachers have both altruistic-beneficent and selfish-narcissistic motivations. Wise teachers recognize the tendency to cling to admiring followers; they try to not allow their own need to be idealized to contaminate their guidance of students.

DISTORTIONS OF DISCIPLESHIP

Sandner views discipleship or apprenticeship as a process of initiation into a new state of individuated existence through a process of submission, fusion, and reemergence.[20] Students submit to the teacher's authority and fuse internally with the mentor in order to derive strength, clarity, and an internal image of perfection that becomes the basis for their own ideals. The completion of the relationship should witness the disciple's reemergence as an independent person. However, Sandner says distortions in this process can occur if the disciple remains bound to the position of submission to the father-master-mentor, and sometimes the relationship can devolve into a sequence of compulsive sadomasochistic acts from which the student can derive pleasure or a sense of security.[21] Here, the student may adopt a masochistic posture of humiliation, which can be reinforced through being physically or emotionally injured, psychically immobilized, severely criticized, or publicly denounced by the teacher.

This is exactly what happened in Robert's case. His teacher had often disparaged him publicly, castigating him for incompetence and physically striking him on several occasions. Apparently he didn't hold that high an opinion of his student, and Robert knew this and it really stung. Robert's response hadn't been to rebel or defend himself, but rather to internalize these harsh criticisms and come back for more, desperate for praise or validation. In the course of therapy, Robert recognized how this abusive relationship was a replica of his relationship with his father, who was an angry alcoholic who intimidated and physically injured Robert, and whose approval Robert had always sought.

This story grimly illustrates the distorted form a relationship between teacher and disciple can sometimes take.

HEALING THE WOUNDS OF SEPARATION

It took Robert several years to work through his anger toward the teacher and his remorse over unfulfilled expectations. Writing about his experiences helped him establish a connection to his own vitality and to expand his thinking and his range of feelings. He started to feel better about himself and eventually published a novel based on experiences in his former community. The wounds of separation finally healed.

Spiritual apprentices eventually realize that their guru's teachings are woefully inadequate in certain respects or that some of the teacher's actions are wrong, destructive, or unethical. The teacher's profound dharma wisdom doesn't make this person the final authority on other matters such as politics or medicine or the stock market. The teacher's instructions about spiritual practice or doctrine may not adequately illuminate issues pertaining to work and livelihood, sexuality and relationships, the need for higher education, or the despair many people feel about ecological destruction and social injustice. We have to look beyond this guru's teaching for guidance in these areas.

Spiritual teachers can only travel so far with us. Sooner or later teachers die or send us away or reject us. We experience disappointment if teachers refuse to give us their approval, or if they're inaccessible to us on a personal level, or if we recognize that in some respects the teacher is a fool. Some teachers disappoint us when we discover how cruel they can be and how immature they are emotionally.

These themes are powerfully addressed in Gail Tredwell's recent book *Holy Hell: A Memoir of Faith, Devotion, and Pure Madness*. Gail "Gayatri" was an early disciple of the Indian guru Ammachi, playing the roles of "personal attendant, handmaiden, whipping post, and unwilling keeper of some devastating secrets." She served Ammachi with devotion; however, the relationship transformed into virtual enslavement, wherein Tredwell was on call nonstop and nearly worked herself to death in the hope of pleasing her guru and finding God. The "Hugging Saint," as Ammachi is known, would apparently come home from public appearances to beat, slap, and insult her devoted attendant. Tredwell's commitment to absolute devotion became a nightmare of physical and verbal abuse so severe that she fled the Amma organization in darkness and secrecy, hiding under a blanket in the back of somebody's truck. She describes her experiences of discipleship and service, disillusionment, and struggle for independence from the guru, writing honestly and humorously, stating the facts about her teacher's flaws but striving to avoid falling into the attitude of a victim. She bravely takes responsibility for her own role in accepting abuse and perpetuating lies about her teacher. Tredwell's riveting account has generated a firestorm of controversy, criticism, and public protests and outcry, as well as waves of admiration from appreciative readers.

DREAMS ABOUT
THE PROCESS OF SEPARATION

Sometimes resolution of the relationship with a spiritual teacher is facilitated through the symbolism of dreams. For example, I began to grapple with an urge to separate from my teacher, Muktananda, and explore new relationships after spending years affiliated with an ashram in which some disciples had taken monastic vows of celibacy. At this time I had two notable dreams. In the first:

> *I was walking through the ashram and noticed several swamis lifting weights, while another swami, who in real life was a very austere monk, was walking hand-in-hand with a woman and wearing an expensive Lacoste tennis outfit. Swami Muktananda stood on the roof of the ashram spraying everyone with a hose.*

In the second dream:

> *I walked into a large meditation hall in which*
> *hundreds of seats were arranged facing away from*
> *the guru's seat at the front of the room.*

The first dream seemed to say that the dry state of my inner world was ready to receive the waters of life. Here the swamis were embracing the life of the body, sexuality, and the company of women. The second dream portrayed my desire to remain reverently connected with the guru, while also turning my attention out into the world.

A twenty-nine-year-old man named Chris was aided by two remarkable dreams. An ardent practitioner of hatha yoga, Chris had studied with many teachers and got something valuable from each of them. But at times he was disillusioned with several of his teachers. Some of them became rigid if he questioned anything they taught. He was particularly upset at one stage because the reckless instruction of one teacher contributed to a serious arm injury from which he was suffering acutely. This teacher denied any responsibility in the matter, so Chris was feeling quite angry. I had a similar experience once so I felt very sympathetic to his plight. Chris had the following dream:

> *A small baby boy with a very large buddha head is lying on*
> *the ground. He appears to be on the verge of an epileptic sei-*
> *zure, trembling and thrashing about spastically, but his par-*
> *ents are nowhere to be found. I try to hold him down while*
> *"Ron" [one of the teachers who'd disappointed him] sprinkled*
> *water on his third eye. Ron says to me, "No, you're not doing it*
> *right," and he insists that he should hold the boy down while*
> *I sprinkle the water on him. The boy's convulsions become*
> *intense and he thrashes around uncontrollably. As he does so*
> *I hear the boy's voice angrily exclaiming "You jerk, you're sup-*
> *posed to be helping me but you can't even prevent this from*

happening to me!" The boy begins smashing every bone in his
body on the ground and twists his head so much that his neck
breaks and his head falls off. Finally all that remains of his
body is one arm bone.

The baby with a buddha's head was an image of the enlightenment
he'd pursued for a number of years, but also reflected back to him that
maybe he was psychologically immature. The dream portrayed frustration at the inability of teachers to help him, and feeling blamed for his
injury ("You're not doing it right"). The dream suggested that his potential for achieving an enlightened state (the buddha's head) was being
destroyed by the bitterness he felt toward teachers who'd failed to initiate and assist him properly; the statement "You're not doing it right"
was also directed at them. The dream's imagery of bodily dismember-
ment evoked the theme of shamanic initiation. The dream implied that
Chris could view his injury (the arm bone) as a shamanic wound suffered in the course of initiation by elders—an initiation that could lead
to integration. Dreams sometimes allow us to touch the most painful
aspects of our existence, and this dream allowed Chris to regress and
have an emotional convulsion that liberated his energy immensely. It's
also interesting to note the similarity between his dream of the decapitated buddha and the image of Chinnamasta Mahavidya discussed in
stage four on pages 125–27.

After some months of reflection and letting go of negative feelings,
Chris had this dream:

I'm in a lush green meadow, standing near a large, very
ancient and beautiful tree. I'm observing a vigil here for my
dead teacher and father, who is buried underneath this tree.
It's a solemn moment, yet I feel very much at peace.

The burial of his dead teacher and father signified the death of the
need for an external spiritual guide and connected Chris to his own

wisdom, vision, and authority. The appearance of the tree, symbol of growth, maturation, individuation and rebirth, aided him in resolving these issues with spiritual teachers. He told me, "With these men fertilizing my roots, I can become my own father."

DISCIPLESHIP AS A CULTURE OF EMBEDDEDNESS

The teacher-student relationship is a transitional relationship that's intended to lead beyond itself. Developmental psychologist Robert Kegan characterizes human development as a passage through a series of holding environments or "cultures of embeddedness," such as the womb, the mother's arms, the family, the schools we attend, and interpersonal relationships, all of which nurture and support us and then release us when we're ready to differentiate from them.[22] For Kegan growth means emergence from "embeddedness cultures" and subsequent reappropriation of the elements of that culture. These structures and systems in which we're embedded become part of the self; they're recognized to be other, apart from the self, yet they're also environments with which a differentiated self can be in relationship. Nevertheless, people tend to actively repudiate a culture of embeddedness, such as the family, in the process of separating from it. Kegan notes, "Growth itself is not alone a matter of separation and repudiation, of killing off the past. This is more a matter of transition. Growth involves as well the reconciliation, the recovery, the recognition of that which before was confused with the self."[23]

As students we're sustained and nourished by a mentoring relationship but must ultimately emerge from that culture of embeddedness into our own independent life in the world. For Otto Rank emergence from Freud's circle was the source of a wound that never healed completely. We've also seen the difficulties my client Robert faced in this process. But such an outcome isn't inevitable. Rather than completely rejecting and repudiating the spiritual guide, it may be possible to inwardly preserve the teacher as a valued part of the self.

A more mature relationship can develop if the teacher is willing to relinquish control and authority and accept our growing independence. This can also mean acknowledging that the teacher's love, power, and wisdom can now be internalized. When the transformational relationship has achieved its purpose, student and teacher can take their leave of each other with mutual affection and gratitude, free to walk their respective paths without regret. When the disciple is ready, the guru disappears.

HOW I LEFT THE ASHRAM

In 1978 I had a reading by the famous Vedic astrologer Chakrapani Ullal at his home in Bombay, India. He told me, "Your relationship with Muktananda will grow stronger once you leave the ashram and go home. That will be the real beginning of your sadhana and discipleship."

Several events helped me transition toward independence. First, after my experiences in Ganeshpuri, described earlier, I experienced a setback: while traveling in northern India, I contracted typhoid and became quite ill. I was hospitalized for five days when I returned to the United States and was dependent on my family to care for me while I recovered for several weeks. Thus I had to confront the reality of who I really was and where I came from, rather than remaining lost in my romanticized fantasy of becoming a swami in India.

> *I remember how I came into my body, age twenty*
> *half dead in a hospital after Montezuma took revenge*
> *at Akbar's castle in New Delhi.*
> *I fell suddenly to earth, like Icarus singed*
> *into the life I tried to flee in ashrams*
> *where I stood in gaudy Hindu temples*
> *chanting Sanskrit*
> *longing to erase my personal history.**

---

*From my poem "Awakening the Flesh."

*Joyful goddesses, a divine couple, and Vishnu in his incarnation
as the divine boar* (varaha avatara). *Vishnu's boar's head and human
body signify union of our human and animal natures. When the demon
Hiranyaksha dragged the Earth to the bottom of the ocean, Vishnu
incarnated as a boar to rescue it on his enormous tusk. He signifies
resurrection of the Earth from* pralaya *(dissolution of the universe) and the
establishment of a new eon. He is shown trampling the defeated demon. His
tall crown signifies that he is king or lord of the universe. Srinageri.*

Also my three-year period of celibacy ended when I became involved
in a relationship and got to experience a moment of sexual Eden. I later
learned that all of this occurred while the planet Pluto was transiting
conjunct my ascendant. Pluto symbolizes death and rebirth. I had a
brush with death, and then experienced a renewal. My ascendant is in
Libra, which represents relationships, lovers, and couples, and from this
time on, relationships became a more vital part of my spiritual life. It
took several years for me to recover fully from typhoid, but I did regain
my health and began to feel a surge of energy and vitality. At this time
I also rediscovered music, songwriting, and poetry.

I decided I could no longer live near the ashram because I wanted more time to pursue my interests in music and writing. Also, one of the swamis in the ashram was on my case because I was letting my hair grow long. I was more interested in playing guitar and reading Tom Robbins novels than sitting in a temple chanting. It was time to leave the ashram. I was twenty-one years old.

I was filled with wanderlust. In January 1980 I departed New York City on a Greyhound bus and spent several years traveling, performing as a street musician in Boulder, Eugene, and Ashland, and living in a tent in the forests of Oregon and Washington. I wandered somewhat aimlessly, hitchhiking around, often unsure where I'd sleep at night. During this period of homelessness, I sought the internal teacher and began to relate to the guru as an internal presence that helped me remain peaceful despite the uncertainty and loneliness I was experiencing during this time of transition.

At one point I wrote Muktananda a letter confessing various transgressions of the ashram discipline. I was living in Colorado, playing music, writing poetry, studying mystical texts, psychology, and astrology, dating women, doing yoga, but not meditating as much. I took a few mushrooms and smoked a little weed. I felt conflicted about the fact that I wasn't adhering to a yogic lifestyle. But my intuition told me these activities weren't detrimental to my spiritual unfoldment. I was developing my mind, my imagination, my creativity, my capacity to love, my understanding of dreams. In my letter I expressed remorse that I wasn't fully following his teachings and was no longer living close to him as a direct disciple. I was concerned that my interests in music, dreams, and metaphysical studies were leading me off the focused path of yoga. My teacher responded by mail that I should continue my current work, viewing this work, like all work, as service to the Lord. He said, "Your heart is very good. Let go of the past. Renew your dedication to your sadhana."

I felt liberated when I received his message, which encouraged me to be independent and to trust my inner voice about the direction my life was taking. I felt he gave me his permission to unfold the energies awakening through shaktipat and my yogic practices in a creative manner. My path wasn't to renounce the world, but to create a spiritual personality, to become a unique expression of universal consciousness.

I recalled how once I was meditating in Ganeshpuri in a room outside Baba's apartment. I heard him come out of his door and walk down the aisle, and I opened my eyes to take a peek at him. Later he scolded me, saying that those who look at the guru with external eyes instead of looking within to find the inner light in meditation are nothing but fake yogis. At the time I didn't like being chastised, but now, as I recalled this episode, it reminded me that my path was to meditate, letting go of preoccupation with my teacher's external form.

For me separating from a spiritual teacher wasn't an angry, bitter process. I learned from my teacher that I need to live my own life. Muktananda actively encouraged me to leave the ashram and to go out into the world to find my own path, my own calling. He encouraged me to discover my destiny. I'm grateful that my teacher had the wisdom not to bind me to him, to recognize that I needed to find my own way. Leaving his physical company was the beginning of a new phase in which I practiced the teachings I'd received, relying on my own judgment, in attunement with the inner spirit of guidance.

SAYING GOOD-BYE

About two years after I left the ashram, I went back to see my teacher. I sat quite far back in the meeting hall amidst hundreds of people. The moment he sat down in his seat, he looked right at me. He didn't say anything, but he looked me over, neither approving nor critical. His long gaze conveyed the awareness that he was always with me and that he was conscious of my development and struggles. I felt he truly saw me and was silently witnessing all. Later, I realized the significance of the fact that he looked at me in this way on this occasion. It was as if he knew what I didn't know at the time—that this would be the last time I ever saw his physical form.

Baba's spirit came to me when he left his body in October 1982. I was living in Colorado at the time. In those days I often practiced meditation in the afternoon and evening but rarely in the morning because I tended to be restless to begin the business of my day. However, one morning I was drawn to meditation from the moment I woke up. Without planning to do so, I sat for over three hours without moving. In my mind's eye, I saw myself sitting in my teacher's presence in the courtyard in Ganeshpuri. Soon after I got up from my meditation, the telephone rang. A friend was calling to inform me that Muktananda had departed from this world. The visitation of his subtle presence had been his parting gift.

WHEN TEACHERS FALL

Earlier I noted that there are both genuine spiritual teachers and charlatans or false teachers. I also noted that a wise or enlightened person may not necessarily be a skillful teacher, able to handle the complexities of a mentoring relationship effectively and responsibly. Conversely, there are teachers whose knowledge or realization may not be perfect but who are gifted in the art of mentoring, instructing, and guiding others.

There are teachers of varying levels of realization whose behavior doesn't live up to the image they've created, the ideals they've taught, and the expectations of their students. They may not truly embody the purity, benevolence, and good judgment that we've come to expect. They may fall from a height of spiritual realization into deluded thinking or impure actions, into greed, lust, or sadistic behavior. Many widely respected teachers have fallen in this way. What do we do if we suspect, or know with certitude, that our teacher has committed some form of misconduct that threatens our feelings of trust and respect? How does the teacher's misconduct affect our spiritual apprenticeship? If we believe a teacher is necessary, then is the seeker who loses trust in a teacher unable to advance further on the path? In this section I'll explore the theme that we can continue to progress on the spiritual path even if our teacher's actions and character fall short of their own standards or our expectations.

In his book *Grist for the Mill,* Ram Dass describes how a teacher of his named Joya became psychologically imbalanced and engaged in deceitful and manipulative behaviors. Nevertheless, Ram Dass asserts that she was the catalyst for a tremendous fire of purification for him and for other students and was thus an important teacher in his life even though her behavior was in some ways tainted.

> These teachings had their positive side. Many underwent incredibly deep experiences of who they really were during an intense sadhana they may not have undertaken without the illusion to draw out the energy and commitment needed to do the work that each must do for himself. . . . The question arises as to whether there is reason to fear taking teachings because the teacher might not be coming from the purest place. I think we need not fear this, for often a student can progress very far, indeed their purification may be greater than their teacher's, because their intention is purer. . . . If your longing for God is pure that will be your strength. Then though you may get lost for a time eventually your inner heart will hear what to do and all the impurities in your world will just become grist for the mill.[24]

It often comes as a complete surprise when teachers fall. Even though they may be inspired conduits or instruments for spiritual power, wisdom, or love, teachers may not be perfectly selfless and desireless. If we recognize a teacher's shadow side, we may choose to continue our practices, regardless of the teacher's conduct. Even if our teacher has misbehaved, we don't necessarily have to abandon the principles of spiritual life; we don't have to abandon the path. At such a moment it's helpful to remember this teaching of Shirdi Sai Baba:

> All the world is full of pulls or problems, you keep on your path. Remain unmoved by the curiosity; remain detached. As you sow,

so shall you reap. As are one's motives, so are the results of one's actions. Your actions go with you. Others' actions go with them.[25]

At this stage we realize that we're responsible for our own evolution and state of consciousness, as our teachers are responsible for theirs. We need to reaffirm that the path of spiritual apprenticeship we've been pursuing is authentic and our motives for following it are pure. The biggest question is whether or not the practices we're doing still feel alive for us and still affect us inwardly. When our trust is shaken, it becomes more difficult to practice guru yoga techniques, but that doesn't mean we should give up on meditation altogether. Spiritual apprenticeship is subject to the cyclical phases of devotion and disillusionment that are found in most relationships. The teacher has become a part of us, yet now we can also see this person more clearly as a human being. Sometimes that can be a little bewildering.

HOLY MADNESS AND A TEACHER'S SHADOW

Nothing is more uplifting than the presence and influence of genuine spiritual masters who turn our minds and hearts toward the light of consciousness within. They guide and illuminate us through both doctrine and transmission, inspiring us to practice yogic and meditative disciplines.

A true teacher isn't an ordinary person whose knowledge can be bought easily in the marketplace, in a bookstore, or at a weekend workshop. A fully expanded being, a saint or siddha, can dynamically awaken latent energies within us and is a radiant fountain of love, wisdom, and grace.

Some rare teachers possess personalities that seem to be flawless. Sometimes an enlightened being truly is a saintly person with a pleasant and kind disposition, with no visible moral flaws or shadow. There are a few great personages, such as Paramahansa Yogananda, Hazrat Inayat Khan, or the current Dalai Lama, whose reputations have survived public scrutiny over time and whose lives and actions appear to be genuinely stainless. Such teachers are both illuminated and integrated. Their personalities are clear and unblemished. They aren't pursued by scandal or allegations of misconduct, and their good reputation is almost universal.

However, there are other teachers who are neurotic and disagreeable, who use unorthodox, outrageous tactics, who don't conform to our images of purity and humility, and who act in ways that can be shocking or reprehensible. Some of these are crazy-wisdom teachers who possess the power to affect the consciousness of others but who are disturbing to us because they seem to operate outside the structures of ordinary consciousness and skirt the borders of ethics. Some gurus don't at all conform to our expectations of moral conduct, and this can be infuriating. One of the reasons why in the West the general public holds such a dim and skeptical view of gurus in general is because so many of them seem to act like scoundrels. Some make impossible demands of students or exhibit insatiable appetites or engage in berserk sexual escapades, financial exploitation, or binges of drug and alcohol use. Crazy wisdom can take a variety of perplexing forms, as we saw in the story of the Sheikh and the Lamb's Bladder. Feuerstein says this about the outrageous behaviors associated with crazy wisdom:

> In its most radical manifestation, holy madness or crazy wisdom transcends the mind and the ego-function; it is a specific expression of the disposition of enlightenment itself. . . . Enlightenment is the shattering of all mental constructs about existence. . . . It is the awakening from the dream in which we mistake our metaphors for the real thing. . . . Holy madness, or crazy wisdom, exists to serve such an awakening; it has no purpose or value beyond that. . . . The crazy-wise adept is a trickster par excellence. Such an adept plays his or her role as "disappointer" of deep-laid conventional notions with gusto. . . . To show that all taboos are human-made and to point beyond them to Reality is the mad adept's self-appointed task. . . . It is natural enough that we should feel offended by some of the

escapades of crazy-wisdom masters. But instead of taking the easy option of righteous indignation, wholesale condemnation, or angry retaliation for our offended sensibilities, our first obligation is to cultivate the light of understanding, including self-understanding.[26]

We're also wise to consider the possibility that some so-called crazy-wisdom teaching is in fact inappropriate conduct. Teachers may fall into traps they hadn't foreseen, even if their strange actions are attributed to crazy wisdom. Sangye Drolma told me, "Teachers can always fall until the moment they die. Sufism acknowledges that you can always lose your state, your level of spiritual attainment. In Christianity you can't be considered a saint until you're dead and your life has been thoroughly examined."

TRANSCENDENTAL DENIAL

A spiritual apprentice needs to be prepared to realistically perceive the teacher's human flaws or improper conduct, and to not ignore or justify these. According to noted journalist Katy Butler, many Western students of spiritual teachers engage in "devotional or transcendental denial," the denial of the teacher's human limitations.[27] Butler sees this at the root of many situations where teachers engage in destructive or addictive behaviors that students refuse to acknowledge or question; at the very least, they don't say anything openly to avoid causing trouble. Butler attributes such behavior to an effort by Westerners to imitate the cultural emphasis found in Asian countries like Japan on acceptance of hierarchy and avoidance of open conflict: "For the Japanese, withholding one's personal feelings in order to maintain the appearance of harmony within the group is seen as virtuous and noble. . . . This attitude is part of the structuring of Japanese social relations—it has a place there. But when imported under the banner of enlightenment and overlaid on an American community, the results are cultish and bizarre."[28]

Butler notes that in Asian societies the behavior of spiritual teachers is circumscribed by vows and obligations to their community or monastery, which constitute systems of reciprocal obligation. In America, however, such social controls don't exist in the same way. Personal freedom and individual choices are favored over shared social ethics and mutual obligation. In Butler's view the tendency of Western students to engage in exaggerated forms of Asian deference toward teachers is combined with an equally exaggerated form of American licentiousness on the part of teachers, a combination that often proves disastrous.

I'll use my own teacher as an example. Toward the end of his life, rumors began circulating that my teacher wasn't celibate as he claimed to be and that he'd been having sexual relations with women and adolescent girls; well-documented accounts of this have followed.[29] For these behaviors he has been widely criticized. Feuerstein writes, "A fallen angel of considerable stature was the late Swami Muktananda. . . . The rumors of sexual exploitation that reached the public after his death did much to disenchant many of his followers and left countless others suspicious and confused." He adds, "There is a clear distinction between a teacher who preaches one thing and lives another and a teacher who openly teaches in crazy-wise fashion."[30] As this statement implies, what upset people the most about Baba's behavior wasn't just the idea that he wasn't celibate, but that he lied about it. He didn't live what he taught. He lied to all of us, which is disrespectful and lacks integrity. His actions also involved underaged adolescents, which most Americans find morally unacceptable.

Rather than defending my teacher or angrily denouncing him, I'm going to share with you as honestly as I can the process I've gone through in sorting out my feelings. When these stories about Baba were made public, I was shocked, like everyone else. Indeed, the entire community of his students was in upheaval, and many departed immediately. Others responded with outright denial that such rumors could be true. Since Muktananda was an enlightened being, it seemed implausible that he could commit such actions, which blatantly contradicted his teachings. In her brilliant paper, "The Heart of the Secret," Tantra scholar and former Siddha Yoga devotee Sarah Caldwell writes, "Baba had spoken so often about celibacy and the need for perfect conformity to impeccable standards of ashram behavior by both guru and disciple, that to accuse him of secret sexual encounters with his devotees seemed tantamount to blasphemy. . . . It seemed one either had to take a stance of loyalty and denial, or leave the ashram."[31]

A lot of people would prefer to believe that none of this ever happened, yet the facts seem to contradict this view, as many women involved have given interviews about their experiences. Caldwell notes that for thousands of Siddha Yoga students, public suppression of the topic over several decades has kept the problem unresolved, and "for some the cognitive dissonance has become so great that they have felt compelled to abandon their spiritual practice entirely."[32] One of the saddest things is that this confusing situation has caused people to become bitter and mistrustful and lose the life-enhancing tonic of meditation that brings devotees and gurus together in the first place.

Because of Baba's actions, many have proclaimed the fall of a great guru, that his entire career as a teacher was a sham, and that he was irreversibly corrupted by his improper actions. Peter Rutter's important book *Sex in the Forbidden Zone* argues that sexual contact between two people involved in any relationship where there's a clear difference of power and status (such as the relationship between doctor and patient, psychotherapist and client, or teacher and student) almost invariably ends up hurting the client, patient, or student, because trust is betrayed; the safety of the relationship is disturbed, and the student or patient ends up feeling discarded and used.[33] By virtue of the fact that his actions may have caused harm or distress to his students, Muktananda failed to live up to his sacred responsibilities as a spiritual teacher.

Others took the position that Baba was actually giving special tantric initiations to these women, who should consider it a great privilege. Some of the women who were later interviewed displayed great variation in their accounts and personal reactions. One woman cited by Liz Harris in her *New Yorker* article "O Guru, Guru, Guru" says that the sexual contact between Muktananda and his female devotees was clearly abusive, while another woman, after recounting intimate details of their encounter, stated, "All I know is that I was in a state of total ecstasy, and whatever happened had nothing to do with sex."[34]

Caldwell concludes that "Swami Muktananda was [a] practitioner of an esoteric form of Tantric sexual yoga."[35] Underneath the public veneer of his teaching an austere, vedantic yogic path, he was actually a follower of the Shaivite Kula system, which "denies antagonism between sensuous joy and spiritual bliss, recognizes the former to be a means to the latter; and emphatically asserts that it is meant for the few."[36] He was apparently imitating practices described by the Shaivite guru Abhinavagupta in his book *Tantraloka,* but lacking "their most essential component, a fully aware, consenting female partner or yogini."

> Whatever Baba was doing, claiming it to be a form of Tantric initiation, seemed rather to retain only the bodily shell of a Tantric practice that once held out the promise of profound enlightenment experience for both the man and woman. . . . . Baba's sexual encounters with young women in a context of totally unequal power, especially with no apparent explanation to the women of the meaning or purpose of these practices, had definite abusive aspects.[37]

Encountering the energy of the goddess. Karntaka.

According to Caldwell's research, Muktananda adopted a more acceptable public self to veil his involvement in the sexual rites of left-handed Shakta tantrics. He had always praised the goddess Kundalini, but nobody suspected that his devotion involved these kinds of practices. Caldwell writes:

Quintessentially antinomian, Tantric traditions radically eschew ordinary forms of morality for soteriological aims. However, when such religious traditions aim to incorporate and publicize themselves, they are forced to develop a carefully guarded secret core and somewhat false, publically acceptable outer identity. . . . The Tantric core of so many of the last century's imported Hindu traditions has successfully been painted over with a more acceptable Shaiva or Vedantic veneer. The storehouse of power that is the Devi, . . . the erotic generatrix of the universe . . . , the coiled Kundalini Shakti herself, is not unleashed, not acknowledged, not known. This denial fuels an unhealthy form of hypocrisy. . . . . We were not ready for this message. We were not ready for Tantra. . . . Many are only now beginning to piece together the complexities of their own feelings about the controversies that still swirl around Baba's name. . . . I, too, have kept silent about my innermost spiritual longings and strivings, . . . never feeling safe to tell the heart of the secret: that my guru was Swami Muktananda, that I gave him my whole heart and soul, that he taught me everything of ultimate value that I know, that I can never express the depth of the love and insight I gained in his presence. Since his death everything else is a pale shadow, even now. The intensity of those years with him will never fade.[38]

In 1997 I spoke about these issues with Master Charles Cannon, one of Muktananda's closest disciples. He told me the following:

A fact that is not very widely known is that Baba never hid anything from the people close to him. We were told about it and he explained that this was his way of celebrating the divine in all forms. What many people don't grasp is that a master is coming from a nondual state of being, so his or her perceptions are nondual. The disciple is coming from a dualistic paradigm of good and bad, right and wrong. Baba had a nondual understanding of celibacy, which was that celibacy meant perceiving no one and nothing as separate from the Self, the one Source that lives in all and everything. For him celibacy meant refraining from dualistic perceptions. He was not having a relationship with anybody. He was worshipping the One present in every form as his own Being. Most people couldn't grasp this nondual understanding.

I find myself unsettled as I consider these various viewpoints. To insist that these reports couldn't possibly be true strikes me as an example of the transcendental denial that Butler notes. For me, after making it clear that I don't condone sexual relationships between adults and underage youth, I must ask myself: Does his bizarre behavior negate Muktananda's contributions as a spiritual teacher? While my image of Baba was seriously shaken by learning of his actions, I still acknowledge him as the guru who awakened me and guided me on the path. Yet no purpose is served by denying that he appears to have engaged in sexually exploitative behavior. At the same time, since he continued to have a transformative influence on others, it's difficult for me to reject him as a complete fraud. My time with Muktananda served my growth greatly. I've never met anyone else like him, and my experiences with him were positive and uplifting. I also recognize that for others he was the cause of disillusionment, emotional pain, and feelings of betrayal. For some he was even the perpetrator of abuse. The reality is that some of his actions caused suffering, not liberation.

All of us have loved ones, parents, spouses, children, and friends, who sometimes get in trouble—trouble at work, trouble in school, trouble with the law. At such times we get an opportunity to truly demonstrate our love, when we stand by them knowing full well that they made mistakes. It's a shame that Muktananda's strange behavior destroyed the trust the world had placed in him and made it more difficult for his successors, swamis Chidvilasananda and Nityananda, to continue the work he started. His actions also damaged the yoga movement in America by confirming the public's cynicism and doubt about the integrity of gurus.

I have felt sadness, anger, and confusion after learning of what Caldwell calls "the heart of the secret," as well as the violent reprisals that some people suffered when they attempted to discuss these matters openly. I personally feel indignation about the idea that my teacher was engaging in sexually exploitative activities. Intuitively, spiritually, and morally, to my mind, this was wrong.

I'm reminded of a memoir by Sufi teacher Irina Tweedie. In her book *The Chasm of Fire,* Tweedie recounts how her teacher crushed her ego, ignored her, and humiliated her during one phase of initiation. Her kundalini awakened furiously and her body was filled with heat. She began to have intense *kriyas* in which she had visions and experientially relived all manner of perversities and sexual experiences, whether involving human, animal, or animate and inanimate objects. The mania within her was so intense that she felt she was going crazy. Her teacher was extremely fierce and worked with her on transforming her experiences of sexuality, but he did it without any sexual contact at all with his student. Her story demonstrates that a teacher can work very deeply with a student without blurring and violating boundaries.[39]

Seeking further depth of understanding, recently I asked one of my current teachers, Dr. Bryan Wittine, a Jungian analyst, about the moral paradox of an apparently saintly and beneficent being who also has a devastating shadow side. Bryan referred me to the book *Being of Two Minds,* by Arnold Goldberg, which expands on Heinz Kohut's concept of a "vertical split" and the defense of "disavowal."[40] For someone who is "of two minds," the vertical split involves shameful and disavowed misbehavior; split-off parts of the self develop as spaces for acting out within the family matrix, where such acting out is silently and unconsciously accepted, while at the same time condemned. Some people live two lives and are divided selves—literally of two minds. This describes a person at odds with himself who behaves in a repugnant manner—the unfaithful spouse, compulsive shoplifters and binge eaters, and out-of-control alcoholics, and the guru who behaves like some sort of tantric sex addict. Dissociation is one result of reliance on disavowal. Goldberg details how others feel repugnance to the offensive behaviors of a person's parallel self, and this repugnance is shared by the person who despises the misbehavior that he's unable to understand. The person's behavior suggests that one side doesn't always know what the other side is doing. Perhaps even an otherwise-evolved yogi such as Swami Muktananda could be psychologically split through disavowal of shameful feelings and impulses.

The idea of the vertical split reminds me of my own need to look at all the disavowed parts of myself that I haven't wanted to claim. Each of us can spend a lifetime shining a light on these wounded parts of ourselves. And the uncovering of disavowed behaviors can lead to remorse and efforts at reparation. In coming to terms with our shadow selves, we're all in need of honesty and compassion. In the next chapter, I'll recount a crucial dream that finally helped me achieve deeper reconciliation with my teacher and his shadow side. It took years of inner work to reach a feeling of closure and completion.

THE NEED FOR OPEN DISCUSSION

There's no way to discuss these issues without arousing strong feelings. I offer these comments because I know that many people are grappling with similar concerns about teachers embroiled in controversy about sexual, financial, or other transgressions. Many have been deeply hurt. The lack of open discussion within communities embroiled in such controversies is one of the most disturbing aspects of the experience of discovering a teacher's shadow side, and may hasten the end of our formal involvement with a spiritual group or organization. Members of leading American spiritual communities such as the San Francisco Zen Center, Vajradhatu, Kripalu Ashram, Himalayan Institute, Anusara Yoga, and Ananda Expanding Light community have all had to grapple with similar difficulties. In several incidents students confronted teachers and invited discussion and dialogue. I know of one spiritual teacher who was pressured to enter Alcoholics Anonymous, and who put his life back together with the support of caring students and friends. Nonetheless, not all teachers will openly admit wrongdoing, express remorse, or improve their conduct. In many instances teachers have responded defensively and defiantly. Several of these teachers were eventually forced to leave the communities they'd founded, and in each instance it caused a very big crisis indeed.

People who try to discuss allegations are often silenced, harshly ushered out of the group, harassed, or threatened with physical harm. As we saw earlier, in some spiritual groups, members are subjected to strict control of their behavior, emotions, thoughts, and access to information. Under these conditions it's difficult for anyone to express their misgivings, to demand answers, or to speak the truth. One positive thing that happened in several instances where groups purged themselves of a teacher's influence is that everything finally came out in the open. This occurred at Zen Center and at Kripalu. In both cases the community took care of the matter of leadership and carried on the teachings of the lineage. Suppressing dialogue serves no one's understanding. Expressing anger toward a teacher doesn't mean that a teacher can no longer be loved or valued, any more than it means this when a child is angry with a parent. It's not unhealthy to feel angry and disappointed. It *is* unhealthy to not be permitted to express or work through these feelings.

It's sad that many teachers accused of misconduct don't meet with students to openly discuss their concerns or receive their reprimand. Obviously this represents a very uncomfortable reversal of roles and power relations, where teachers who may have been unquestioned are now made to answer to the students as clients who are unhappy with

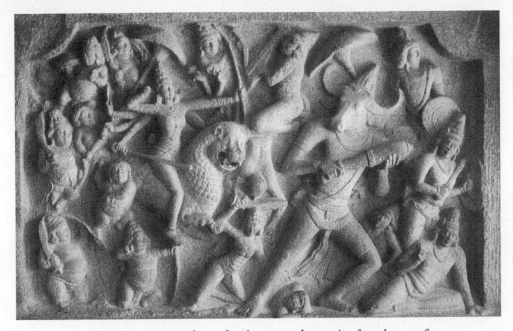

Everyone experiences days of reckoning, when we're forced to confront the evil forces within us. This is no less true for gurus, who may be forced to face their own shadow sides. This scene, from the Temple of Mahabalipuram, portrays the embattled soul undergoing testing.

their services. In a recent exception to this trend, the American spiritual teacher Andrew Cohen, after a period of discord with some of his students, responded to feedback about his conduct and demeanor by resigning from leadership and going into retreat for the purpose of self-examination. I admire teachers who show a willingness to learn from their mistakes. Amrit Desai, founder of Kripalu, experienced a fall from power and subsequently went into exile for a period of retreat and purification and then reemerged as a teacher. My attitude is that everyone falls sometimes, and everyone deserves a chance for atonement and redemption.

In addition to adopting from American culture a greater emphasis on openness, perhaps teachers from the East also need to be better educated about Western views of morality. For example, in America we have a relatively open ethic about sexuality compared to many other countries, but we also have our own cultural conceptions and laws defining when someone is mature enough to engage in adult sexual relationships. We also have an intolerance for dishonesty and violation of relationships of trust. Author Peter Lamborn Wilson offers this eloquent commentary:

> The gurus arrive here (actually or psychologically) from traditions which contain strong anti-sexual codes—combined in some cases with social customs that mitigate the religious laws through tacit tolerance of deviance. Our society, by utter contrast, has a *code* of tolerance and a *discourse* of "freedom," along with a social praxis of horrified rejection of all deviance and even of all pleasure. The guru's first temptation therefore will almost certainly be a sexual one—but once he's arrived at a good esoteric excuse for disciple-boffing, he may as well go all the way and cheat and lie and steal as well—all in the name of his "transcendence" of mere religious and moral codes. The rejection of petty morality might perhaps be defended as spiritual revolution, except that the freedom *never* extends to the guru's disciples. . . . Let me be clear: personally I do not disapprove of sexual intercourse nor of "deviant" desire and pleasure. I do, however, disapprove of hypocrisy, power-tripping, and the self-aggrandizement of self-proclaimed avatars. I can even imagine erotic love as an integral aspect of spiritual/pedagogic companionship, but only on condition of its open consensuality. I reject (for myself) the moral/sexual codes of outdated and reactionary ideologies, but I accept (for myself) the best ethics I can imagine, based on a perception of the other as an aspect of the self, so that my desire to some extent depends on the other's desire and not on the other's loss. If I can do this for myself, then I can demand of anyone who claims to be able to reach self-realization that he too follow this minimal ethics of mutuality.[41]

An obvious question that arises is whether or not the student truly benefits from such secret "initiations." For further insight let's listen to the voice of a woman who experienced these kinds of intimacies with her teacher. June Campbell gives an illuminating account of her long-time role as the secret consort of the Tibetan lama Kalu Rinpoche. Campbell concludes that the system of Tibetan tantric practice was built on the subjugation of women. In Tibetan culture:

> Women were excluded from the sacred domain, except under conditions laid down by men, and "tantra" was used as a means of polarizing male and female as opposites. As a result, women and their role in the system had to remain hidden. . . . [T]o have an actual sexual consort is considered the most important ingredient in the path of tantra. That's where so much of the confusion and ambivalence and misogyny come into play because you have both: the emphasis on male monastic society, and at the same time, the need for women, but without the acknowledgment of the role women play. . . . My relationship with Kalu Rinpoche was not a partnership of equals. When it started, I was in my late twenties. He was almost seventy. He controlled the relationship. I was sworn to secrecy. What I am saying is that it was not a formal ritualistic relationship, nor was it the "tantric" relationship that most people would like to imagine. . . . [P]eople rationalize these acts as beneficial. . . . I've got no doubt now that when a male teacher demands a relationship that involves secret sex, an imbalance of power, threats, deceptions, the woman is exploited. You have to ask, "Where does the impulse to hide sexual behavior come from?". . . Of course, there are those who say they are consensually doing secret "tantric" practices in the belief that it's helping them become "enlightened". . . . That's up to them, and if they're both saying it, that's fine. But there's a difference between that and the imperative for women not to speak of the fact that they're having a sexual relationship at all. What's that all about if it's not about fear of being found out? And what lies behind that fear? These are the questions I had to ask.[42]

Reading this passage I don't get the impression that Campbell felt she was liberated by her experiences as consort to her spiritual guide. While it's possible that such a relationship could lead a student to the highest freedom, the evidence from Campbell's account doesn't support that idea. Regardless of whether the teacher intends this as crazy-wisdom instruction, if the student isn't liberated by the teaching, then it's not an expression of *skillful means* or *upaya*. I believe that it's the teacher's responsibility to use skillful means in the guidance of students.

CONFRONTING MISCONDUCT

When you know for yourselves: These things are not good, these things are faulty, these things are censured by the intelligent, these things, when performed and undertaken, conduce to loss and sorrow—then do you reject them.

GUATAMA BUDDHA

Those entering into a relationship with a spiritual teacher are always advised to do so cautiously and with their eyes open. As the Dalai Lama states, it's best if we test a teacher thoroughly before accepting this person as our guide. And if the teacher does or says something that we strongly feel is ethically wrong, it's our responsibility to say or do something about it. For example, Buddhist teacher Jack Kornfield traveled to India to confront an Asian meditation teacher who had committed acts of sexual misconduct, informing him that he'd no longer be welcome as a teacher in the United States until he publicly acknowledged that his behavior was improper.[43]

Sangye Drolma offers these comments concerning situations in which a teacher is accused of misconduct:

Some people think that a teacher can be enlightened without being moral. But we don't need to throw away our judgment. Discrimination is the name of the game. It must continue throughout our relationship with a teacher. Sufism and Christianity both say the jury is out until after a teacher is dead. As the immortal Yogi Berra said, "It ain't over till it's over." There are teachers who have so much power and wisdom and claim to be enlightened and then fall flat on their faces. These teachers often have a total lack of awareness of the consequences of their sexual behavior and fool themselves into thinking it's okay to do it and to lie about it. Power without love and wisdom is nothing. If a teacher openly admits, "Yes, I'd give a tantric initiation to some students of the age of consent," then some of us might be able to live with that. Instead they violate our trust and sexually exploit students. This is hypocrisy. You have to use the same moral standards for an enlightened being as you do for a normal person. Enlightenment is no justification for sociopathic behavior.

If you feel a teacher is acting improperly, I think it's better to voice your feelings and let your teacher respond. Recall the example of Doug and Lama Z, noted earlier. If you feel you're not safe to speak for fear of rejection, intimidation, or retaliation by the teacher or the teacher's followers, reconsider your association with that teacher.

I once spoke to a teacher about some concerns I had about his methods. Students were getting injured in his hatha yoga classes, and I felt he was overly aggressive in his instructions. He reacted defensively, as if my feedback and concern were an attack on him. His reaction told me much about the man's character, and it became clear that I could no longer study with him.

We may reach a point where we no longer trust a teacher's judgment. The best way to regain trust in a teacher is to have an open conversation about our doubts and misgivings. It's when we're unable to communicate directly with a teacher that we may feel the most confusion and anger. A willingness to listen to our own intuition and inner voice is essential to our spiritual evolution. We need to listen to it now if it tells us that something is amiss.

CONTINUING OUR PRACTICES

Someone once asked Ramana Maharshi, "If the Guru happens to turn out to be incompetent, what will be the fate of the disciple who has implicit faith in him?" Maharshi's response: "Each one according to his merits."[44] As spiritual aspirants we make a commitment that goes beyond devotion to a particular teacher. We become disciples of the path, the eternal way of initiation and spiritual unfolding that seekers have walked since time immemorial. Even if a teacher stumbles or falls, if our teacher proves to be an imperfect role model, we can focus on fulfilling our commitment to the spirit of discipleship. We can revere teachers for what they've offered us with awareness of both their strengths and limitations as instruments of truth and instruction. This is the moment for each of us to become a disciple of the universal teacher and of the lineage of all awakened beings.

If we abandon our practices at this point, disgusted with the teacher, then we were probably never committed to begin with. This becomes the perfect excuse we need to stop practicing. But this can also be the moment to become more committed practitioners.

I choose to believe that masters from subtle planes come to the assistance of students who sincerely wish to proceed toward enlightenment. During a period when I was experiencing doubts about my teacher's integrity, I sat to meditate one day. I felt the presence of Sri Yukteswar, guru of Paramahansa Yogananda, and heard his voice instruct me to remain steadfast in discipline and aspiration. I was to remain a disciple, regardless of whatever my teacher had done.

In some cases it's helpful to enact self-created ceremonies of severance or completion of a relationship with a teacher.[45] I know several people who found it cathartic and healing to burn pictures of their gurus. Others need exit counseling to work through conflicted feelings about the teacher. While experiencing doubts about my own teacher, I installed pictures of other great beings on my altar, all of whom evoked in me feelings of devotion to the process of spiritual awakening. I tried

Dedicated practitioners continue to receive the steadying and guiding influence of their sacred lineage. Srinageri.

to imagine myself under the care of a lineage of yogis who supported and guided my progress on the path.

At a certain point, preoccupation with the teacher's ethics diverts attention from the need to continue our own spiritual practices, regardless of how a teacher has behaved. Of course, there are times to repudiate not just a teacher but also the doctrine and way of life he or she teaches. However, if the teachings and practices we've learned are authentic, they will withstand the tests of time. They'll be based in traditions and lineages that outlive the personality of the individual teacher. Recall how earlier, during the stage of initiation, the spiritual apprentice took refuge in the teacher and the lineage—the Buddha and the sangha—thereby becoming a link in an unending chain. Now we need the power and wisdom preserved in our lineage to sustain us through our period of doubt and confusion. Connection to a reliable lineage can be a helpful refuge in cases where a teacher has become imbalanced. For example, after the downfall of Buddhist teacher Osel Tendzin, who committed many acts of sexual misconduct, infected a student with the AIDS virus, and eventually died of AIDS himself, senior Tibetan Buddhist lamas played an important role in guiding the Vajradhatu Buddhist community.[46]

When we feel betrayed by a spiritual teacher, it's important to express our rage or indignation, but we must also face our illusions and see the teacher as a human being who is capable of error, not infallible. In some cases we may seek another guide more worthy of our devotion. Even if we're not ready for another devotional relationship, we can reaffirm our quest for enlightenment by focusing attention on those who convincingly embody that ideal.

WORKING THROUGH ANGER

If a teacher turns out to be an impostor and a charlatan, we may need to work through feelings of betrayal and anger. Many people get stuck at this stage of angrily repudiating the teacher or feeling that all spiritual teachers are charlatans. This attitude isn't freedom or liberation; not all teachers are charlatans. With the proper understanding, we can continue on our path free of bitterness and regret, motivated by the longing for truth that impelled us to seek a spiritual teacher in the first place. In this way we become disciples of the inner light. A sincere seeker will not be deterred in the quest for enlightenment just because the teacher has committed acts of misconduct.

There's a stage when expressing feelings of betrayal and anger toward the teacher may be a healthy response. But eventually we must move on and stop considering the teacher responsible for our evolution. Most spiritual guides teach us to unfold our consciousness through prayer, meditation, yoga, service, and so forth. Even when a teacher is a source of grace or shaktipat, if the student doesn't do any practices, actively purifying mind and heart, then no inner awakening will occur.

There may be important personal reasons why we need to leave the teacher, such as a need to work on our vocational skills and find better employment, or to address unresolved issues about our families. In the process we benefit from continuing to practice what all great gurus teach us: to harmonize ourselves, balancing our bodies, calming our restless minds, doing daily tasks with love and inner peace, plunging into the ocean of consciousness within. At this stage we're called on to live in accordance with spiritual teachings and ideals, even if a particular teacher hasn't always done so.

If the student has truly learned from the spiritual guide, then separating from the teacher is really no separation. The two are ultimately one. Yet they're also two—separate, distinct manifestations of the divine, with their own destinies and lives to unfold.

The path of spiritual apprenticeship eventually leads away from a teacher's physical company to our own tasks of living an enlightened life. Separation is a crucial phase even for those who remain devoted

Temple corridor, Kanchipuram.

and committed to the teacher. Dilgo Khyentse Rinpoche told Sangye Drolma, "You don't need any more initiations. You don't need any more teachings. You know what you need to do. Now go do it." She told me, "You have to go away from the teacher to practice. He had explained everything to me. I knew everything I needed to know. Now it was up to me."

My own spiritual life deepened steadily after I left my teacher and continued to practice meditation and hatha yoga regularly. I trusted my inner nature and the course my life was taking, a path focused on my interests in meditation, mysticism, psychology, dreams, and music. My awareness focused less on Baba and more on the Self, the silent witnessing consciousness. I sought out new teachers and found the guidance I needed from within.

❧

Finding
the Teacher Within

Creating Your Own Synthesis
and Paths of Self-Liberation

At times you will think of your Guru.
Whenever such yearning arises
Visualize Him upon your head
And for his blessings pray.
Visualize him sitting
In the center of your heart,
And forget Him never.
But you should know that ever your Guru
Is delusory and dream-like.

The Guru who indicates the true knowledge from without is
 your Outer Guru;
The Guru who elucidates the Awareness of Mind within is
 your Inner Guru;
The Guru who illuminates the nature of your mind is your
 Real Guru.

I am a yogi who has all three Gurus,
Is there a disciple here who wishes to be faithful to them?
THE HUNDRED THOUSAND SONGS OF MILAREPA

Spiritual apprenticeship is a path that gradually transforms us. Receiving a teacher's guidance and blessings and sustaining our spiritual practices prepare us to become more independent as we experience an awakening of our potentials, including greater constancy and depth in meditation, the emergence of creative urges, and the discovery of our own life's work.[1] As our eyes shift away from the guru's fascinating form, our evolving awareness unfolds through developing key life structures and forming new commitments and intentions.

The transition away from a teacher is a delicate moment and is often handled badly, both by students in this stage of evolution and by the teachers and communities who guide them. This is an opportunity for us to reach the next level of development. Some people remain in a state of relying on a teacher or feel they can't function in the world independently. Conversely, others are frozen in bitterness, rebellious defiance, and angry denunciation of a spiritual teacher and need to resolve these feelings to move forward. In some cases our further growth requires a radical termination of discipleship or our involvement with a group. But separating from a spiritual teacher isn't the end of the path; it's a new beginning. Our awakening consciousness can be expressed in our careers, relationships, and families, and by contributing to the evolution of our communities and our planet.

Peter Lamborn Wilson questions the notion that spiritual growth and realization requires the mediation of an external authority such as a spiritual teacher or church. In Wilson's view the exercise of authority is rarely innocent, but almost inherently implies inequality, betrayal, or the abuse of power.[2] In contrast Wilson emphasizes inner spiritual authority and contends that enlightenment is possible without the external authority of a teacher, through "imaginal auto-

initiation," through attending to our dreams, visions, and spontaneous inner directives. Two examples of this are the imaginal initiation
of a Sufi mystic described in Henri Corbin's book *Avicenna and the
Visionary Recital* and the visionary initiation of Jung by an ancient
Gnostic teacher named Philemon.[3] In this chapter I consider this idea
of internal initiation and suggest how each of us might access, and be
guided by, our own inner light.

MERGING AND SEPARATING

The process of discovering the inner teacher may be obstructed if we
have lingering issues about merging and separating. An emphasis on
merger in the student-teacher relationship can take either healthy or
unhealthy forms. We saw earlier that inwardly merging with a teacher's state of consciousness through guru yoga can be an illuminating
and catalytic practice. But merging can also be unhealthy if by idealizing a teacher and negating self in devotion we're unable to individuate.

A man named Ted couldn't let go after the death of his teacher,
Rajneesh, and the demise of the spiritual community with which he'd
been affiliated. Ted missed the ecstasy, the songs and music, the com-
radeship and fun, the aura of drama and mystery that surrounded his
teacher. When Rajneesh died the community disbanded, and most of
Ted's friends went elsewhere to begin following another teacher. Now
Ted was depressed and his life felt empty and meaningless. He needed
to find a new sense of purpose and let go of the past without guilt. I
suggested that he bring the elements of life in the community that he
loved into his current life, into his own home. He could bring alive that
same spirit here and now. I suggested that he meditate, sing devotional
songs, prepare food consciously, and peacefully meditate and dance.
After several months of this practice, Ted reported more happiness and
satisfaction in his daily life, and he also felt less separation from his
teacher.

The ecstatic Sufi poet Rumi said:

After being with me one whole night,
you ask how I live when you're not here.
Badly, frantically, like a fish trying to breathe
dry sand. You weep and say,
But you choose that.[4]

FINDING NEW TEACHERS

Gurus are like parents. There are good and bad parents.
No parent is perfect. But we cannot dispense with parents
altogether because of the failures of some. . . . It is possible
for good disciples to transcend inadequate gurus and move
on to a better teacher. Not everyone follows the same teacher
for life, just as in school we do not stick with the same
teacher throughout. Yet we should not discard our teachers
carelessly. . . . Good disciples may grow even through a
lesser teacher. Good disciples find what is truthful in the
teacher and benefit from it.

DAVID FRAWLEY, *ALL GURUS LARGE AND SMALL*

In Tibetan Buddhism teachers work together to further a seeker's evolution. The disciple usually has a primary, root teacher, but periodically may be directed to seek out another teacher for a specific initiation or empowerment. The same model can be applied to contemporary spiritual apprenticeship. Even if we have a primary teacher, we may still wish to approach others for instruction. Our needs change over the course of time. Sometimes we need to have no teacher for a while. At other times we're ready for someone who will offer new information and perspectives and who may also serve different psychological needs for us. The interest in finding new teachers at this stage can be a sign of maturation.

In my case I realized I needed instruction in several areas. After I left the Siddha Yoga ashram and began traveling, I sought out another teacher, not to be my guru, but to teach me hatha yoga. I wanted personal, in-depth instruction. In 1979 I was fortunate to meet Allan Bateman, who was an impeccable guide for me at that stage. He exuded confidence and gracefulness and was an exceedingly skillful mentor. He never demanded that his opinions be accepted on faith, and he insisted that we question him, test his methods for ourselves, and reach our own conclusions. "This gives students room to grow on their own," he told me, "and it respects their judgment." He always treated me like an equal and encouraged me to challenge him.

Allan taught me that my path to liberation is through the body. Hatha yoga postures soften physical and energetic blockages and liberate streams of vitality and joy. Allan taught me to work deeply with the breath within each posture, to move my awareness through every region of the spine, to elongate the spine to increase the space between each vertebra, to find precise alignment of the spinal column. Although he never stated it in exactly these words, I can summarize the essence of what I learned from him: *free the breath, free the spine, free the mind.* These have been extremely helpful principles. Allan showed me a truly effective, transformative yoga practice and helped me at several critical junctures on the path.

For example, in 1983, for several months I was vigorously practicing postures from the book *Light on Yoga* by B. K. S. Iyengar, including the yogic *bandhas* (literally "locks"), which involve contractions of the muscles of the abdomen, anus, and perineum. Ostensibly, I was trying to transmute my sexual energy and release blocks in my lower chakras. In reality I was becoming increasingly jittery and wired. I went to visit Allan after not seeing him for two years. I went into his yoga studio and warmed up for five minutes. Without my saying a word about what I'd been doing, Allan walked over to me and said, "You're a complete mess. Don't do anything to your sexual energy. Practice a full workout of postures without any stress or binding or locking of your energy and you'll open all of the chakras naturally, without any strain." He went on to explain:

When you lock, you block. You restrict the movement of prana (life energy). Why would you want to do that? In Hindu yoga you try to block your sexual energy because it's seen as a reservoir that's exhausted through expenditure. But in Chinese Taoist yoga the principle is to keep energy circulating, knowing that if the reservoir is empty it will fill up again naturally. You never want to block the circulation of energy.

Allan Bateman used yoga in his own unique way to become a remarkable person, a teacher who was highly focused and serious in purpose and also full of humor and energy for service. On every occasion when I met him, he was always kind to me. I have always respected his skillful yoga instruction and his warm and benevolent demeanor. Allan taught me how to liberate myself, step by step, through the practice of yoga.[5]

After leaving New York in 1980, I traveled to Boulder, Colorado, where I had a marvelous darshan with Chögyam Trungpa at a sunrise ceremony. I was living in a tent at the time, and I looked exceedingly scruffy. I had long hair and my clothes were dirty. I was the only person present that wasn't clean and sharply dressed. I felt many people's eyes on me as I clearly looked somewhat out of place. But I was glad to be there, and ultimately I didn't care what others thought of me. I waited in line and finally got my chance to go before Trungpa Rinpoche to receive his blessing. As I did so, our eyes met, and he treated me with complete kindness, dignity, and respect—with a genuine sense of welcome. He met me with the warmth of buddha nature, and I felt my own clear buddha nature in his presence. At a time when I was just starting out in search of my own path and experiencing many uncertainties, I was grateful for this affirming moment, which stirred a feeling of self-respect and appreciation of what Trungpa called "basic goodness."

Soon thereafter I met another unusual teacher. For nine months in 1981, I became the apprentice to a mystic and scholar named Andres Takra, a sidereal astrologer, a wise and funny man. Son of a prominent family, Andres was a notorious activist in Venezuela in the 1960s, promoting vegetarianism, communal living, UFO research, and ancient metaphysical teachings. He'd been employed for several years as a diplomat stationed in New Delhi, during which time he hobnobbed with various yogis and jyotishas. Andres hired me as his assistant and English-language ghost writer, and I spent my days receiving instruction and devouring his extensive library of rare, leather-bound mystical and metaphysical books. He fed me protein drinks and drove me around in his red Jaguar. This nine months in his company transformed me. Andres taught me the art of spiritual guidance, training me to assist others using the sacred art of astrology. He taught me tools I could use to help other people, the greatest gift. He and I have an undying friendship.

Later I studied for four years at the Iyengar Yoga Institute of San Francisco, where I took classes from many excellent instructors and refined my understanding of the transformational power of yoga. I was trained to teach hatha yoga in the tradition of B. K. S. Iyengar, whose potent book *Light on Yoga* had set me on fire so many years earlier. Judith Lasater was especially helpful to me, teaching me how to learn from an injury—a big setback in my life—and to experience it mindfully. I'd been practicing hatha yoga intensively for several years, reaching new levels of strength and flexibility. Then one day I injured myself, tearing intercostal cartilage while overzealously practicing back bends. The injury was slow to heal, and I repeatedly reinjured it by trying to return to my previous level prematurely. Many feelings surfaced in me. I was ashamed because I knew better than to push my body beyond its limits as I had done. In addition I was angry because I felt that another teacher I'd taken classes from had encouraged me to try to exceed my limits. At first I wanted to deny my own responsibility for the injury by projecting blame onto the teacher. I was also depressed, as I recognized that I'd now have to work within certain constraints.[6]

When I started taking Judith Lasater's yoga classes, she told me to stop practicing so much and encouraged me to do nothing but meditation, pranayama, and seated relaxation poses.[7] She got me to quiet down

The author demonstrating Virabhadrasana II, pose of the warrior, in the presence of B. K. S. Iyengar, whose teachings revolutionized the practice of hatha yoga. The pose of the warrior requires focused will, precise alignment, energy, and determination. Tilden Park, spring 1987.

for several months so my body could repair itself. She shone a gentle spotlight on the competitive, grasping, ambitious quality of my yoga practice. A factor that contributed to my injury was that I'd secretly been imitating another practitioner I viewed as more advanced. I felt that I should be able to do all the postures he could do and had given myself deadlines to learn certain difficult poses. Judith taught me to accept my body's limitations, practice more quietly and meditatively, and experience innate contentment. This wise teacher rescued me from a serious pitfall and set me back on the right path.

In 1983 I began corresponding with Dane Rudhyar, the metaphysical philosopher, mystic, and composer, who was also the founding visionary of a new humanistic astrology. Rudhyar guided me through a difficult transition in my life in which I made the decision to follow the spiritual vocation and profession of an astrologer despite the ridicule and social disapproval this often provoked. My parents were absolutely aghast, but I was committed to my path and the form of work that felt to me like right livelihood. At this time I was struggling to cope with the pressures of the world while remaining intently focused on the inner quest. He wrote:

> Yes, being "in" the world but not "of" it is very difficult. It is man's supreme power that he can live consistently at more than one or two levels. Polyphonic, counterpunctual living—Caesar *and* God (say the Gospels). Yet there are periods when singleness of purpose and an all-absorbing focus of vision are required to move safely through the rite of passage. Keep on with your work and do not be impatient if the field of transhuman activity and consciousness seems enveloped in mist. Clarity comes only most gradually, and one has to build means of formulation that emerge out of one's own experiences, indeed out of crises courageously and nobly passed through. May you reach in your own time, and with the help of those of who have gone before you, the "other shore." And may peace, deep peace, be with you.

In March 1985 I met Rudhyar at his home in Palo Alto and gave a talk about the significance of his work at a conference on the occasion of his ninetieth birthday,[8] and I was present when Rudhyar gave his final public talk. Though physically frail and experiencing great discomfort, he was completely lucid. He concluded by saying:

> He who treads the path is in a way alone, and yet not alone. Our implicit divinity comes to meet us, as we reach towards it. In India it was the guru who was supposed to be a clear lens to give us a feeling, a reflection of what the divine state was. However, if we are individualized enough already, free from biology and our culture, we

need not have that kind of physically embodied guru. Yet, we almost always need at first a mentor to dissolve the structure of the individual culture-mind as well as to introduce us to the basic principles of the new mind organization. . . [that incites and gives] strength to our will to metamorphosis. This new mind is only a structural foundation. But it is necessary. In my whole life I have tried to provide such a foundation in terms which could inspire the generation following mine. I have done all I could under difficult circumstances, and now it is your full responsibility. The power that held my being as a lens to bring ideas to some focus will be released when I go. Perhaps, when the person that I appear to be is gone, it may be easier to tune up to the wholeness of the spirit, to the freed seed. As it is now, I have stated what I know is my truth, and for me incontrovertibly reality. Do with it what you will, as you will, as you are able to. May you live, think, and *act,* in terms of the wholeness you are. . . . May you act, feel, think, and have faith—faith, courage, patience, and endurance. May these be, every day, your companions, as will still be my love and sustainment in whatever state of being I shall be in the years ahead. . . . And now please go, in peace and silence. I bless you all. The whole universe is waiting for you. Be true to yourself.[9]

As he spoke these final words, something extraordinary happened: Rudhyar sat up in his chair and started to radiate light. What I saw, and what others present also witnessed, was that his body was transfigured so that he became luminous. The essential light of Being was shining through him, soon to be liberated from his ninety-year-old shell. This was one of the most intense and extraordinary experiences I've ever had with a teacher.

A few months later, and right before Rudhyar died, I had a dream about him: I was trying to hold on to him, but he pushed me away, as if he were shooing away a cat. Since that dream I've never had any conflict about holding on to a teacher. I had reached a stage where I no longer needed the physical form of the Wise Old Man.

CREATING OUR OWN SYNTHESIS

Each of us can evolve our own forms of spiritual discipline that are less dependent on the authority of an external teacher. I like to have fun inventing my own variations on traditional practices. For example, I like to do what I call the Great Nature Walking Meditation. It's based on the traditional Buddhist walking meditation, in which one gives full attention to the act of walking and all the movements it involves. The Great Nature Walk begins with centering in serene awareness of conscious physical movement—rhythmic breathing, the sensation of feet lifting, extending forward, and softly touching the Earth. Then I expand the sphere of awareness outward, progressively through each of the senses, registering the odor and freshness of the environment, the sounds, the full, rich tapestry of patterns and forms, the color of leaves and flowers and sky, the texture of wind, sky, tree bark, and wildflowers. I am the growing leaf, the inching worm, the barking dog, the scurrying squirrel. I am nature, unceasing growth and evolution, always reaching toward the light.

I enjoy combining hatha yoga with music. Practicing asanas and breathing while listening to uplifting music, my mind grows calm, my inner energy unfurls, and my body moves fluidly through long sequences of poses, becoming supple and alive.

The synthesis of spiritual practices I've evolved for myself consists of five components: (1) *dreamwork,* the yoga of the unconscious, integrating archetypal material and subpersonalities; (2) *hatha yoga,* the path of transformation through integrating the body, breath, and mind; (3) *meditation,* the yoga of cultivating tranquility through focusing and calming the mind, leading to Self-realization; (4) *astrology,* the study of cycles in human experience, the yoga of time, which describes our passages through the many phases of life; and (5) receptivity to the mystery of *grace,* the direct transmission of the divine presence, the revealing or self-disclosure of the sacred, the inner light of consciousness. Sadhana, spiritual practice, is a process of removing physical, emotional, and energetic obstacles so that the love, light, and power that flow from above can fill us and transform us.

SELF-LIBERATION THROUGH YOGA, PRANAYAMA, MEDITATION

Yoga is the art of self-liberation through freeing the body, breath, and mind of constrictions and limitations. I have practiced hatha yoga since I was fourteen years old, and it has been an unfailing source of guidance, clarity, strength, energy, and inspiration. Whenever I'm upset or confused, yoga practice restores my equilibrium and returns me to a place of centered calm so I can find the answers that I need. The fruits of yoga are poise, serenity, a clear mind, and the courage to face life with balance and confidence; my consciousness grows calmer, wider, vaster. While it's essential to receive good instruction in the techniques, the practices of yoga are transformative without being dependent on the presence of a teacher.

The challenging physical discipline of hatha yoga also nourishes the spirit. The practice of asanas systematically releases areas of constriction and contraction, creating a lithe, toned, flexible body that moves through the world gracefully. Our body awareness grows more subtle as we systematically expand our range of motion and access limitless inner space. For example, right now I'm aware of a block in the region of my upper thoracic spinal column encompassing the heart, upper lungs, and the base of the throat. I'm practicing postures that open my throat and chest, increasing elasticity in this region, and opening up my breathing. This ease of breathing enhances my ability to quiet down and plunge inward. I have some of my deepest meditations after an intensive session of hatha yoga practice.

In yoga meditation begins with the body. When we open up the body by altering movement and breathing patterns, expanded states of consciousness emerge spontaneously. We become more awake, porous, oceanic, and translucent. Energy and spiritual light begin to course through our cleansed body and psyche. Yoga psychology teaches that the quality of our embodiment both affects and reflects our state of consciousness. Postural limitations and contraction co-arise with unhealthy emotional and mental conditions, and these can be alleviated by changing one's posture, breathing, and movement. Yogis recognize that states of emotional agitation, anxiety, or fear are reflected in shallow, unsteady, jerky breathing. Changing the quality of our breathing and our posture brings about immediate expansion of our state of mind-body presence.

Awareness of the breath is fundamental to nearly all spiritual practices—Buddhist mindfulness meditation, Sufi Zhikr, Christian Hesychasm prayer, shamanic journeying, rebirthing, and holotropic breathwork. For me pranayama, yogic breathing, is the path to natural meditation. Many people have told me they find it difficult to meditate. But it's easy if you approach it through the process of gentle breath release, through pranayama. If you were to ask me what's the most effective practice for bringing the most enlightenment with the least effort and the least strain, I'd undoubtedly choose pranayama. In a moment I'll describe several breathing techniques that flow into deep meditation. I get such good results with these practices that I teach them to all of my psychotherapy clients to counteract stress, anxiety, and depression, and to reach a calm, expansive state of consciousness. These methods are free of charge and completely safe, assuming you don't overdo it or perform intense practices on a full stomach.

Pranayama is best practiced in a relaxed manner free of strain and tension. It's very powerful; even a brief practice of these methods will activate meditation and higher energetics in yoga. You don't need to go off on retreat. You can practice for five minutes and you'll get immediate benefits. You can also do it for longer periods at any time. It's important to rest and relax after doing these practices.

For the reader's benefit I'll briefly describe five techniques that you can try for yourself: *ujjayi, nadi shodhana, kapalabhati, bhastrika,* and *sitali.* It's best to get personal instruction in these techniques from a qualified yoga teacher, but if you do decide to try this on your own, I hope you'll follow these instructions closely and approach the practices with caution.

For Each Pranayama Exercise

Sit comfortably.

Allow your mind to be tranquil, spacious, and full.

Feel your breath, feel your center.

◈ Ujjayi, Ocean Breath

Draw a full breath through your nose with a quiet hissing sound, actively inflating your lungs.

Inhale fully, keeping your nose, lungs, and nasal passages soft, liquid, easeful, without straining your shoulders or facial muscles.

Pause briefly at the top of the breath.

Then softly exhale through your nose, a long, smooth out-breath.

Fully expel the air. Pause for a moment.

Take another breath and repeat.

Start with three or four breaths; gradually increase.

Now meditate in silence for a few moments.

Next, try *nadi shodhana,* the cleansing of the subtle nerve channels, or *nadis,* through alternate nostril breathing. You can do profound inner yoga through alternate nostril breathing. It's an internal elixir. *Nadi shodhana* is a quiet, calming, balancing breath. This practice balances the two sides of the brain and facilitates the spiraling, serpentine movement of energy through *ida* and *pingala,* the moon and sun energy channels, one on either side of the spinal column, the left being the ida and the right the pingala. This spiraling energy is depicted in the symbol of the caduceus.

◈ Nadi Shodhana, Alternate Nostril Breath

Using your right thumb, cover your right nostril and breathe in through the left nostril.

Fill your lungs gently and pause.

Using your right pinky and ring finger, close the left nostril, and open your
   right nostril.

Breathe out fully through the right side.

Keeping your left nostril covered, breathe in through the right nostril.

Fill your lungs gently and pause.

Using your right thumb, close the right nostril and breathe out fully through
   the left side.

Pause for a moment.

This completes one round of alternate nostril breathing. Try three or four
   rounds.

Then take a few normal breaths and sit quietly in meditation.

The next practice is dynamic and activating: *kapalabhati,* the "skull-shining" breath. Here you emphasize the active out-breath, allowing the in-breath to take care of itself. Kapalabhati clears the lungs, nasal passages, and the mind. Kapalabhati, along with its more advanced cousin bhastrika pranayama, is sometimes called the "breath of fire" because it heats us up energetically, raising and charging the prana, the flow of vital energy.

◇ *Kapalabhati, Skull-Shining Breath*

Using your abdominal muscles and diaphragm, gently exhale, exhale, exhale,
   exhale, exhale—through your nose. The in-breath is shallow and easy.

Emphasize the out-breath. Keep your lungs soft—no strain.

After ten or twenty out-breaths, inhale deeply, pause, then fully exhale
   though your nose.

Take a normal breath and relax.

Then do another round of ten or twenty or thirty out-breaths, as desired.

Take a normal breath.

Be still and silent for a few moments.

Try two or three rounds to begin. Increase gradually as desired. The goal is
   a gently emphatic out-breath that isn't rushed, frantic, or excessive.

Keep your lungs and nasal passages as soft, liquid, and relaxed as they were in *ujjayi* and *nadi shodhana*. Be gentle; pump the air through you.

Oxygenate. Out-breath, out-breath, out-breath. Then deeply inhale, pause, and gently, smoothly exhale.

Be completely still and feel your body vibrate. Let your mind dissolve.

Don't break a blood vessel or bust a gut doing this too vigorously. Fan a gentle fire.

And don't practice this on a full stomach.

After several months or years of practicing kapalabhati, you'll develop greater strength and vitality in your lungs and solar plexus center. This prepares you to practice *bhastrika* pranayama, the bellows breath. This practice awakens kundalini energy, but it is best practiced responsibly, gently, without too much intensity. It will take the practitioner quickly into states of spontaneous meditation.

◈ Bhastrika, Bellows Breath

Here, you inhale and exhale with equal intensity, instead of solely emphasizing the exhalations, as in kapalabhati.

Using your abdominal muscles and diaphragm, gently inhale and exhale, inhale and exhale, inhale and exhale—through your nose. Get a steady rhythym going.

Start slowly and gradually accelerate the pace of your steady breath cycles.

Pump the air in and out like a bellows stoking a fire. Keep your lungs and nasal passages soft—no strain.

After ten, twenty, or thirty breaths, inhale deeply, pause, then exhale though your nose.

Take a normal breath and relax.

Then do another round of ten, twenty, or thirty breaths.

Take a normal breath.

Be still for a few moments.

Practice the rapid cycles of inhale-exhale-inhale-exhale with ease in your body, with no strain in the face, eyes, jaws, or shoulders, and no tightness in the lungs. Breathe and release.

You can also gain immeasurable benefit from *sitali* pranayama, the cooling breath. This breath is centering and also an excellent practice in hot weather or when the body or psyche is heated and would like to gently cool down.

◈ Sitali, the Cooling Breath, or Tongue-Hissing Breath

Stick out your tongue, curl it into a tubular shape.

Suck the breath in through your curled tongue.

As you fill your lungs, feel the energy connection to your solar plexus center.

Breathe out through your nose.

Repeat several times. Then sit quietly and relax. Close your eyes and meditate.

By practicing these breath exercises, either separately or as a series, it's possible to access meditation naturally, without strain. A few gentle rounds of pranayama can lead directly to the gates of meditation. The practitioner holds the keys to self-liberation.

Bhagavan Ramana Maharshi said this about pranayama:

The aim is to make the mind one-pointed. For that pranayama is a help, a means. Not only for *dhyana* [meditation], but in every case where we have to make the mind one-pointed, it may even be for a purely secular or material purpose, it is good to make *pranayama* and then start the other work. The mind and the *prana* are the same, having the same source. If one is controlled, the other is also controlled at the same time. If one is able to make the mind one-pointed without the help of *pranayama,* he need not bother about *pranayama.* But one who cannot at once control the mind may control the breath, and that will lead to control of the mind. It is something like pulling a horse by the reins and making it go in one direction.[10]

DREAMWORK

If yoga frees the body and breath of contractions and blockages, then dreams help us become more conscious by revealing information, in symbolic form, from the depths of our being. Dreams are integrative, healing, and anticipatory. They help us integrate our subpersonalities, our shadow side and our emotional complexes. They help us resolve past traumas so that they have less power over us. And they portend what's arising within us, the direction our unfoldment is taking.*

I was guided through the process of separation and individuation from my teachers by a series of dreams. In one an infant was being held by his father, who simultaneously embodied my teachers Swami Muktananda and Allan Bateman, plus a third man I'd met named Charles Bebeau, a Jungian analyst. The message of this dream was that these men represented my own spiritual potential—that the seed of wisdom was within me, and that I would "grow up" to become my own teacher. The dream also portended a major project I'd soon undertake in my life: the blending of yoga with the practice of depth psychology, symbolized by the Jungian analyst. I discerned that my path was to combine meditation, hatha yoga, psychotherapy, and the yoga of dreams and the unconscious.

In a second dream, I walked through a park, where I saw a procession of swamis looking very solemn. I was dressed in punk-looking clothes—a black leather jacket and tie-dyed headband. I looked like a punked-out hippie dude. The swamis were surprised to see me, a bit shocked at my appearance, and they kept their distance. It was obvious that I was not one of them and wouldn't become a renunciate. This dream was an inward confirmation of the fact that my spiritual path was leading me from the ascetic, ashram stage, back into the world, where I would assume a very different persona.

In a third dream, Muktananda's successor, Gurumayi Chidvilasananda, told me, "It's okay for you to live your own life." The

_____

*These themes are extensively discussed in my book *Dreamwork and Self-Healing*.

internal messages from my unconscious mind affirmed that I needn't feel guilty about finding my own path.

I have continued to do ongoing inner work with my teacher, Swami Muktananda, through dreams. In February 1999, after struggling for many years with misgivings about his sexual behavior, I had a dream that helped me heal and resolve my feelings. In this dream

> *Baba appears before me. I'm so happy to see him! He looks small, old, but immensely powerful. His head is shaved. His eyes are partially closed and his awareness is drawn inward. He doesn't gaze outward or interact with me, but he allows me to view him. The moment I see him, my whole being lifts up and I feel a magnetic pull into the divine presence. I feel myself merging into consciousness, the Self-revealing light of the divine. I intuitively know that he has grappled with the consequences of his actions, that he has undergone penance and purification. I have the awareness that he is reconciled with himself for his actions, that I am reconciled with him—I have forgiven him; and that he has forgiven me for having doubts and being upset with him.*

I awakened from this dream feeling grateful for this dream darshan, this glimpse of my teacher. It gave me a powerful feeling of closure and blessings. The transmission I received here was intense; it was one of my strongest experiences of shaktipat.

In 2003 I had another dream of Baba, at a time when I was in trouble at work and my boss was upset with me. I was afraid I was about to get fired. I dreamed that Swami Muktananda was standing in my dining room. He was there to express his love, his concern, and his reassurance. I could feel him behind me, looking at me with immense compassion. He was completely there for me. I felt inwardly blessed.

It was comforting that my teacher was thinking about me and was concerned about my situation. This strengthened my confidence and faith. I felt as though he was actually there in the room with me. I tangibly felt his bodily presence, the current of his vibrational influence. This experience, twenty-nine years after first meeting Baba, showed me that the connection between us is timeless and unbroken. I couldn't get over the fact that in the spiritual world of my unconscious, he cared and showed up for me.

Then, in 2008, I experienced a minor flap within academia when I came up short in my quest for a hotly contested faculty seat. The morning after I received the disappointing news that I hadn't been selected for the job, I had another dream:

> *I was in an apartment with Swami Muktananda and offered him a container of mixed nuts. He grabbed them from me. I asked, "Would you like me to prepare you something for lunch?" He said no, he just wanted his own stash of nuts. I saw his face, his shaved head, his body, his freedom beyond form, beyond the world.*

Once again my teacher came to me at one of the worst moments in my life, when I was at an absolute low point. Offering to feed him signified feeding the part of myself that's unconditioned by form, by success and failure. This dream showed me that my real existence is outside the play of this world; it reconnected me to an inward moving stream of consciousness. My teacher appeared to me as an *avadhut,* a being who is radically detached and free from worldly ties. In the dream he shows me his state of freedom and unconditioned awareness. This was one of my greatest experiences, as my teacher directly revealed and bestowed the experience of union within divine consciousness.

In 2009 Baba appeared in a fourth dream darshan:

> *He was sitting right next to me. He said he was leaving on a trip to India, and I asked him if he was going to Kerala, where he was born. He said no and named another destination.*

*Then he put his forehead right up against mine and continued
talking to me very quietly and intimately. I couldn't understand a word he said, but what was silently conveyed was the
current of his blessing, his approval, his interest in me. He
had a big smile and closed his eyes ecstatically. I was all lit up
and felt waves of energy running through my body.*

In the dream the guru isn't returning to the place of his childhood
origins but is traveling to another destination. I felt the message here
was that I was too preoccupied with the past and needed openness to
future possibilities. At first I didn't grasp a word he was saying; our
relationship was beyond my conceptual understanding, but we met on a
caring, feeling level. Being face to face with him, forehead to forehead,
was an experience of receiving a mind-to-mind transmission.

INNER GUIDANCE
THROUGH ASTROLOGY

To find the teacher within and a vision of one's identity and potential,
it can be immensely helpful to study astrology and the symbolism of
one's natal chart. Astrology is an impartial teacher that illuminates the
cycles and archetypal structures and energies that organize our lives. As
I once wrote:

Astrology is the Yoga of Time. It is a form of sacred knowledge
that teaches us to live consciously as embodied beings in a tem-
poral world. Study of the birth chart enables us to find our next
step in evolution—whether this means choosing a career, forming a relationship, physical or emotional healing, building a business, social activism, or deepening our meditation practice. It can
be a reliable guide through life's changes, a means of sanctifying
earthly existence and fulfilling its challenges with courage, clarity,
and joy.[11]

Astrology is the study of time and change, the cycles and phases of life. It uses cyclical principles rooted in nature and archetypal symbolism rooted deeply in the human psyche to create a map of personal growth and life-cycle development. The basic symbolism of a natal chart includes zodiacal signs, representing the seasons of life and nature; the planets, representing core functions and motivations of the personality; and the astrological houses (i.e., the areas of space surrounding us at the birth moment), representing the twelve realms of life:

First house: personal identity
Second house: finances
Third house: learning and communication
Fourth house: family, home, residence, and property
Fifth house: children, play, and creativity
Sixth house: health, employment, and job training
Seventh house: relationship attractions and dynamics
Eighth house: sexuality and shared resources
Ninth house: education and philosophy of life
Tenth house: career development and occupational role
Eleventh house: groups and community involvement
Twelfth house: spirituality and interior life

Astrologers also study transits, the ongoing movements of planets that indicate areas of past, present, and future emphasis. Transits allow us to identify our most pressing tasks and areas for personal growth and expanding consciousness. As yogis our focus in astrology is not on prediction, but on informed, well-timed action and clarity in defining our intentions.

Astrology is a form of contemplative knowledge that can awaken inner peace and wisdom and aid us in achieving enlightenment. Reflection on the language of the sky teaches us to discern the will and intention of the cosmos, to attune ourselves to the "cosmic guru," the spirit of guidance. It helps us to become centered in the here and now and to understand the meaning of events, including painful ones. Since a full elucidation of this subject would take us somewhat far afield of our current topic, I refer those interested to several books I've written that explore this knowledge at length.[12] I consider knowledge of one's birth chart and current planetary transits an important tool for every spiritual apprentice.

EXPERIENCING THE POWER
OF SACRED IMAGES

The teacher can appear in the form of a spiritual icon or image that inwardly affects us. One day in 1993, I spontaneously walked into an art store on Telegraph Avenue in Berkeley. I have no idea why, but something pulled me in there. Seated on an antique wooden cabinet was the radiant form of a meditating Shiva. I was magnetized by it. My immediate response was to bow down on my knees. Something inside me said, "Oh, this is my guru." I looked into Shiva's eyes and saw the bliss of his inner state. I fell into a deep meditation and sat there in front of the statue for a long time. Its price was $500, which was way over my budget at that moment. But over the next few weeks, I couldn't get the image out of my mind. I was obsessed with the idea of bringing Shiva home with me and installing him in a place of honor.

Eventually I went back to the store, determined that if I could bargain the owner down to $375, I'd purchase the statue. Without my saying a word, the owner walked up to me and said, "I'll sell it to you for 375." I picked up the statue, and as I held it I saw golden light emanate from it. Then I could have sworn that Shiva smiled at me! In that moment I was committed. He was definitely coming home with me.

Years later the meditating Shiva still sits in my living room. He has four arms. In one he holds a drum, symbolic of the power of music, rhythm, tone, and dance, the primary expressions of Spirit's power of unending expansion, emanation, and creativity. The drumbeat sends the shaman into visionary trance states. The drum is also a symbol of the cosmic rhythms and cycles that govern and organize our lives.

Meditating Shiva

It represents our consciousness of time, the changing of seasons, the marking of transitions. The drum also represents the time it takes for everything to unfold to completion. In another hand Shiva holds a trident, symbol of his fierceness and fearlessness. Shiva is lord of the wild animals, the tamer of beasts, the tamer of our passions. In his third hand his palm is lifted, facing outward in benediction, symbolizing the bestowal of grace. In his fourth hand he holds a begging bowl. Shiva is an ascetic and a renunciate. He has fully surrendered and is merged in the ocean of consciousness. He doesn't grasp or cling.

Shiva's hair is long and matted and filled with snakes. He's ever-delighted in the presence of his consort, Kundalini, the serpent goddess, who is coiled around his neck. His eyes are filled with bliss, lifting up into the vast inner sky. Energy lifts from his root chakra up to his crown chakra, where he's fully merged in the sea of tranquility and eternal being. For me contemplating this image is a powerful catalyst for inner awakening.

DISEMBODIED TEACHERS

We may also find ourselves drawn to a teacher who is no longer physically alive, feeling the presence of a being we meet on the subtle planes in meditation or in a dream state. We might feel a strong connection to a particular lineage of teachers such as the Tamil siddhas of South India, Christian or Sufi mystics, or Tibetan Buddhist yogis. We can feel a connection to a deceased teacher through books, lecture transcripts, or audio or video recordings, and through our willingness to contemplate the teacher's life and practice what he or she taught. We may also resonate with disembodied teachers as a result of experiencing their subtle presence or essence. One man had a vision of the Indian saint Swami Sivananda, who left his physical body in 1963:

> I was staying at my mom's condo in Florida. I was sitting by the pool feeling sad because I didn't have anyone to talk to and I'd been eating too much and hadn't practiced yoga in a week or so. Suddenly I saw the subtle form of a very large, tall man with an orange robe and a shaved head. I know he wasn't physically present, yet I saw him quite distinctly. He spoke to me, saying, "Rise up and practice! Rouse the serpent energy with vigorous practice!" I went to my room and started doing my yoga routine. After an hour I was in a quiet, blissful state and meditated deeply. And as I sat there I had the sensation of a serpent moving around at the base of my spine, and I began to feel electricity rising up my back.

As I've continued on my own path, I've been strongly influenced by a number of disembodied teachers, for example, the Indian siddha

Nityananda, whose silent, oceanic consciousness is transmitted through his pictures. I feel connected to mystics such as Nisargadatta, Rumi, and Ramakrishna when I read their written words. I've also been influenced by Sri Yukteswar, guru of Paramahansa Yogananda, whose austere, stern presence reminds me of discipline and ethics, especially when I'm on the brink of committing some act of incredible stupidity and poor judgment.

One can feel the power of great beings long after their physical bodies have departed. Many seekers have powerful experiences doing sadhana at the shrines or samadhi places of great saints and siddhas. In 1996, while meditating next to the tomb of Sri Aurobindo at his ashram in Pondicherry, India, I felt an immediate connection with the exalted consciousness of this sage. I was instantly gripped by meditation. Forming an internal relationship with a teacher who isn't in a physical body forces us to locate the presence of the teacher within.

It's also possible to form a connection with beings on other planes of existence through the phenomenon of channeling.[13] Some say that adherence to the teachings of disembodied spirit guides isn't an authentic path because it could leave us susceptible to our own delusions. But many aspirants report that they receive valuable guidance in this manner. For example, for more than a decade, my friend Laura has received rich personal instruction through a series of channeled conversations with a wise nonphysical guide:

One day I saw a vision, an inner picture of a man. Looking into his eyes was like looking straight into the cosmos. I said to myself, *Oh, he's not human.* It was an overpowering experience. I began having sessions with a channel, who told me, "He's your teacher." At first I got very into the idea that I had a guru. But the next time I had a session this being came through the channel and told me, "I'm not your guru." The force of that sent me reeling. I felt tremendous shame, dependency, and fear. I felt rejected and complete abandonment. I worked through it and then I understood the teaching, which was a refusal to take that role with me. The next time I talked to my guide he said, "I knew that was going to have a strong effect on you. You've done that in many lives and it has held you back. My task is to make you a teacher, to bring you to my level, not to keep you a disciple." People who follow gurus often don't become gurus. It was a direct severing of that kind of bond I was trying to make with him, and it forced me to confront those parts of me that would like to hide out in that disciple stance. His refusal to do that with me has been a great gift. I've come to see that the guru-disciple setup was a prison for me. I need to keep moving out of that way of relating to the guru, in terms of dependency needs and inability to separate and individuate. I need to step up next to the guide instead of being a supplicant, which is what I've tended to do.

I understand from my teacher that I've been under his care for a very long time. We had one life together in physical bodies, and he's been with me ever since. He waited to reveal himself to me until a time in this life when I was ready. And now we're continuing our work together. This doesn't preclude my having other, living teachers and following the practices they recommend. But it doesn't make any sense to me that things don't continue after you die. A lot of traditions speak of visitations by disembodied teachers, and I don't feel like it's anything particularly out of the ordinary. In Tibetan Buddhist tradition, it's common to have visitations, dreams, and visions in which long-dead teachers come and give teachings. These beings are considered part of the refuge tree. We're to honor all the Buddhas that have ever been, all the dakinis, and all the teachers. It's not just imagination. It's assumed that these nonphysical beings are really there to help you.

THE FORMLESS GURU, GNOSIS, AND THE INVISIBLE GUIDE

At times we sense a formless but tangible presence guiding our lives. Yogis call it Shiva, Krishna, the eternal guru, the witness, the Self. Sufis call it the Spirit of Guidance. In the Islamic tradition there's a legendary figure known as Khidr, "the guide of the mystics,"[14] an invisible spirit of assistance and grace that's said to come to the aid of seekers of truth. Khidr, the patron saint of travelers, is also known as the prophet Elijah. As Schimmel stated earlier, "Sometimes the mystics would meet him on their journeys; he would inspire them, answer their questions, rescue them from danger."[15]

I believe that once I may have encountered this mysterious figure. One night, in 1980, while I was wandering in the woods near Mt. Ashland in southern Oregon, I was lonely and scared. I was camped under a tree, and as I sat there under the stars, tears came to my eyes. I began to rock gently back and forth, which felt very soothing. It was as if there were an invisible presence reassuring me and looking after me. I closed my eyes and became quiet. Suddenly I began uttering the word Elijah. I knew absolutely nothing about the figure of Elijah, but the name resounded like a mantra. I repeated it numerous times and felt stillness and inner peace. I have no idea why. I've never done it again. Something was with me there that night as I vocalized the name of the guide and protector of travelers.

Henri Corbin has written at length about Islamic texts that describe the visitations of the invisible guide:

> In the charming book entitled *The Shepherd of Hermas,* . . . which was formerly part of the Biblical canon, the epiphany of the personal angel takes place. . . . Hermas is at home, sitting on his bed, in a state of deep meditation. Suddenly a person of strange appearance enters, sits down beside him, and says: "I have been sent by the most reverend angel to dwell with you the rest of the days of your life." Hermas thinks that the apparition has come to tempt him: "But who are you? for . . . I know to whom I was handed over.' He said to me, 'Do you not recognize me?' 'No,' I said. 'I,' said he, 'am the shepherd to whom you were handed over.' While he was still speaking, his appearance changed, and I recognized him, that it was he to whom

I was handed over." In this dialogue we clearly discern the familiar Gnostic figure of the angelic Helper and Guide, who is the celestial archetype of the human being entrusted to him.[16]

In the Islamic mystical tradition, the guide is an archetypal figure discovered within the seeker's inner world. Islamic philosophers, mystics, and poets such as Avicenna and Suhrawardi wrote the mystical texts known as *visionary recitals*, which describe a series of inner initiations that mystics experience.[17] These texts are works of gnosticism, the search for liberation or salvation of the soul through sacred knowledge. Gnosticism appeared in the Hellenistic era in Jewish, Christian, and Islamic forms, and was central in the Hermetic tradition.

There are two themes common to all gnostic texts and teachings: the motif of estrangement, and the motif of return to one's true origin. Gnostics experience a consciousness originating in realms of light beyond the physical and astral worlds, a spark of light that has become estranged from its divine nature, trapped in the physical world, hidden and encased in the tomb of the body. The motif of estrangement suggests that the soul must find its way back home to the Pleroma, the realm of light and splendor, the fullness and unity of Spirit, with the help of an invisible, celestial guide. Corbin writes:

> The soul must find the way of Return. That way is Gnosis and on that way it needs a Guide. . . . There is synchronism between the soul's awakening to itself and its visualization of its guide. . . . At the moment when the soul discovers itself to be a stranger and alone in a world formerly familiar, a *personal* figure appears on its horizon, a figure that announces itself to the soul *personally* because it symbolizes with the soul's most intimate depths. In other words, the soul discovers itself to be the earthly counterpart of another being with which it seemingly forms a totality that is dual in structure. The two elements of this *dualitude* may be called the ego and the Self, or the transcendent celestial Self and the earthly Self. . . . It is

from this transcendent Self that the soul originates in the past of metahistory. . . . The Self is neither a metaphor nor an ideogram. It is . . . the heavenly counterpart of a pair, or a syzygy made up of a fallen angel, or an angel appointed to govern a body, and of an angel retaining his abode in heaven. The idea of syzygy . . . corresponds to a fundamental gnostic intuition, which . . . individualizes the Holy Spirit into an individual Spirit, who is the celestial *paredros** of the human being, its guardian, angel, guide, helper, and savior. . . . The soul cannot emerge from this cosmos without its Guide, and reciprocally, the Guide needs the soul in order to perform and celebrate his divine service.[18]

Moments of visionary illumination reveal that each of us is, in essence, a spiritual intelligence, or "angel," appointed to govern a body, yet at the same time connected with an angelic presence retaining its center of awareness in the heaven of formless, infinite Spirit. This invisible Guide is the one who has from the beginning accompanied the aspirant, leading the soul on an inner voyage out of Egypt, out of exile, back toward its true home in the realms of light. The Guide is the seeker's spiritual twin, still rooted in its divine nature. The realization dawns that the Guide and the individual soul are eternally wedded; the two now become conscious of each other and merge into one. The Guide is the rainbow bridge linking our human nature and our higher spiritual nature, and leads us into realms of light, revealing our true identity as the celestial Self, the tranquil field of consciousness. The Guide is both the goal and the method that leads to the goal, which is to abide in the real. The Guide is the one who has always been with us, who has always walked beside us, who never left us.

Sri Aurobindo, the sage of modern India, eloquently describes the aspirant's growing awareness of the formless inner guide:

---

*Paredros means "one who sits beside."

But in proportion as this contact establishes itself, the Sadhaka must become conscious that a force other than his own, a force transcending his egoistic endeavor and capacity, is at work in him, and to this Power he learns progressively to submit himself and delivers up to it the charge of his Yoga. In the end his own will and force become one with the higher Power; he merges them in the divine Will and its transcendent and universal Force. He finds it thenceforward presiding over the necessary transformation of his mental, vital, and physical being with an impartial wisdom and provident effectivity of which the . . . ego is not capable. . . . When the human ego . . . learns to trust itself to that which transcends it, that is its salvation. . . . The inner Guide, the World-Teacher . . . destroys our darkness by the resplendent light of his knowledge; that light becomes within us the increasing glory of his own self-revelation. . . . This inner Guide is often veiled at first by the very intensity of our personal effort and by the ego's preoccupation with itself and its aims. As we gain in clarity and the turmoil of egoistic effort gives place to a calmer self-knowledge, we recognize the source of the growing light within us. . . . We feel the presence of a supreme Master, Friend, Lover, Teacher. We recognize it in the essence of our being as that develops into likeness and oneness with a greater and wider existence; for we perceive that this miraculous development is not the result of our own efforts; an eternal Perfection is moulding us into its own image.[19]

Here Aurobindo expresses with utmost profundity the essence of the mystery we're exploring in this book.

SACRAMENTAL PLANTS

Once I encountered another teacher that impacted me powerfully: the peyote cactus. Many mystical traditions employ entheogens, mind-altering, psychedelic substances, as agents of profound healing and teachings for those who are properly prepared for the experience.[20] To the

Huichol and Tarahumara peoples of Mexico, peyote is the grandfather, the teacher of the people, the healer, the one who reveals a sacred path. The Huichol make an annual sacred pilgrimage to Wirikuta, the land where peyote grows. For centuries these peoples have eaten the cactus as part of collective celebrations, dances, and feasts. Its usage was fully integrated into social customs and relationships. Indeed, it was an essential spiritual core that held the tribal group together. As the use of peyote migrated north to the Native American tribes of the United States, it became associated with more introspective, meditative ceremonies such as those practiced in the contemporary Native American Church. Members of this church revere peyote as their teacher, receiving visions from the cactus that they use to guide themselves and their tribal affairs. They eat the cactus only in the context of group meetings and ceremony. Thus, use of the sacred cactus is both a shared ritual that promotes social cohesion and a tool for individual vision questing and inner initiation.[21]

My experience with peyote occurred in April 1980 when I visited Eden hot springs near Safford, Arizona, which was the place where the warrior chief Geronimo went to mend his wounds between battles. The morning I arrived, a man named Noah, who lived on the premises, offered me some fresh, juicy cactus. I chowed two of them for breakfast and wandered out to soak in the pools. I walked around the desert hills gazing at the beauty of the colorful spring wildflowers, and I experienced a deep feeling of love for a hummingbird that seemed to remain suspended in space for eternity. Then I returned to the water and began to meditate. My legs locked into the lotus posture and I began to do spontaneous bhastrika pranayama, the full breath of fire, the same breath that had made me pass out one night when I was fifteen. I felt myself rising up, ascending through all the colors of the spectrum into white light. I lifted my chin up so that my throat began to open, and as I did so I began to roar and breathe fire like the Plumed Serpent, Quetzalcoatl. I felt myself become the Plumed Serpent, the dragon of Spirit, the ascending snake of coiled power. I still feel that flying bird–serpent alive within me to this day. Later a song came to me: "Peyoooooteeee, father of visions, keeper of the door." I sang it over and over as that magical day's sun finally set. As a special seal of this remarkable experience, later that evening Noah gave me the gift of an eagle feather.

A year later I had another dream that connected to this experience of the plumed serpent: A very powerful, ancient golden bird with an enormous wingspan descended from the sky and landed on the branch of a tree and slowly lowered its wings. It rested there, emanating presence and power. It would stay on the ground for a while. Later it would take flight again.

This dream showed me my spiritual potential, evident in the bird's enormous wingspan and its emanating presence. But I felt that the dream was a message from my unconscious that right now wasn't the time for visionary journeys, full kundalini awakening, or the rising of the phoenix. The dream made me aware that my work at that moment was to become more grounded, trusting that the liberating, ascending current would return in its own good time.

RELATIONSHIP PARTNER AS GURU

We receive some of the most important lessons and teachings through our personal relationships, in the company of those we love.[22] Sri Ramakrishna was ecstatically in love with all women as embodiments of the Divine Mother and would go into trance at the sight of women. In contrast the great Indian poet-saint Tukaram was sexually fixated on his wife, who told him, "If you only loved Ram [God] as much as you love my body, you would be enlightened by now." This statement forced Tukaram to look at himself closely and awakened a spirit of renunciation and one-pointed devotion to the divine that sparked his urge for enlightenment. My own wife, Diana, has a special knack for revealing my imperfections—my egotism, carelessness, stinginess, defensiveness, and my sloppiness in daily living. I no longer need a spiritual teacher to expose my ego because she does it for me every day.

Once Diana taught me a marvelous lesson. We were cleaning

spiderwebs out of the house with a broom and dust rags. While searching through a drawer, Diana found a worn-out, faded, baggy orange
swami shirt that I bought in Benares in 1978. When she attempted to
use it as a dust rag I objected vehemently. This shirt had sentimental
value, I said. It was an important symbol of my first journey to India
and my commitment to the spiritual path. I couldn't just use this as a
rag to clean up spiderwebs. She asked me, "How long has it been since
you actually wore that shirt?" It had only been fifteen or sixteen years.
She said, "Well, if you're such a swami, you should know the importance
of nonclinging and not being attached to material possessions—which
is exactly what you need to practice right now." And with that she tied
my swami shirt to the end of the broom.

> Delight in the presence of your own Shakti or Shiva.
> With your human partner
> the great tantric feast is consummated.
> This is the burning grounds of the ego, its place of
>   cremation.
> Pick up the ashes of yourself that you are handed
> and offer them
> at the feet of the eternal.
> This is your companion
> on the journey to the stars.[23]

Over the years Diana has tried a number of the spiritual disciplines
I'm involved with, but most of them haven't felt right for her. For a
long time I encouraged her to try various techniques because I had the
concept (or hang-up) that "spiritual" people practice a discipline of consciousness expansion. When I start talking like this, she always gives
me a funny, slightly disgusted look and says, "Greg, *you* want to do that
practice. You *need* to do that practice. But I don't need to. I have my
own path." Diana likes to perform rituals of attunement to the four
directions, to the elements, and to the spirits of trees and animals. After

Divine couple, Srinageri.

a few hours working outside with plants in the garden, she exudes the same clarity, peacefulness, and expanded awareness as anyone I've ever seen after a meditation retreat. She has her own way of "being peace."

The essence of wisdom is attention and care in our relationships. Recall what Joshu Sazaki Roshi told me: "The highest discipline of Zen is to manifest silence when you meet others." This attitude serves us well as we continue our journey and begin to share with others what we've learned along the way.

STAGE NINE

Teaching Others

Sharing Knowledge Gracefully

*I am a tide in the sea of life, bearing toward the shore all
who come within my enfoldment.*

THE COMPLETE SAYINGS OF HAZRAT INAYAT KHAN

In all forms of apprenticeship, the student eventually achieves sufficient
mastery of a particular skill or body of knowledge that he or she becomes
capable of practicing independently of the teacher. And at some point we
may be asked by other aspiring seekers to provide guidance, instruction,
and mentorship. As a variety of contemplative practices and lineages take
hold in the West, increasing numbers of people are seeking guidance on
the path. Thus more people, as a natural stage in their own maturation,
are being called on to serve as guides and teachers. Even if we aren't fully
evolved, we can help others along the way, whether informally or in our
roles as yoga instructors, meditation teachers, and spiritual counselors.
Whatever level we've reached in our own practice, becoming a teacher
will challenge us to deepen ourselves on every level.

There are several factors that make it more likely we'll be successful
in this work and that we'll actually be helpful to others. First it's impor-

tant that we're immersed in our own spiritual practice and continue this once we've begun teaching, rather than relying only on past experience. Our integrity as teachers derives from the intensity of our own self-discipline. Indeed, teaching others ideally inspires us to practice more, not less. Also it's important to receive either the encouragement or blessing of a qualified teacher or a strong inner calling before we begin teaching. It's especially helpful if a teacher who is familiar with our character recommends or requests that we begin to teach.

Nyogen Sensaki, the first Zen master to teach in America, attended the famous conference on world religions in Chicago in 1895 and stayed on in America, working as a "house boy" for twenty years before he began teaching. His teacher had instructed him to wait twenty years before commencing to teach. He faithfully obeyed his roshi's instructions and waited until he had time to fully mature. But very often an urge to teach may come from within. When impelled by this inner sense of calling, we need to rely on the principle of self-appointment, discussed in stage seven. If we examine our own motives and sincerely believe we're undertaking the work of spreading spiritual truth with right intention, then we may be self-appointed to the role. Teacher training is helpful, such as courses in spiritual direction, counseling methods, or yoga instruction. It's essential that we have the right attitude, not making inflated claims about our level of attainment and understanding our limits and the scope of our competency and knowledge. When the teacher is ready, the students will appear. The way the universe shows us that we're ready to begin teaching is that students start appearing.

Recently I spoke with a woman named Suniti, who began studying with her teacher, Amrit Desai, in 1970 and moved to the Kripalu community in 1981. She has been there ever since, serving for many years as a yoga teacher. Life changed dramatically for her when her teacher was accused of sexual misconduct and forced to leave the community. Her comments demonstrate how we can gracefully meet the challenges of separating from a teacher while continuing to evolve. The interview I conducted with her illustrates how a maturing spiritual apprentice can assume the function of teaching and leadership for others:

When my teacher resigned, it was a sad time for me, but I don't feel responsible for his life or his karma. I'm grateful for the teachings he gave. I don't believe other people betray us. I believe we get stuck where our karma sticks us. He never said that he was completely evolved; to the contrary he was in the thick of it. And I took him literally to mean that. My intention in being involved was always my growth in service, not to monitor where the master is or his level of evolution. I listened to the teachings and absorbed them, and I thought he spoke them quite eloquently.

I've matured tremendously through his leaving. I always believed in internalizing the teachings, and I have a great opportunity to do that now. I feel very strong inner guidance come through in my meditation. I've had to empower myself because there isn't the same sense of community anymore. In our group we don't speak about our spiritual values the way we used to. A lot of people were very disillusioned. We've become much more business-oriented. I'm challenged to accept the changes that God is bringing me and to be grateful for these changes. I miss the structure to support inner work that used to be much more visible. But I also see that this is an opportunity for me to grow.

When my mind becomes quite silent, I find there's always instruction and inner guidance there for me. I've recently begun to write that down as I hear it. I've also begun to read it to myself as a reminder of how my life is unfolding and what my cutting edge is—to serve and care for the people around me.

When we lose a teacher or when a relationship with a teacher changes, it's often incredibly liberating.

Yes, it is grace. But it has to be after you have a solid grounding in the teachings; otherwise it's devastating.

How do you counsel others who may not have had as deep a relationship with the teacher and who may have been interrupted at a different stage of the process?

I teach them classical Ashtanga yoga, especially the *yamas* and *niyamas* [moral precepts and recommended acts of self-purification] because I consider these the foundation to absorbing the practices of asana, pranayama, and meditation.

It sounds like you're finding inspiration in the age-old traditions and practices of yoga.

I feel more connected to my lineage now than I did when I had a teacher; it feels more pure because it's just their energy, rather than taking the teaching through a human being. I'm inspired by the teachings my teacher gave, but I don't consider them his. If any other teacher of this lineage spoke, it would be the same teachings.

So you're stepping into a role of spiritual leadership as part of the natural process of your own spiritual growth.

The vacuum will be filled by a number of us who are already stepping in.

You have maintained a positive feeling about your teacher despite his trangressions, preserving the memory of the positive experiences, the grace, the guidance, and the transmission you received.

My teacher's teacher said, "See the strengths in others, and the weaknesses in ourselves." I've chosen to work with that. The bottom line is that my path is inside of myself. Focusing on the weaknesses of others doesn't facilitate my sadhana at all.

A couple of months before my teacher left, I was in a darshan with him, and I shared with him how deeply I'd taken the teachings in, and I felt that the work had been done. I felt that the guru was inside. I expressed my gratitude for that. So it was as if he came into my life and I did the work, and he left just after I finished it. He is part of that energy that took me through that process, but he is no longer a distinct human being in my life. That's not true for other people, but that's true for me. Other people have been left less complete in the process than I was.

You seem to have come through this with a sense that you received teachings that have transformed your life. You accept what has happened and you're moving forward, unimpeded by blame. Some people never get over these situations. They remain stuck in losing their teacher, not seeing that this is just another stage of discipleship.

The guru is an opportunity for us to look at ourselves. But if we stay stuck in thinking our process is all about the external human being, the outer teacher, then we won't grow. We have to learn to get beyond being reactive and feeling betrayed. Feelings of betrayal come out of fear, and I don't choose to live in fear.

Suniti has matured in spiritual practice to the point where others entrust her with the responsibility of leadership. Her story illustrates how a student can develop into a teacher with a high degree of integrity in the role.

Not every spiritual apprentice ultimately becomes a teacher, but for those who do, it's helpful to have some basic guidelines. The suggestions I offer here are similar to principles that are implicitly followed by any successful and effective educator.

BASIC GUIDELINES FOR TEACHERS

- A spiritual teacher is dedicated to the welfare and progress of students and keeps their best interests uppermost in her or his awareness. This doesn't mean that we never challenge, surprise, or sometimes irritate people. But it does mean that we don't deliberately and recklessly injure, exploit, or endanger anyone. We remain accountable for our actions and consider how they'll impact others.

- Wise teachers don't put themselves above students. As we share knowledge with others, we'll also learn something from each of them. Effective teachers don't claim to know everything, and they remain open to questions, exploring these in an atmosphere of open inquiry. One of the benefits of teaching is that it spontaneously draws forth from us insights we may have never articulated previously.

- The ultimate reason to teach is to accelerate and further our own evolution. The best teachers are always learning through the act of teaching. A person in this role is constantly challenged to manifest new levels of truth, clarity, and tolerance. A teacher is asked to bring wisdom to bear on the problems of students with widely varying needs and those who are facing practical challenges in life.

- It's advisable to be mindful of the dynamics of transference within the relationship. If students idealize us and become very enthused, does that make us feel inflated and self-important? It's also possible to be openly devalued or negatively idealized, as when somebody decides we are the worst person who ever lived. We need to be able to identify these projections. Teachers with balanced self-esteem know the value of what they offer others without grandiose atittudes; they also don't collapse or become enraged whenever someone questions them.

- Skillful, compassionate teachers don't treat students with disdain just because they disagree with or struggle to grasp a teaching. Students want to be challenged and receive instruction; but at times they'll resist and be afraid, or become very argumentative. It's important to acknowledge people's fears and their differing viewpoints, knowing these are an intrinsic part of the learning process.

- Teachers need to curb their aggression and cruelty. Being in a position of authority sometimes activates unconscious tendencies toward condescending, abusive, or tyrannical behavior. A teacher is a companion, not a queen or king. I believe even the student with the thickest ego will usually respond better to a gentle teaching than an annihilating or humiliating one. This isn't to say a teacher shouldn't challenge people sometimes. Recall the story, recounted earlier, of

Like these temple guardians, dedicated teachers greet
wayfarers with friendliness, humor, balance, and tranquillity.
Temple entrance, Tanjore.

Karl, whose teacher yelled and cursed at him, but who received this as a test and ended up learning a great deal about himself. But one can take provocative behavior too far. I've heard stories about some so-called spiritual teachers who hit students, hurl dangerous objects at them, publicly embarrass and insult people, or financially exploit them. I believe that there's a difference between fierce teaching and injurious behavior. Inayat Khan said, "It takes years to make an ideal, and it takes but a moment to break it."[1]

• The best spiritual teachers avoid the pedagogy of humiliation. One famous teacher is known for his harsh, humiliating treatment of students, who often feel mocked and criticized for asking sincere questions or because of their fears. I'd avoid such a teacher like the plague. It's rarely helpful to humiliate a student unless the person is grossly arrogant and conceited. The habit of browbeating students is a sign that the teacher has unresolved psychological issues that need to be examined. Such a person has a lot more inner work to do.

TESTS OF CHARACTER

A good reputation is as fragile as a delicate glass. . . . A good reputation is a trust given to a man by other people, so it becomes his sacred duty to maintain it.
THE COMPLETE SAYINGS OF HAZRAT INAYAT KHAN

All teachers go through tests of character, to determine their worthiness to guide others. Teachers are forced to examine their true motivations for teaching: Sex? Power? Money? Fame? It will all be exposed. If a person is vain, cruel, or disinterested in students, it's obvious to everyone. People's character is completely transparent, fully visible to others.

Teachers sometimes have to admit when they've made mistakes. It's common for students to confront teachers about some insensitive, critical, or hurtful statement they've made in a class or other teaching situation. A woman with whom I hadn't spoken in ten years called me and said, "In the last yoga class I took from you, I felt that you were impatient with me. And I've been a bit angry at you ever since." Imagine having someone harbor angry thoughts about you for ten years! After our conversation she said, "I'm not angry anymore, but I just needed to tell you." We learn through experience the importance of remaining mindful of our actions and how they'll impact others.

MONEY

Teachers need to keep policies about money fair and clear. I believe that it's totally acceptable for us to want to fulfill certain personal goals and desires—for example, to want adequate financial reward from teaching.

In some cultures spiritual teachers are supported financially by the generosity of followers and by institutions such as monasteries, so often it isn't necessary for them to charge money for teachings. In America, however, it's difficult to survive without money. Thus, teachers can feel justified in charging reasonable fees for their knowledge and guidance. I don't think we have to be completely selfless saints.

Some people may disagree with me on this point, believing that wisdom should be available to everyone free of charge. My policy is to charge what I feel my services (yoga classes, counseling, private instruction) are worth, but if someone wants to work with me and can't afford to pay the requested fee, I try to accommodate them. Sincerity of interest is more important to me than the ability to pay in full.

EXPECT COMPLICATIONS

Our work as teachers brings us into many complex relationships in which we sometimes have to resolve conflicts with others. For example, a woman once called me to say that she had been injured in a yoga class because I encouraged her to do a twisting pose that turned out to be too difficult for her. My first impulse was to dismiss her claim. I hadn't physically touched her, nor had I forced her body into the twist. Wasn't she responsible for her own body? She said that I'd encouraged her to do a posture that was too difficult for her, and therefore, she'd exceeded her capacity and that now her back was sore and she had to visit the chiropractor and it was all my fault. She said, "I told you I had a history of back problems, but you had me do that posture anyway."

For a moment I felt irritated with her. There had been many students in the class, and I didn't remember the complete medical history of each person. Then she became even more upset with me because in the few minutes we'd been speaking on the phone, I hadn't yet offered to refund her money for the series of classes for which she'd registered.

The situation was escalating slightly, but I took a breath and backed off from my initial defensive reaction, trying to listen and empathize with her. I told her I was sorry she'd gotten hurt in class and that I'd send back her money. The situation was resolved harmoniously.

This interaction reminded me of the importance of allowing the student to express complaints and negative feelings, and reacting nonpunitively. I truly didn't feel that I did anything to hurt her, but her experience was that I had. I had to accept some responsibility. It's entirely possible that she'd explained her physical limitations and that I hadn't listened or didn't take her seriously. She later told me that it meant a lot to her that I responded without becoming angry, took her feelings into account, and refunded her money. This experience taught me to not be too quick to dismiss claims of injuries. It taught me to look at myself and my actions carefully, to admit mistakes, and to make amends if necessary.

We can't hide behind our role or reputation as a way to avoid conflict or confrontation with the effects on others of our words or actions. Even masters of spiritual, contemplative disciplines have personalities with shadows and flaws that need to be examined and transformed. The work of teaching others demands continuous exposure and purification of the teacher's own imperfections. Those not willing to keep working on themselves shouldn't become teachers. We don't have to be perfect. We do, however, need to be open to feedback from others. True humility, not false humility, is all that will cut it.

Of course, there are also students who are chronic complainers, who look for any excuse to find someone they can blame for their unhappiness. Such students teach the teacher the lesson of patience. On the other hand, sometimes we need to ask such a student to find another teacher.

AVOID SEXUAL MISCONDUCT

It's important for teachers not to violate the trust that students place in them through sexual misconduct. Life is much simpler for teachers who avoid sexual intimacy with students, and they're less likely to cause pain to themselves or to others.

In reality attractions occur between students and teachers. Some people adamantly insist that a wise teacher will never become intimate with any student. But what about when the student wants to make love with you, and you want to too? Teachers may have many opportunities to get involved with students, so they'd better look closely at their motives and their feelings. It's not that I'm opposed to the idea of spiritual teachers having a social life and their own vibrant relationships. We're all physical beings and sometimes need an outlet for the fulfillment of basic drives and the desire for love and affection. Yet we need to be very clear about what we're doing. In some professions, such as law, medicine, and psychology, there are legal constraints on sexual involvement with clients. In these fields sexual contact between client and practitioner is considered unacceptable behavior on the part of the professional and is often punishable by serious civil or criminal penalties.

For spiritual teachers there are no such explicit and formal laws, except relating to the age of consent. Yet the careers of many highly respected teachers have been tarnished by sexual misconduct. It's not just the fact of engaging in sexual intimacies with students that has led to the downfall of such teachers, but also a broader pattern of deceit and mistreatment of students, who end up feeling used and betrayed, and whose trust in the teacher is often seriously compromised. If a teacher does get involved with a student, then he or she has to prove himself or herself responsible to the other, just as anyone else involved in a caring relationship needs to do. It's exploiting rather than cherishing the other person that often becomes the central issue. Think back to what June Campbell told us earlier. For her the most damaging part of her intimate involvement with her guru, Kalu Rinpoche, was the forced secrecy and hypocrisy that surrounded the relationship.

If a teacher and student discover that they love each other and want to be together and it's not injurious to anyone, that's one thing; but what often happens is the relationship becomes wrapped in secrecy and lies. People had less trouble with the sexual behavior of a teacher such as Chögyam Trungpa because he was open about it, he never hid it, and he never said that he was celibate. He even told his wife about his love affairs, and this was part of their agreement. It's the inconsistency between a teacher's words and deeds that causes others to lose trust in them. And the entire student-teacher relationship is based on trust; without trust the stream of transmission ceases.

It's astonishing how many teachers engage in various forms of sexual harassment and coercion. One renowned yoga teacher fondled students during classes—sometimes while they were lying prone with their eyes closed relaxing at the end of a class. This was an inexcusable violation of boundaries. Swami Rama, a very accomplished yogi, groped his secretaries and awkwardly pounced on them in his quarters. Another teacher was sued in court by several female ex-devotees who claimed he'd forced them to go to bed with him, saying, "You'll never achieve enlightenment unless you do this with me."

AN ARROGANT TEACHER'S DOWNFALL

All who aspire to become spiritual teachers should learn from the cautionary tale of Chögyam Trungpa's disciple and chosen successor, Vajra Regent Osel Tendzin, mentioned in stage seven. An American student of Trungpa's, a prince of the dharma, the inheritor of a powerful lineage, the regent failed completely as a spiritual leader. First there were his irresponsible sexual indiscretions, which were horrendous. There were reports of abuse of cocaine and other drugs. But these were not the only problems. According to Trungpa's wife, Diana Mukpo:

> There were reports of Osel Tendzin being very demanding and heavy-handed with people. People found the Regent to be an accomplished teacher, but he was also extremely critical of students at

times, in ways that they found demeaning and excessively negative.
. . . He had moments when he really shone, . . . but he also had a
kind of street fighter's mentality that dumped a lot of aggression on
others. . . . [H]e seemed to get carried away with who he was. . . .
[S]everal [Vajradhatu] board members took Rinpoche aside and
began complaining to him about the Regent's conduct and their
fears that he was becoming an egomaniac.[2]

Trungpa tried to talk to the regent about his concerns but was
unsuccessful.

[S]till unable to get the Regent's attention, Rinpoche smashed his
hand down on the coffee table . . . and screamed "No!". . . . and the
Regent crumbled at his feet. Rinpoche placed his hands together in
front of the Regent's face. He held up his two hands, cupping them
as if they were holding a treasure. Indicating the space between
hands, with everyone as a witness, he said to the Regent, "This is
the dharma. This is unbelievably precious. And if you pervert the
dharma, I will destroy you. You have to understand that I made you,
and I can destroy you."[3]

In this incredibly powerful moment, Trungpa reminded his student of
the special privilege it is to be a teacher representing a spiritual lineage.
I believe everyone who teaches should think of Trungpa's words and
carry their wisdom treasures with reverence and sufficient humility, as
those who fail to do so may reap the whirlwind—and nobody wants
that.

In 1985 Trungpa planned to move to Nova Scotia with his family, and the regent found a very expensive mansion for his own family
to move into and proceeded to spend hundreds of thousands of dollars of community funds to renovate this house, despite the fact that
Vajradhatu was experiencing financial difficulties. He was apparently
planning to live quite a lavish, opulent lifestyle.

I think that he felt that he was going to assume Rinpoche's role as the head of the community, . . . and this was the kind of house that he envisioned for himself when *he* was in charge. . . . Rinpoche had heard all the complaints . . . but he had not done anything. . . . Then, in one fell swoop, he dealt with the whole problem. He sent a senior student . . . to deliver the message to the Regent that Rinpoche was moving to Halifax and would need his house. Then Rinpoche phoned the Regent to confirm this. Of course, the money had already been spent, but the Regent didn't get to live in the luxurius palace he had built for himself. As it turned out, he was building it for his teacher, a twist that was not lost on many of us. . . . [T]he Regent suffered terribly after Rinpoche's phone call. . . . [H]e became angry and distraught and descended into a depression that lasted for days. He didn't want to give up his house, but Rinpoche was the one person he couldn't say no to. I heard that he threw things around that night after the call, he was so angry. . . . [Later, Rinpoche] said, "The situation with the Regent is terrible. We've got to dismantle him."[4]

Trungpa's fierce crazy wisdom was directed toward a disciple whose ego had run amuck with hubris, greed, and presumptuousness. These are always dangers for anyone who carries the enlivened energy and expansive presence that spiritual practices can generate. Therefore, spiritual guides who wish to never fall prey to such behaviors will see the value of always continuing to look at their own shadows. Here someone psychologically unprepared for the mantle of leadership became deluded into thinking he was impervious to the consequences of his actions, thinking he could put his own comfort above the well-being of his community. Even highly accomplished and fully initiated teachers can fall into the pit of conceit, arrogance, and inflation. Fortunately, Tendzin's teacher was still monitoring his student's progress and tested him and effectively exposed his ego and self-cherishing attitude. Wise teachers always remember that they're here to serve, not to lord it over others.

The mansion of honor is reserved for those teachers who truly love their students and the practices they undertake together.

THE ART OF SPIRITUAL DIRECTION

A final insight emerges through reflection on the nature of spiritual direction within the Christian tradition. In Catholicism the teacher-student relationship takes the form of the Act of Confession. Here a clergyman serves as an impartial listener, providing an experience of purification by allowing the person's expression of conscience, and also providing specific moral, behavioral, and spiritual guidance. Monks and nuns receive more in-depth guidance in contemplative prayer from a spiritual director who oversees the novice's inner spiritual life. Catholic priests William Barry and William Connolly write:

> Spiritual direction is concerned with helping a person directly with his or her relationship with God. . . . The ministering person helps the other to address God directly and to listen to what God has to communicate. . . . The focus of this kind of spiritual direction is the relationship itself between God and the person. The person is helped not so much to understand the relationship better, but to engage in it, to enter into dialogue with God. Spiritual direction of this kind focuses on what happens when a person listens to and responds to a self-communicating God.[5]

Barry and Connolly suggest that spiritual direction shouldn't focus on the personality of the teacher or director, who is there only as a reminder, to point the student inward, toward direct communion with the true source of blessing and guidance. This understanding of spiritual guidance contrasts with the tendency to focus excessively on the teacher's personality. The teacher shouldn't become the primary focus of the student's attention. Instead, the teacher's job is to help the aspirant become receptive to the inner revelation of the great mystery. Moreover, spiritual direction need not involve enslavement of the student to the will of the teacher. Barry and Connolly note, "The person who receives direction must always retain personal responsibility, and the mode and content of sound direction will help him to retain and develop personal responsibility, not make it more difficult for him to do so."[6]

I find this approach quite healthy, both in emphasizing the student's responsibility and in providing a helpful guideline for teachers. We've seen that there are some teachers who, as a result of their advanced spiritual attainment, are able to serve as agencies for transmission. The rest of us, who know that we can best serve others as "helpful guides," direct the attention of our students toward the truth within themselves.

❧

The greatest test of teaching others is maintaining transparency to the light of Being, which is always the ultimate source of guidance. This is the high road on which one strives, by example and vibrational influence, to move forward with others toward a more evolved state of consciousness. The teacher is an instrument and visible embodiment of the eternal archetype of the Sage—a messenger of the truth that's greater than any human guide.

The Cycle of Apprenticeship Complete

This book has explored the full cycle of spiritual apprenticeship and mentorship. We approach a teacher for instruction and then learn that the guide is none other than our own spacious and serene awareness. We have reached the destination always sought, transformed by knowledge of our innate Being, inwardly illumined by the methods and practice of self-liberation, emerging from the chrysalis with an open heart that honors and respects all beings. Nisargadatta Maharaj said:

> Life itself is the Supreme Guru; be attentive to its lessons and obedient to its commands. When you personalize their source, you have an outer Guru; when you take them from life directly, the Guru is within. Your own self is your ultimate teacher. . . . It is only your inner teacher that will walk with you to the goal.[1]

The company of Sages bestows a luminous transmission. Looking back, I'm amazed at how deeply my life has been touched by this process, and I feel fortunate to have experienced being part of this timeless sacred tradition of initiatory relationship, a tree of knowledge that ceaselessly extends its climbing branches.

Notes

INTRODUCTION.
THE CATALYZING ROLE OF TEACHERS

1. Feuerstein, *Holy Madness.*
2. Levinson, *The Seasons of a Man's Life* and *The Seasons of a Woman's Life.*
3. Rossman, *New Age Blues,* 54–55.
4. Kramer and Alstad, *The Guru Papers,* 41.
5. Ibid., 99.
6. Harvey, "Teachers and Seekers."
7. Welwood, "On Spiritual Authority," 293.

STAGE ONE. CHOOSING A TEACHER

1. Chang, *The Hundred Thousand Songs of Milarepa,* 51.
2. Halifax, *Shamanic Voices.*
3. Schimmel, *Mystical Dimensions of Islam,* 237.
4. Ibid., 100–101.
5. Scholem, *On the Kabbalah and Its Symbolism,* 18.
6. Wilber, "Pathologies of the Spiritual Path."
7. De Bary, *Sources of Indian Tradition,* 329.
8. Mascaro, *Bhagavad Gita,* 64.
9. Prem, *The Yoga of the Bhagavat Gita,* 34–36.
10. De Bary, *Sources of Indian Tradition,* 16.
11. Krishna, *Kundalini: The Evolutionary Power in Man*; Avalon, *The Serpent Power.*
12. Frawley, "All Gurus Great and Small," 28.
13. Murphy, *The Future of the Body.*
14. Ibid., 47.

281

15. Renard, "Islamic Tradition of Spiritual Guidance," 62.

16. Ibid., 62, 64.

17. Cited in Feuerstein, *Yoga,* 25.

18. Dass, *Grist for the Mill,* 81.

19. Godman, *Living by the Words of Bhagavan,* 278.

20. Dabholkar, *Shri Sai Satcharita,* 44, 59, 107, 150–51, 154–55.

21. Khan, "What Is Initiation?," 10.

22. Rumi, *This Longing,* 18.

23. Islamic saying, cited in Schimmel, *Mystical Dimensions of Islam,* 190.

24. Nikhilananda, *The Gospel of Sri Ramakrishna.*

25. Welwood, "On Spiritual Authority," 292–93.

26. Frawley, "All Gurus Great and Small," 28.

27. Muller-Ortega, *The Triadic Heart of Siva,* 164–66.

28. Govinda, *Foundations of Tibetan Mysticism,* 90.

29. Lerner, *Journey of Insight Meditation.*

30. Kapleau, *The Three Pillars of Zen,* 96.

31. Ibid., 54, 93, 94.

32. Goleman, "Early Warning Signs," 127–28.

33. Scholem, *On the Mystical Shape of the Godhead,* 127.

34. Scholem, *The Messianic Idea in Judaism,* 4.

35. Scholem, *Sabbatai Sevi,* 132.

36. Wiesel, *Souls on Fire,* 13.

37. Ibid., 7–8.

38. Buber, *Tales of the Hasidim.*

39. Wiesel, *Souls on Fire,* 19–20.

40. Ibid., 26–27.

STAGE TWO. INITIATION

1. Schimmel, *Mystical Dimensions of Islam,* 102, 234.

2. Khan, "What is Initiation?," 7.

3. Khan, "The Link with the Spiritual Hierarchy," 8–9, 23–25.

4. Schimmel, *Mystical Dimensions of Islam,* 105–6.

5. Feuerstein, *Yoga,* 25, 27.

6. Ibid., 28–29.

7. Tirth, "Signs of an Awakened Kundalini," 94–97. For more on the symptoms of awakened kundalini, see Sannella, *The Kundalini Experience.*

8. Poonja, *Truth Is,* 75.

9. Khan, *The Path of Initiation,* 62 ff.

10. Ibid., 74.
11. Ibid., 67.
12. Ibid., 68.
13. Ibid., 77, 97.

STAGE THREE. DISCIPLESHIP

1. Lorenzen, *Kabir Legends.*
2. Heruka, *The Life of Milarepa.*
3. Feuerstein, *Yoga,* 26.
4. Khan, *The Complete Sayings of Hazrat Inayat Khan,* 127.
5. Cited in Needleman, *On the Way to Self Knowledge,* 109.
6. Godman, *Living by the Words of Bhagavan,* 335.
7. Maharshi, *Talks with Sri Ramana Maharshi,* 370, 501.
8. Hixon, *Great Swan.*
9. Happold, *Mysticism,* 56–57, 59.
10. St. John of the Cross, *The Dark Night of the Soul.*
11. Ibid.
12. Roy and Devi, *Pilgrims of the Stars.*
13. Khan, *The Complete Sayings of Hazrat Inayat Khan,* 128.
14. Mansfield, "The Guru-Disciple Relationship."
15. Frawley, "All Gurus Great and Small," 34.
16. Sayle, "Nerve Gas and The Four Noble Truths."
17. Singer, *Cults in our Midst.*
18. See Lifton, *Thought Reform and the Psychology of Totalism;* and Lifton, "Cults: Religious Totalism and Civil Liberties."
19. Hassan, *Combatting Cult Mind Control,* 7.
20. Ibid., 54–55.
21. Ibid., 61.
22. Ibid., 62.
23. Ibid., 64.
24. Ibid., 5.
25. Ibid.

STAGE FOUR. TESTING

1. Guenther, *The Life and Teaching of Nāropa,* 80.
2. Feuerstein, *Holy Madness,* xxiii, 3, 204.
3. Asher, "When Hippies Battle."
4. Ouspensky, *In Search of the Miraculous,* 351–56.
5. Taimni, *The Science of Yoga,* 142.

6. Shankara, *Crest Jewel of Discrimination*, 80–81.

7. Arguelles and Arguelles, *The Feminine*, 46.

8. For more see Benard, *Chinnamasta*.

9. Heruka, *The Life of Milarepa*.

10. Khan, *The Complete Sayings of Hazrat Inayat Khan*, 16, 20.

11. Eckhart, "The Talks of Instruction," 15–16, 115–17, 121–22.

12. Radha, "Dispelling Illusions," 8.

13. Welwood, "On Spiritual Authority," 296–97.

STAGE FIVE.
GRACE AND GURU YOGA

1. Feuerstein, *Yoga*, 25.

2. Ibid.

3. Otto, *The Idea of the Holy*, 11–13.

4. Ibid., 20.

5. Ibid., 26.

6. Ibid., 31.

7. Anthony, "The Anthony Typology," 82 ff.

8. Ibid.

9. Hughes, *Self Realization in Kashmir Shaivism*, 32.

10. Eliade, *A History of Religious Ideas*, 342, 347–48.

11. Schimmel, *Mystical Dimensions of Islam*, 205.

12. Richard Gale, personal communication.

13. Schimmel, *Mystical Dimensions of Islam*, 103, 237.

14. Taimni, *The Science of Yoga*.

15. Ibid., 22–23.

16. Muktananda, *Play of Consciousness*, 38 ff.

17. Kane, "The Art of Spiritual Guidance."

18. Govinda, *Foundations of Tibetan Mysticism*, 96–97.

19. Khyentse, *The Wish-Fulfilling Jewel*, 56.

20. Ibid., 8–9.

21. Ibid., 70–71.

22. Rinbochay, *Tantric Practice in Nying-Ma*, 179.

23. Rick Amaro, personal communication. The quotation from Padmasambhava is from Evans-Wentz, *The Tibetan Book of the Great Liberation*, 232.

24. Trungpa, *Crazy Wisdom*, 25–30.

25. Ibid., 18.

26. Ibid., 34.

STAGE SIX. AT THE THRESHOLD OF AWAKENING

1. Shankara, *Crest Jewel of Discrimination*, 4.
2. Deikman, "Deautomatization and the Mystic Experience."
3. James, "The Varieties of Religious Experience," in Happold, *Mysticism*, 138–39.
4. Shankara, *Crest Jewel of Discrimination*, 52–54, 91.
5. White, *What is Enlightenment?*, xii–xiv.
6. Conze, *Buddhism*, 204.
7. Maharshi, *Day by Day with Bhagavan*, 52, 101, 111, 191, 195–96.
8. Brunton, in Maharshi, *Day by Day with Bhagavan*, 97–98.
9. White, *What is Enlightenment?*, xv.
10. Shankara, *Crest Jewel of Discrimination*, 36, 42–43.
11. Nelson, "Living Liberation in Sankara and Classical Advaita."
12. Godman, *Living by the Words of Bhagavan*, 259–60.
13. Eliade, *Autobiography*, 185.
14. Ibid., 198.
15. Ibid., 198–99.
16. Bogart, *Finding Your Life's Calling*.

STAGE SEVEN.
SEPARATING FROM A SPIRITUAL TEACHER

1. Levinson, *The Seasons of a Man's Life*, 101.
2. Ibid., 147.
3. Wilber, "The Spectrum Model," in Anthony, Ecker, and Wilber, *Spiritual Choices*, 249.
4. Progoff, *The Death and Rebirth of Psychology*, 188.
5. Ibid., 192–95.
6. Engler, "Therapeutic Aims in Psychotherapy and Meditation," in Wilber, Engler, and Brown, *Transformations of Consciousness*.
7. Wilber, *The Atman Project*.
8. See Needleman, *On the Road to Self Knowledge;* Welwood, "Reflections on Psychotherapy"; Welwood, "On Psychotherapy and Meditation"; Kornfield, Ram Dass, and Miyuki, "Psychological Adjustment Is Not Liberation"; Kornfield, "Even the Best Meditators Have Old Wounds to Heal"; and Bogart, "The Use of Meditation in Psychotherapy."
9. Wittine, "Basic Postulates for a Transpersonal Psychotherapy."
10. Kohut and Wolf, "The Disorders of the Self and Their Treatment."
11. Jacoby, *The Analytic Encounter*.

12. Kohut and Wolf, "The Disorders of the Self and Their Treatment," 421.

13. Sandner, "The Split Shadow and the Father-Son Relationship."

14. Ibid., 180.

15. Progoff, *The Death and Rebirth of Psychology,* 189.

16. Hillman, "Senex and Puer."

17. Bogart, *Finding Your Life's Calling.*

18. Menaker, *Otto Rank.*

19. Ibid., 35.

20. Sandner, "The Split Shadow and the Father-Son Relationship."

21. Ibid.

22. Kegan, *The Evolving Self.*

23. Ibid., 129.

24. Ram Dass, *Grist for the Mill,* 71–72.

25. Ruhela, *Sri Shirdi Sai Baba,* 109.

26. Feuerstein, *Holy Madness,* 213, 215, 228, 229.

27. Butler, "Encountering the Shadow in Buddhist America."

28. Ibid., 18.

29. Rodarmor, "The Secret Life of Swami Muktananda."

30. Feuerstein, *Holy Madness,* 142.

31. Caldwell, "The Heart of the Secret," 18.

32. Ibid., 30.

33. Rutter, *Sex in the Forbidden Zone.*

34. Harris, "O Guru, Guru, Guru," 97.

35. Caldwell, "The Heart of the Secret," 10.

36. K. C. Pandey cited in Caldwell, "The Heart of the Secret," 13.

37. Ibid., 25, 36.

38. Ibid., 35.

39. Tweedie, *The Chasm of Fire.*

40. Goldberg, *Being of Two Minds.*

41. Wilson, *Sacred Drift,* 106.

42. Campbell, "The Emperor's Tantric Robes," 40, 42–43.

43. Kornfield, *A Path with Heart.*

44. Maharshi, *Talks with Sri Ramana Maharshi,* 241.

45. Hine, "Self-Created Ceremonies of Passage."

46. Butler, "Encountering the Shadow in Buddhist America."

STAGE EIGHT. FINDING THE TEACHER WITHIN

1. Bogart, *Finding Your Life's Calling.*

2. Wilson, *Sacred Drift,* 103–19.

3. Corbin, *Avicenna and the Visionary Recital;* and Hoeller, *The Gnostic Jung and the Seven Sermons to the Dead.*

4. Rumi, *Unseen Rain,* 25.

5. Bogart, "Profile of Allan Bateman."

6. Bogart, "How to Learn From an Injury."

7. Lasater, *Relax and Renew.*

8. Bogart, "Rudhyar's Astrology in Plain Language," 81–116.

9. In Barbara Somerfield's, "To Dane Rudhyar, Who Inspired My First Steps on the Path."

10. Maharshi, *Day by Day with Bhagavan,* 82.

11. Bogart, *Astrology and Spiritual Awakening,* 1.

12. See my books *Astrology and Spiritual Awakening, Astrology and Meditation,* and *Planets in Therapy.*

13. Some good resources: Klimo, *Channeling;* and Hastings, *With the Tongues of Men and Angels.*

14. Schimmel, *Mystical Dimensions of Islam,* 102.

15. Ibid., 105–6.

16. Corbin, *Avicenna and the Visionary Recital,* 22–23.

17. Ibid.

18. Ibid., 20–21, 44.

19. Aurobindo, *The Essential Aurobindo,* 139–40, 142–43.

20. See Forte, *Entheogens and the Future of Religion.*

21. Anderson, *Peyote.*

22. See Vissell and Vissell, *The Shared Heart;* and Welwood, *Challenge of the Heart.*

23. This is a passage from one of my unpublished poems.

STAGE NINE. TEACHING OTHERS

1. Khan, *The Complete Sayings of Hazrat Inayat Khan,* 131.

2. Mukpo, *Dragon Thunder,* 293, 303, 309.

3. Ibid., 311

4. Ibid., 374–75, 378.

5. Barry and Connolly, *The Practice of Spiritual Direction,* 5–8.

6. Ibid., 10, 43.

EPILOGUE.
THE CYCLE OF APPRENTICESHIP COMPLETE

1. Maharaj, *I Am That,* 131, 51.

Glossary

apocalypticism: The belief in the imminent end of the world

Atman: The Self or soul, the changeless reality, all-pervasive consciousness

axis mundi: The world axis, world pillar, or world tree

bhastrika: Bellows breath, a form of pranayama

bhikkhu: A monk; *bhikkhuni,* a nun

bodhicitta: The intention to develop a clear mind and compassion and to strive for enlightenment for the benefit of all sentient beings

bodhisattva: In Buddhism an enlightened being who, motivated by great compassion, has generated bodhicitta, the spontaneous wish to attain buddhahood for the benefit of all sentient beings

brahmacharin: The chaste student; celibate for spiritual purposes

Brahman: The Absolute

crazy wisdom: A Buddhist path and form of conduct that includes what is perceived by ordinary people to be seemingly irrational, unconventional, or outrageous actions, but which are in fact part of the enlightened master's methodology to reach liberation

darshan: The beholding of a sacred person (or deity or sacred object), said to confer blessings

dharmakaya: "Truth body" or "reality body"; a Tibetan Buddhist term signifying the unmanifested, inconceivable aspect of a buddha, out of which buddhas arise and to which they return after their dissolution

diksha: In the Indian yogic tradition, an initiation, also called *shaktipat diksha*

dokusan: An interview where the teacher examines the student's experiences in meditation and tests the student's understanding of the dharma

guru tattva: The guru principle or the guru function in the Indian yogic tradition of Kashmir Shaivism

guru yoga: Deliberate psychic merger or union with the teacher

hierophany: The manifestation of the divine or the sacred, especially as a sacred place, object, or occasion

kenshō: Initial insight or awakening but not yet complete enlightenment

kirtan: Chanting of divine names

koan: In Zen Buddhism paradoxes to be meditated on to train in abandoning ultimate dependence on reason and to force the meditator into gaining sudden intuitive enlightenment

mala: A string of prayer beads

maya: Sanskrit term for illusion or deception

messianism: The hope for the advent of a religious and political leader who will be the savior and liberator of the people

murti: The sacred form of perfect being, consciousness, and bliss

ngöndro: Tibetan Buddhist preliminary or foundational practices

prajna: Buddhist term for wisdom

pranayama: Yogic breathing

roshi: A highly venerated senior teacher in Zen Buddhism

sadguru: The "true guru" or saint

sadhu: A holy man

samsara: The cycle of birth, death, and eternal rebirth

satori: A deeper spiritual experience of enlightenment; often used interchangeably with *kenshō,* but satori is a more profound or stabilized experience

satsang: The company of a guru; the company of the "highest truth"

shakti: Spiritual power

shaktipat: "Descent of the power"; in the Indian yogic tradition, the conferring of spiritual energy on one person by another; transmission of spiritual power that awakens the student's dormant kundalini energy

shastra: Sacred scriptures and teachings

siddha: One who is accomplished, "perfected one"; an adept who has been transformed through spiritual practice and realization to such an extent that extraordinary powers and psychic abilities manifest through this person

siddhis: Yogic powers

sunyata: The space of emptiness, openness, spaciousness beyond the ego, wherein one perceives a union of form and emptiness

tapas: "Heat" or "burning"; in yoga vigorous practices such as asanas, chanting, mental concentration exercises, or physical cleansing regimens that eliminate impurities of body and mind and prepare the body and psyche to hold the energies of intensive meditation

thangka: A religious painting on a fabric scroll, usually depicting a religious deity, scene, or mandala

tulku: In Tibetan Buddhism a reincarnated lama

tzaddik: "The righteous one"; Jewish spiritual figure and visionary possessing extraordinary powers who provides spiritual and prophetic leadership to his community

upaya: A concept of Buddhism that refers to any activity, skill, experience, or practice that helps someone toward the realization of enlightenment; sometimes called *skillful means*

vidyadhara: A powerful tantric master believed to be endowed with magical or supernatural powers

vipassana: Insight meditation

yidam: An enlightened being or chosen deity who is the focus of meditation

zazen: In Zen Buddhism seated meditation involving focusing on the breath, contemplation of a koan, and eventually just sitting in a state of nonthinking

Bibliography

Anderson, Edward. *Peyote: The Divine Cactus.* Tucson, Ariz.: University of Arizona Press, 1980.

Anthony, Dick, Bruce Ecker, and Ken Wilber, editors. "The Anthony Typology: A Framework for Assessing Spiritual and Consciousness Groups." In *Spiritual Choices: The Problem of Recognizing Authentic Paths to Inner Transformation.* New York: Paragon House, 1987.

Arguelles, Miriam, and Jose Arguelles. *The Feminine: Spacious as the Sky.* Boston: Shambhala Publications, 1977.

Asher, Levi. "When Hippies Battle: The Great W. S. Merwin/Allen Ginsberg Beef of 1975." *Literary Kicks*, www.litkicks.com. Originally published November 17, 2005.

Aurobindo, Sri. *The Essential Aurobindo,* edited by Robert McDermott. New York: Schocken, 1973.

Avalon, Arthur. *The Serpent Power: The Secrets of Tantric and Shaktic Yoga.* New York: Dover, 1974.

Barry, William, and William Connolly. *The Practice of Spiritual Direction.* San Francisco: Harper and Row, 1982.

Benard, Elizabeth Anne. *Chinnamasta: The Aweful Buddhist and Hindu Tantric Goddess.* Delhi, India: Motilal Banarsidass, 2000.

Bogart, Greg. *Astrology and Meditation: The Fearless Contemplation of Change.* Bournemouth, UK: Wessex Astrologer, 2002.

———. *Astrology and Spiritual Awakening.* 2nd ed. Tempe, Ariz.: American Federation of Astrologers, 2014.

———. *Dreamwork and Self-Healing: Unfolding the Symbols of the Unconscious.* London: Karnac, 2009.

———. *Finding Your Life's Calling: Spiritual Dimensions of Vocational Choice.* Berkeley, Calif.: Dawn Mountain Press, 1995.

———. "How to Learn from an Injury." *Yoga Journal,* May-June 1992, 28–29.

———. *Planets in Therapy: Predictive Technique and the Art of Counseling.* Lake Worth, Fla.: Ibis Press, 2012.

———. "Profile of Allan Bateman." *Yoga Journal,* September-October 1988, 32–33.

———. "Rudhyar's Astrology in Plain Language." Chapter 3 in *Planets in Therapy: Predictive Technique and the Art of Counseling.* Lake Worth, Fla.: Ibis, 2012.

———. "The Use of Meditation in Psychotherapy: A Review of the Literature." *American Journal of Psychotherapy* 45 (1991): 383–412.

Buber, Martin. *Tales of the Hasidim.* New York: Schocken, 1947.

Butler, Katy, "Encountering the Shadow in Buddhist America." *Common Boundary,* May-June 1990, 14–22.

Caldwell, Sarah, "The Heart of the Secret: A Personal and Scholarly Encounter with Shakta Tantrism in Siddha Yoga." *Nova Religio* 5, no. 1, 2001.

Campbell, June. "The Emperor's Tantric Robes: An Interview with June Campbell on Codes of Secrecy and Silence." *Tricycle,* Winter 1996, 38–46.

Chang, Garma, trans. *The Hundred Thousand Songs of Milarepa.* New York: Harper and Row, 1962.

Conze, Edward. *Buddhism: Its Essence and Development.* New York: Harper Colophon Books, 1975.

Corbin, Henri. *Avicenna and the Visionary Recital.* Dallas, Tex.: Spring Publications, 1980.

Dabholkar, Govind. *Shri Sai Satcharita: The Life and Teachings of Shirdi Sai Baba.* New Delhi: Sterling, 1999.

Dass, Ram. *Grist for the Mill.* Santa Cruz, Calif.: Unity Press, 1977.

De Bary, William Theodore, editor. *Sources of Indian Tradition.* New York: Columbia University Press, 1958.

Deikman, Arthur. "Deautomatization and the Mystic Experience." *Psychiatry* 29 (1966): 324–88.

Eckhart, Meister. "The Talks of Instruction." In *Meister Eckhart: A Modern Translation,* translated by R. B. Blakney. New York: Harper and Row, 1941.

Eliade, Mircea. *Autobiography.* Vol. 1, *1907–1937, Journey East, Journey West.* New York: Harper and Row, 1981.

———. *A History of Religious Ideas.* Vol. 2, *From Gautama Buddha to the Triumph of Christianity.* Chicago: University of Chicago Press, 1982.

Engler, Jack. "Therapeutic Aims in Psychotherapy and Meditation." In Ken Wilber, Jack Engler, and Daniel Brown, editors, *Transformations of Consciousness.* Boston: Shambhala Publications, 1986.

Evans-Wentz, W. Y. *The Tibetan Book of the Great Liberation*. New York: Oxford University Press, 1970.

Feuerstein, Georg. *Yoga: The Technology of Ecstasy*. Los Angeles: Jeremy Tarcher, 1989.

———. *Holy Madness*. New York: Paragon House, 1991.

Forte, Robert, editor. *Entheogens and the Future of Religion*. Rochester, Vt.: Park Street Press, 2012.

Frawley, David. "All Gurus Great and Small." *Yoga Journal*, March-April 1997, 28–35.

Godman, David. *Living by the Words of Bhagavan*. Tiruvannamalai, India: Sri Annamalai Swami Ashram Trust, 1995.

Goldberg, Arnold. *Being of Two Minds: The Vertical Split in Psychoanalysis and Psychotherapy*. Hillsdale, N.J.: Analytic Press, 1999.

Goleman, Daniel. "Early Warning Signs for the Detection of Spiritual Blight." *Yoga Journal*, July-August 1985, 23.

Govinda, Lama Anagarika. *Foundations of Tibetan Mysticism*. New York: Samuel Weiser, 1969.

Grof, Stanislav. *Beyond the Brain*. Albany, N.Y.: State University of New York Press, 1985.

Guenther, Herbert, translator. *The Life and Teaching of Nāropa*. New York: Oxford University Press, 1963.

Halifax, Joan. *Shamanic Voices*. New York: Dutton, 1979.

Happold, F. Crossfield. *Mysticism: A Study and an Anthology*. Middlesex, England: Penguin, 1963.

Harris, Liz. "O Guru, Guru, Guru." *The New Yorker*, November 14, 1994, 92–109.

Harvey, Andrew. "Teachers and Seekers: An Interview with Andrew Harvey." *Yoga Journal*, August 1995, 56–63, 152–53.

Hassan, Steven. *Combatting Cult Mind Control*. Rochester, Vt.: Park Street Press, 1990.

Hastings, Arthur. *With the Tongues of Men and Angels*. Ft. Worth, Tex.: Holt, Rinehart and Winston, 1991.

Heruka. *The Life of Milarepa*, translated by Lobsang Llalungpa. New York: Penguin, 1992.

Hillman, James. "Senex and Puer." In *Puer Papers*, edited by James Hillman. Dallas, Tex.: Spring Publications, 1979.

Hine, Virginia. "Self-Created Ceremonies of Passage." In *Betwixt and Between: Patterns of Masculine and Feminine Initiation*, edited by Louise Mahdi, Steven Foster, and Meredith Little. LaSalle, Ill.: Open Court, 1987.

Hixon, Lex. *Great Swan: Meetings with Ramakrishna*. Boston: Shambhala Publications, 1992.

Hoeller, Stephen. *The Gnostic Jung and the Seven Sermons to the Dead*. Wheaton, Ill.: Quest Publications, 1982.

Hughes, John. *Self Realization in Kashmir Shaivism: The Oral Teachings of Swami Lakshmanjoo*. Albany, N.Y.: State University of New York Press, 1994.

Iyengar, B. K. S. *Light on Yoga*. New York: Schocken, 1965.

Jacoby, Mario. *The Analytic Encounter: Transference and Human Relationship*. Toronto: Inner City Books, 1984.

Kane, Atum. "The Art of Spiritual Guidance." In *Sufism, Islam, and Jungian Psychology*, Joseph Spiegelman, editor. Scottsdale, Ariz.: Falcon Press, 1991.

Kapleau, Roshi Philip. *The Three Pillars of Zen: Teaching, Practice, and Enlightenment*. Garden City, N.Y.: Anchor, 1980.

Kegan, Robert. *The Evolving Self: Problem and Process in Human Development*. Cambridge, Mass.: Harvard University Press, 1982.

Khan, Hazrat Inayat. *The Complete Sayings of Hazrat Inayat Khan*. New Lebanon, N.Y.: Sufi Order Publications, 1991.

———. "The Link with the Spiritual Hierarchy." In *Initiation*. New Lebanon, N.Y.: Sufi Order Publications, 1980.

———. *The Path of Initiation*. Katwik, Holland: Servire, 1979.

———. "The Sacred Link." In *Initiation*. New Lebanon, N.Y.: Sufi Order Publications, 1980.

Khan, Pir Vilayat Inayat. "What Is Initiation?" In *Initiation*. New Lebanon, N.Y.: Sufi Order Publications, 1980.

Khyentse, Dilgo, Rinpoche. *The Wish-Fulfilling Jewel*. Boston: Shambhala Publications, 1988.

Klimo, Jon. *Channeling: Investigations on Receiving Information from Paranormal Sources*. Los Angeles: Jeremy Tarcher, 1987.

Kohut, Heinz, and Ernest Wolf. "The Disorders of the Self and Their Treatment: An Outline." *International Journal of Psychoanalysis* 59 (1978): 413–25.

Kornfield, Jack. *A Path with Heart: A Guide through the Perils and Promises of Spiritual Life*. New York: Bantam, 1993.

———. "Even the Best Meditators Have Old Wounds to Heal." *Yoga Journal*. September–October 1989, 46.

Kornfield, Jack, Ram Dass, and M. Miyuki. "Psychological Adjustment Is Not Liberation." *Zero: Contemporary Buddhist Life and Thought* 2 (1979): 72–87.

Kramer, Joel, and Diana Alstad. *The Guru Papers: Masks of Authoritarian Power*. Berkeley, Calif.: Frog Ltd., 1993.

Krippner, Stanley. *Dreamtime and Dreamwork*. Los Angeles: Jeremy Tarcher, 1990.

Krishna, Gopi. *Kundalini: The Evolutionary Power in Man*. Boston: Shambhala Publications, 1970.

Lasater, Judith. *Relax and Renew: Restful Yoga for Stressful Times*. Berkeley, Calif.: Rodmell Press, 1995.

Lerner, Eric. *Journey of Insight Meditation: A Personal Experience of the Buddha's Way*. New York: Schocken, 1977.

Levinson, Daniel. *The Seasons of a Man's Life*. New York: Ballantine, 1978.

———. *The Seasons of a Woman's Life*. New York: Ballantine, 1996.

Lifton, Robert Jay. *Thought Reform and the Psychology of Totalism: A Study of "Brainwashing" in China*. New York: Norton, 1961.

———. "Cults: Religious Totalism and Civil Liberties." In *The Future of Immortality and Other Essays for a Nuclear Age*. New York: Basic Books, 1987.

Lorenzen, David. *Kabir Legends and Ananta-Das's Kabir Parachai*. Albany, N.Y.: State University of New York Press, 1991.

Maharaj, Nisargadatta. *I Am That*. Durham, N.C.: Acorn Press, 1973.

Maharshi, Ramana. *Day by Day with Bhagavan*. Tiruvannamalai, India: Sri Ramanasramam, 1968.

———. *Talks with Sri Ramana Maharshi*. Tiruvannamalai, India: Sri Ramanasramam, 1984.

Mansfield, Victor. "The Guru-Disciple Relationship: Making Connections and Withdrawing Projections." Unpublished paper. Available at www.lightlink.com/vic/guru.html.

Mascaro, Juan, translator. *The Bhagavad Gita*. Middlesex, England: Penguin Books, 1962.

Menaker, Edith. *Otto Rank: A Rediscovered Legacy*. New York: Columbia University Press, 1982.

Mukpo, Diana. *Dragon Thunder: My Life with Chögyam Trungpa*. Boston, Shambhala Publications, 2006.

Muktananda, Swami. *Play of Consciousness: A Spiritual Autobiography*. 1st ed. Oakland, Calif.: SYDA Foundation, 1974.

Muller-Ortega, Paul. *The Triadic Heart of Siva: Kaula Tantricism of Abhinavagupta in the Non-Dual Shaivism of Kashmir*. Albany, N.Y.: State University of New York Press, 1988.

Murphy, Michael. *The Future of the Body*. Los Angeles: Jeremy Tarcher, 1992.

Needleman, Jacob, and Dennis Lewis, editors. *On the Way to Self Knowledge*. New York: Alfred Knopf, 1976.

Nelson, Lance. "Living Liberation in Sankara and Classical Advaita." In *Living Liberation in Hindu Thought*, edited by Andrew Fort and Patricia Mumme, 17–62. Albany, N.Y.: State University of New York Press, 1996.

Nikhilananda, Swami. *The Gospel of Sri Ramakrishna*. New York: Ramakrishna Vedanta Center, 1974.

Otto, Rudolph. *The Idea of the Holy*. New York: Oxford University Press, 1950.

Ouspensky, P. D. *In Search of the Miraculous*. New York: Harcourt Brace and World, 1949.

Poonja, H. W. L. *Truth Is*. Huntington Beach, Calif.: Yudhishtara, 1995.

Prem, Krishna. *The Yoga of the Bhagavat Gita*. Baltimore: Penguin Books, 1958.

Progoff, Ira. *The Death and Rebirth of Psychology: An Integrative Evaluation of Freud, Adler, Jung, and Rank and the Impact of Their Culminating Insights on Modern Man*. New York: Julian Press, 1956.

Rinbochay, Khetsun Sangpo. *Tantric Practice in Nying-Ma*, translated by Jeffrey Hopkins. Ithaca, N.Y.: Snow Lion Press, 1982.

Radha, Swami. "Dispelling Illusions: The Guru-Disciple Relationship." *Ascent*, Spring 1992, 4–11.

Renard, John. "Islamic Tradition of Spiritual Guidance," *The Way* 28, no. 1, January 1988, 60–68.

Rodarmor, William. "The Secret Life of Swami Muktananda." *CoEvolution Quarterly*, Winter 1983, 104–11.

Rossman, Michael. *New Age Blues: On the Politics of Consciousness*. New York: Dutton, 1979.

Roy, Dilip Kumar, and Indira Devi. *Pilgrims of the Star*. New York: Dell, 1973.

Rudhyar, Dane. *An Astrological Mandala*. New York: Vintage, 1973.

Ruhela, S. P. *Sri Shirdi Sai Baba: The Universal Master*. New Delhi: Sterling, 1994.

Rumi. *This Longing*, translated by Coleman Barks and John Moyne. Putney, Vt.: Threshold Books, 1988.

———. *Unseen Rain*, translated by John Moyne and Coleman Barks. Putney, Vt.: Threshold Books, 1986.

Rutter, Peter. *Sex in the Forbidden Zone: When Men in Power—Therapists, Doctors, Clergy, Teachers, and Others—Betray Women's Trust*. New York: Fawcett, 1991.

Sandner, Donald. "The Split Shadow and the Father-Son Relationship." In *Betwixt and Between: Patterns of Masculine and Feminine Initiation*, edited by Louise Mahdi, Steven Foster, and Meredith Little, 175–88. LaSalle, Ill.: Open Court, 1987.

Sannella, Lee. *The Kundalini Experience*. Lower Lake, Calif.: Integral Publishing, 1987.

Sayle, Murray. "Nerve Gas and The Four Noble Truths." *The New Yorker*, April 1996, 56–71.

Schimmel, Annemarie. *Mystical Dimensions of Islam*. Chapel Hill, N.C.: University of North Carolina Press, 1975.

Scholem, Gerschom. *The Messianic Idea in Judaism*. New York: Shocken, 1971.

———. *On the Kabbalah and Its Symbolism*. New York: Schocken, 1969.

———. *On the Mystical Shape of the Godhead: Basic Concepts of the Kabbalah*. New York: Schocken, 1991.

———. *Sabbatai Sevi: The Mystical Messiah*, translated by R. J. Zwi Werblowsky. Princeton, N.J.: Princeton University Press, 1973.

Shankara. *Crest Jewel of Discrimination*, translated by Swami Prabhavananda and Christopher Isherwood. Los Angeles: Vedanta Press, 1975.

Singer, Margaret Thaler. *Cults in our Midst: The Continuing Fight against Their Hidden Menace*. San Francisco: Jossey-Bass, 1995.

Somerfield, Barbara. "To Dane Rudhyar, Who Inspired My First Steps on the Path." *Planet Earth*, Spring 1995, 53–55.

St. John of the Cross. *The Dark Night of the Soul*, translated by E. A. Peers. Garden City, N.Y.: Image Books, 1959.

Stryk, Lucien. *The World of the Buddha*. New York: Grove, 1968.

Taimni, I. K. *The Science of Yoga: The Yoga Sutras of Patanjali*. Wheaton, Ill.: Theosophical Publishing, 1961.

Tirth, Vishnu. "Signs of an Awakened Kundalini." In *Kundalini, Evolution, and Enlightenment*, John White, editor, 94–97. Garden City, N.Y.: Anchor, 1979.

Tredwell, Gail. *Holy Hell: A Memoir of Faith, Devotion, and Pure Madness*. Kihei, HI: Wattle Tree Press, 2013.

Trungpa, Chögyam, Rinpoche. *Crazy Wisdom*. Boston: Shambhala Publications, 1991.

Tweedie, Irina. *The Chasm of Fire: A Woman's Experience of Liberation through the Teachings of a Sufi Master*. Rockport, Mass.: Element Books, 1993.

Vissell, Barry, and Joyce Vissell. *The Shared Heart: Relationship Celebrations and Initiations*. Aptos, Calif.: Ramira Publishing, 1984.

Welwood, John. *Challenge of the Heart*. Boston: Shambhala Publications, 1985.

———. "On Psychotherapy and Meditation." In *Awakening the Heart: East-West Approaches to Psychotherapy and the Healing Relationship,* edited by John Welwood, 43–54. Boston: Shambhala Publications, 1983.

———. "On Spiritual Authority: Genuine and Counterfeit." In *Spiritual Choices: The Problem of Recognizing Authentic Paths to Inner Transformation,* Dick Anthony, Bruce Ecker, and Ken Wilber, editors, 283–303. New York: Paragon House, 1987.

———. "Reflections on Psychotherapy, Focusing, and Meditation." *Journal of Transpersonal Psychology* 2 (1980): 131–42.

White, John. *What is Enlightenment? Exploring the Goal of the Spiritual Path.* New York: Paragon House, 1998.

Whitmont, Edward, and Sylvia Perera. *Dreams: A Portal to the Source.* New York: Routledge, 1989.

Wiesel, Elie. *Souls on Fire: Portraits and Legends of Hasidic Masters.* New York: Simon and Schuster, 1982.

Wilber, Ken. *The Atman Project: A Transpersonal View of Human Development.* Wheaton, Ill.: Quest, 1980.

———. "The Spectrum Model." In *Spiritual Choices: The Problem of Recognizing Authentic Paths to Inner Transformation,* edited by Dick Anthony, Bruce Ecker, and Ken Wilber, 237–77. New York: Paragon House, 1987.

Wilber, Ken, Jack Engler, and Daniel Brown. *Transformations of Consciousness: Conventional and Contemplative Perspectives on Development.* Boston: Shambhala Publications, 1986.

Wilson, Peter Lamborn. *Sacred Drift: Essays on the Margins of Islam.* San Francisco, Calif.: City Lights, 1993.

Wittine, Bryan. "Basic Postulates for a Transpersonal Psychotherapy." In *Existential-Phenomenological Perspectives in Psychology,* Ron Valle and Steen Halling, editors, 62–80. New York: Plenum, 1989.

Index

Page numbers in *italics* refer to illustrations.

About the Author

Photo by Diana Syverud

Greg Bogart, Ph.D., MFT, is a psychotherapist in private practice in the San Francisco Bay Area. He attended college at Wesleyan University, where he majored in religious studies. He went on to receive his master's degree in counseling psychology at California Institute of Integral Studies (CIIS) and his doctorate in psychology from Saybrook University. He is also a graduate of the Iyengar Yoga Institute of San Francisco, where he received his yoga teacher training and certification. He is currently a lecturer in the department of psychology at Sonoma State University and an adjunct faculty member at CIIS. Previously he taught for twenty years in the field of counseling psychology at schools including John F. Kennedy University and the Institute of Transpersonal Psychology. He has published research on therapeutic benefits of meditation, yoga, and dreams, most notably in his book *Dreamwork and Self-Healing*. Greg is also the author of *Astrology and Spiritual Awakening, Planets in Therapy: Predictive Technique and the Art of Counseling,* and *Astrology and Meditation: The Fearless Contemplation of Change.*

BOOKS OF RELATED INTEREST

The Path to the Guru
The Science of Self-Realization according to the Bhagavad Gita
by Scott Teitsworth

The Heart of Yoga
Developing a Personal Practice
by T. K. V. Desikachar

Sadhus
Holy Men of India
by Dolf Hartsuiker

Autobiography of a Sadhu
A Journey into Mystic India
by Rampuri

The Science and Practice of Humility
The Path to Ultimate Freedom
by Jason Gregory

Chakras
Energy Centers of Transformation
by Harish Johari

The Complete I Ching — 10th Anniversary Edition
The Definitive Translation by Taoist Master Alfred Huang
by Taoist Master Alfred Huang

The Science of the Rishis
The Spiritual and Material Discoveries of the Ancient Sages of India
by Vanamali

INNER TRADITIONS • BEAR & COMPANY
P.O. Box 388
Rochester, VT 05767
1-800-246-8648
www.InnerTraditions.com

Or contact your local bookseller